CAR BUYER'S AND LEASER'S

NEGOTIATING BIBLE

Second Edition

CAR BUYER'S
AND LEASER'S
NEGOTIATING BIBLE

Second Edition

W. James Bragg

Random House
New York

Car Buyer's and Leaser's Negotiating Bible, Second Edition
Copyright © 1999, 1996 by Cogito Ergo Sum, Inc.
Copyright © 1993 by Fighting Chance ®

This book is available for special purchases in bulk by organizations and institutions, not for resale, at special discounts. Please direct your sales inquiries to Random House Premium Sales, toll-free 800-800-3246 or fax 212-572-4961.

Please address inquiries about electronic licensing of this division's products, for use on a network or in software or on CD-ROM, to the Subsidiary Rights Department, Random House Reference, fax 212-940-7352.

This is a revised and updated edition of *Car Buyer's and Leaser's Negotiating Bible,* published in 1996 by Random House, Inc.

Visit the Random House Reference Web site at www.randomwords.com

Typeset and printed in the United States of America

Library of Congress Cataloging-in-Publication Data

Bragg, W. James (William James)
    Car buyer's and leaser's negotiating bible / W. James Bragg —
2nd ed.
      p.   cm.
    Includes bibliographical references and index.
    ISBN 0-375-70466-3
    1. Automobiles—Purchasing.   2. Automobile leasing and renting.
3. Negotiation. I. Title.
TL162.B7297   1998
629.222'029'6—dc21   98-49712
                                          CIP

Second Edition
0 9 8 7 6 5 4
August 2002

ISBN 0-375-70466-3

New York   Toronto   London   Sydney   Auckland

DEDICATION

- To every man who's ever bought a new car or truck and wondered whether the next guy got the same vehicle for a lot less.

- To every woman who's suffered through the purchase process and wondered whether she was a victim of gender-based price discrimination.

- To every member of a minority group who's wondered whether he or she has encountered race-based price discrimination when buying a new car or truck.

- To everyone who's about to buy that first new vehicle and wonders whether he or she will end up asking the same questions.

This book is for all of you. After reading it, you'll wonder why no one ever told you this before.

Acknowledgments

- Difficult as this project is, it would be impossible to accomplish without the support, encouragement, and love of my wife, who loses a husband for several weeks with each new edition. Thank you, Ricky, for understanding that perfection is the enemy of excellence and accepting me as I am.

- I must also acknowledge the patience and love of my young daughter, who loses a daddy and Disneyland buddy for the same period. Thank you, Casey, for understanding that grown-ups can't come out to play every day and for giving me those rain checks. I promise to use them all.

- To my three grown children, Laurie, Karen, and John, who have watched their father write a book and start a demanding national business at a time in life when other fathers are cutting back and kicking back. Thank you for the encouragement and love I needed when I couldn't see the light at the end of the tunnel.

- Finally, I am grateful to my editors at Random House—partly for curing my tendency to overpunctuate, but mostly for believing this was a book worth doing.

W.J.B.

Contents

element affecting over nine out of ten vehicles sold that nobody talks about.

yourself by phone or fax to hiring a stand-in. Why auto brokers and Internet car-buying services may not be the best answer.

If a little is knowledge is dangerous,
where are those who have so much
as to be out of danger?
> —Thomas Huxley

Among new car buyers, it's those
who've read this book.

Introduction

I f another book covered car buying and leasing well, we wouldn't have written this one—neither the first two versions nor this updated, expanded third version*. But no business is as dynamic as the automobile business, which continues to change dramatically. For the car shopper, some of these changes are good news, other bad news.

- Spurred by the huge popularity of sport utility vehicles, the light truck market segment (which also includes minivans and pickup trucks) has exploded from just over one-third of the business to account for about half of all new-vehicle sales. As a result, consumers

*This is technically the second edition of the book under the title *Car Buyer's and Leaser's Negotiating Bible*. It was first published under the title *In the Driver's Seat*.

have more makes and models of cars and trucks to choose from than ever before.

• Competition has become even more intense as international automakers fight for pieces of the U.S. market—the largest and most lucrative in the world. Most of the major Japanese and European players have established manufacturing beachheads here to insulate themselves from the pricing dilemmas caused by unpredictable fluctuations in international monetary exchange rates and, in some cases, to escape higher labor costs in their countries.

• Detroit's Big Three—GM, Ford, and Chrysler—face a particularly tough challenge. Millions of baby boomers have matured driving Hondas and Toyotas and Nissans, and they are unlikely to turn to Buicks and Mercurys and Chryslers and Lincolns as they age. One key reason: Import makes generally score higher on measures of initial quality and long-term reliability, so they hold their value better as used cars. With the imports continuing to encroach on the minivan, sport utility, and full-size truck segments that were once Detroit's exclusive domain, the competitive pressures will intensify.

• In addition, the United States is a more mature auto market today. With sales increases usually in the low single digits, and the market stagnant or even down a little in some years, it's become a pitched battle for a share of a pie that's not growing much—similar to that in the fast-food business, which has put a hamburger store on every corner. In this environment, customer and dealer sales incentives and subsidized financing and leasing offers have become the equivalent of those 99-cent burgers. The automakers would love to dump them, but they can't if they want to remain competitive.

Overall, these changes have benefited the new-vehicle shopper. A super-competitive marketplace tends to stimulate continuous product improvement and keep prices in line. But there have been other changes that are not so consumer-friendly.

• Leasing has grown from relative infancy to become a major factor in new-vehicle sales. Leasing is a great idea for some people. Unfortunately, many shoppers don't understand the language of leasing or how the monthly payment is determined, and they end up paying much more than they should. (There's nothing a car salesman likes more than customers who ask, "How much per month to lease that car?" It's as if they walk in with a sign reading, "I Just Fell off the Turnip Truck.")

• The Internet has exploded as a source of automotive information, much of it free. You can even buy a new car on the World Wide Web. But our periodic checks indicate that much of the "free" automotive information there—particularly the dealer invoice pricing, the incentive data, and the information on holdback—is either out-of-date or wrong. And those dealers you get through Internet auto-buying services have typically paid for the exclusive right to all the prospects from your zip code. The price you get from them may or may not be a good one, but it's likely to be better when there's more than one dealer competing for your business.

• Perhaps most important, there's a revolution under way at the retail level—one aimed at reducing the number of car stores and making the business less competitive. Detroit's Big Three have been eliminating smaller dealers and consolidating dealerships in several markets. In addition, some big, publicly held companies have been buying many of the largest and most successful dealerships, as well as launching chains of used-car "superstores." Many of these stores have adopted a one-price, "no-dicker" sales policy, and there is a growing body of evidence indicating that no-dicker buyers pay significantly more than people who shop for the same vehicle at stores where prices are negotiable.

• The automaker's aggressive promotion of leasing over the past several years has created a steady stream of attractive vehicles for the used-car buyer. But dealers get used cars from several sources, and one used car can be a much smarter buy than its identically priced twin on the same lot, depending on who owned it first.

YOU'LL LEARN FROM MORE THAN 28,000 AUTHORS

In this more complex market environment, the consumer must be better informed than ever to avoid getting taken. *The Car Buyer's and Leaser's Negotiating Bible* is loaded with inside information that will empower you in today's changing automotive market. Much of this information you won't find in any other book. Indeed, much of what we know about this business comes from the actual shopping experiences of the thousands of Fighting Chance customers we've talked to—more than 28,000 at the time this third edition was published and increasing by at least 5,000 each year. In a sense, this book was written by over 28,000 new-car shoppers. This gives us an unfair advantage over every other book in the category—and you an unfair advantage over those car salesmen.

OUR SUBJECT IS MONEY, NOT CARS

There's an old maxim that applies here. We call it the 80/20 Rule of Life. Simply stated, it says that 20 percent of the people account for 80 percent of the activity, no matter what it is. For example, 20 percent of moviegoers buy 80 percent of the tickets; and 20 percent of readers buy 80 percent of the books.

When the subject is the money dealers make from selling new cars, the rule says that 20 percent of the customers account for 80 percent of the profits. And when we walk into that showroom, every car salesman views every one of us as a prime candidate to join that unfortunate group. This book's reason for being is to keep you out of that group.

The one sure way for anyone to avoid getting taken is to become an informed and disciplined shopper, period. This book can help you become that shopper. We will *not* be steering you to any specific car or truck. *You* are the best judge of which vehicle fits your requirements. Do you like the way the vehicle looks? Is your body comfortable in the seat? Do you like its handling characteristics? Is it big enough for your needs? Is it too noisy, or too quiet? Some of these are very personal questions, and many are quite subjective.

And we are not experts on fuel economy, long-term reliability, maintenance and repair costs, or insurance ratings. These important issues are well covered in lots of all-purpose books and magazines.

Our focus here is primarily on the elements that influence the *financial* outcome of the purchase process—elements those all-purpose books and magazines often cover only superficially. Our job is to provide you with the knowledge that will give you real negotiating leverage in a transaction that traditionally has been stacked against the buyer.

We'll do that by bringing together all the relevant information, distilling and synthesizing it into one coherent presentation. We'll demystify the automotive purchase process thoroughly (in English, not AutoSpeak) and teach you how to use that information to negotiate from a position of strength, in the driver's seat.

SEVERAL SUBJECTS YOU'LL BE GLAD WE STUDIED

To illustrate, here are some important aspects of today's market reality—things you must know about to deal from strength.

1. **Today the average vehicle has $500 to $1,000 or more built into its price for incentives—customer rebates, reduced-rate financing and subsidized leasing offers, and secret factory-to-dealer incentives.**

Since you'll pay for them, you ought to be informed so that you can benefit from them.

2. Research shows that, compared to Caucasian males, women and minorities (who buy more than half of all new cars) face significant price discrimination in the purchase process—discrimination that may cost them over $1 billion a year. No other book we've seen even mentions this landmark study. This book presents these research results in chapter 2 and teaches readers how to turn the tables.

3. The fortunes of auto companies and their dealers ebb and flow from month to month, affecting price flexibility for each make and model. Disappointing sales typically lead to excess inventories and a greater willingness to deal. Chapter 3 explains this in detail, and chapter 25 provides a mechanism for obtaining a current sales and inventory picture to help you identify the more vulnerable makes.

4. In this super-competitive auto market, there's one thing no dealer wants you to know: Most dealers make several slim-profit deals every month with knowledgeable customers. In chapters 15 and 21, you'll learn why that's true and how you can turn this fact to your advantage. We'll even give you some overall target price guidelines for cars in different price ranges.

5. Leasing now accounts for a major percentage of new-vehicle purchases. While leasing isn't right for everyone, manufacturer-subsidized offers make it a very attractive alternative for many new-car shoppers. Chapter 22 is, hands down, today's bible on leasing.

6. The success of GM's Saturn division has encouraged many other dealers to adopt Saturn's one-price, "no-dicker" sales policy. But these Saturn wanna-bes don't have Saturn's crucial pricing umbrella working for them, and they don't offer the consumer the same pricing reassurance. Chapters 13 and 14 take you behind the curtain for a revealing look at how no-dicker pricing really works and why it's not as consumer-friendly as they'd like us to believe.

7. The Customer Satisfaction Index (CSI), an advertising staple for makes that score well in national surveys, also has implications for your shopping behavior. Manufacturers now conduct surveys to rate each of their dealers on customer satisfaction, and everything else being close to equal, you should want to buy from a dealer with an above-average CSI score. Chapter 20 teaches you how to identify those dealers.

BUYING A CAR ISN'T ROCKET SCIENCE

In fact, buying a car ought to be fun! Our objective is to make this the most comprehensive, interesting, and useful information package available for helping new-car and -truck shoppers save money. We won't talk down to you or tell you things you already know (such as, dress comfortably but conservatively when visiting showrooms). We'll just explain, as simply as we can, how the process works, and how you can take advantage of it, instead of letting it take advantage of you.

We think you'll find this book fun to read, which may be a first for books in this category. It should help you relax about the entire car-shopping process, which is going to be much easier than you think because you'll know exactly how to complete the task successfully. And believe it or not, you'll find car dealers much easier to negotiate with when they know that you know what you're doing.

COMPLETING THE LOOP: FIGHTING CHANCE®, A UNIQUE INFORMATION SERVICE

To negotiate successfully, you'll need the most current, vehicle-specific information for the cars or trucks on your shopping list. When you're ready, our company, Fighting Chance, offers you an easy way to get that data by calling (800) 288–1134, ordering through our web site on the Internet, or writing to us. The Fighting Chance information package contains the factory invoice pricing for the vehicles you're shopping, a current report on manufacturers' incentive programs (including factory-to-dealer cash offers), and an updated sales and inventory picture for each make—including vehicle-specific pricing targets based on the feedback we've received on actual transaction prices from thousands of Fighting Chance customers. Fighting Chance is also the only service in the category that gives you a "coach," someone to talk to (via a customer service number) as you go through the buying or leasing process. See chapter 25 for ordering details.

1

In a time of turbulence and change, it is more true than ever that knowledge is power.
— John F. Kennedy

Everybody's Problem: An Uneven Playing Field

Quick! Can you name three things that are more fun than driving home in a brand-new car or truck? For most people, that's a tough call.

Now, can you name three things that are less fun than shopping for and negotiating the price of that new car or truck? For most people, that's even tougher.

We all suffer world-class anxiety in this process, with good reason.

Over the years, car prices have gone up faster than take-home pay. The average new car's actual transaction price is now over $20,000. That's more than six months' wages for a typical household, enough to make anyone anxious. And there's little relief in sight. Despite evidence that "sticker shock" hurts new-car sales, you can expect automakers to continue hiking prices. (One key reason: the expanding number of costly built-in safety systems such as side- and head-level airbags and anti-lock brakes.) If the annual increases averaged only a "modest" 2 to 3 percent, they would add $400 to $600 a year to the cost of the average car.

All automakers are focused on reducing production costs, but you can squeeze only so much juice from an orange. And the United Auto Workers union seems to fight every effort of Detroit's Big Three to improve productivity.

The vagaries of international monetary exchange rates can also have a major impact on auto pricing. In this arena, the Japanese manufacturers pull the strings. As the yen strengthens against the dollar, the Japanese receive fewer yen for each dollar they make here. For example, they took home over 250 yen for each dollar in the mid-1980s, but a decade later the yen was much stronger and the exchange rate went to 80 yen per dollar. In response, the Japanese were forced to raise U.S. prices continuously over that period to avoid big losses. The domestic makes should have seen this as an opportunity to gain a pricing advantage and recapture market share. But Detroit's response was to use the Japanese increases as an "umbrella" under which to raise prices and reduce incentive offers on domestic cars.

Conversely, as the dollar strengthens against the yen and the Japanese get more yen for each dollar they make here, there is no pressure to raise prices and the Japanese tend to hold the line. In that environment, Detroit must exercise price restraint or risk losing more market share to Tokyo.

Of course, the Japanese want to keep improving their results here. They could do that by aggressively increasing their share of a market that's expanding quite slowly. But they're very concerned about the political hornet's nest they'd stir up if they garnered a significantly higher market share. The pressure to avoid escalating U.S. trade tension has forced them to shift their focus from increasing share to increasing profits per car sold. Which means increasing prices, at least symbolically, as a way to show Detroit and Washington that they are not predatory.

What's the prognosis for the consumer? *The cost of the average new car will continue to increase by at least $500 a year and probably more.* Is it any wonder that many of us would rather visit a dentist for root canal work than visit a showroom to shop for a new car or truck?

THE REAL PROBLEM: AN UNEVEN PLAYING FIELD

The gut-level issue, of course, is that the price of that expensive machine is negotiable, and therefore different for each buyer. By contrast, the price of just about everything else we buy is firmly established, and therefore the same for each buyer. That puts the pressure on us. We've got to do something we're not used to doing: negotiate the price of the second most expensive purchase most of us will ever make. And we're operating on unfamiliar turf, in a position of weakness, because we do it only once every few years.

But those salesmen we have to negotiate with are on very familiar turf, the car store, and in a position of strength, because they do it every day. (Yes, they call the dealership "the store." There are more than 22,000 of them nationally, and the average store for a Top Six automotive brand moves 500 to 900 new cars and trucks each year. Many sell thousands!)

Those salesmen are trained to do one thing really well: maximize the car store's profit on each sale by separating us from as much of our money as possible. Their job is to determine how much is "as much as possible" for each prospect and, if the number is high enough, to close the sale at that price before the prospect gets away.

We make that job easier than it should be by giving them lots of important information they can use. We tell them exactly which car we want, and how much we can pay per month, and which vehicle we're trading in. In return, they give us no information we can use, such as how much that car really cost them, how low they'll really go to sell it, and what our trade-in is really worth. As a result, a playing field that was uneven from the start tips even further toward them. And when the transaction is over, most of us don't know whether we got a good deal or got taken.

EVERYONE DESERVES A FIGHTING CHANCE

As a *Motor Trend* writer said in an annual auto review issue, "Negotiating with terrorists is easier than bargaining with car dealers." That's why we wrote this book. We wanted to give the average new-vehicle shopper a fighting chance by making the playing field a little more level.

Our goal is to make the purchase process less painful and costly for you. To do that, we must change something important in that process. Since we can't change those salesmen and what they do, we've got to help change you and what you do.

THE OBJECTIVE: TO MAKE YOU MORE KNOWLEDGEABLE THAN THE CAR SALESMAN

That's not Mission Impossible. The average car salesman isn't that knowledgeable. He's trained to qualify, control, and close most of the people who walk in, prospects who just don't know much. But he's not well prepared to control and close people with solid knowledge of his business, a well-planned, disciplined approach, and insights that even he may not understand. Those shoppers can have real negotiating leverage.

(Incidentally, when we say "salesmen," assume we mean both sexes. There are successful auto saleswomen, but the male stereotype is still dominant. Also, when we say "cars," assume we're referring to both cars and trucks.)

How can we make you more knowledgeable than the car salesman? By giving you the attitude, facts, up-to-date insights, and advice you need to negotiate from a position of greater strength.

We can't guarantee, of course, that you'll save hundreds or thousands more with this information than without it. That's up to you and what you do with it. The supply and demand conditions in your market for the vehicles you're interested in will also influence the outcome.

But remember, knowledge is power. The main advantage the salesman has over most buyers is that he thinks he's got all the knowledge. If you absorb the information we give you, you'll know more than most car salesmen. If you act on this information, you'll go into the process with real confidence in your ability to negotiate effectively. And if you believe you can, you will.

NO PAIN, NO GAIN

Most people work harder planning a $2,000 vacation than planning the purchase of the $20,000 car they'll be vacationing in for years. Why? For two reasons: (1) planning a vacation is more fun; and (2) they know how to plan a vacation, but they don't know how to shop for a car. If smart shopping were easy, everyone would do it.

The facts say everyone doesn't. Incredible as it seems, in a national survey conducted by the Dohring Company of Glendale, California, *one out of seven prospective new-car buyers was not aware that new-vehicle prices were negotiable!* And we'd bet that most of the other six frequently pay more than they realize, simply because they aren't focused on all the ways a car store can make money on a deal (more on this in chapter 5).

Smart shopping requires homework. Studying this book and acting on it intelligently will require more of your time than simply going out and buying a car next Saturday. The trade-off is between time and money, perhaps as much as several thousand dollars.

We'll assume that you wouldn't have bought this book if you weren't willing to trade time for money. Let's get on with your education.

2

The Other Problem: Price Discrimination

Our civil rights laws focus on the areas of employment, education, housing, and public accommodations. When it comes to the prices we pay for the things we buy, there's a comfortable assumption that good old American competition at the retail level tends to eliminate price discrimination.

Try telling that to women, who know they pay more for shoes than men do for theirs, even when the materials and workmanship are the same. Or to inner-city residents, who know that stores in their neighborhoods often charge higher prices for lower-quality goods than similar stores elsewhere.

Women and minorities will not be surprised to learn that they also face significant price discrimination in the automotive marketplace. *We believe a conservative estimate of the cost of this discrimination is over $1 billion a year, compared to the prices paid for the same vehicles by white males.*

WOMEN MAKE THE WHEELS GO ROUND

The female working population has grown dramatically over the last few decades, sparking a revolution in auto design and marketing strategies. With three out of four women between twenty and fifty-four years old in the labor force, women have become a key target for automakers.

Manufacturers now spend as much money researching women's automotive needs as men's, with good reason. Women purchase half of the new passenger cars sold and more than one-third of the light trucks, including some very profitable segments (minivans like the Dodge Caravan, for instance, and sport utility vehicles like the Jeep Grand Cherokee).

Many vehicles are designed to appeal primarily to women. Female designers play important roles at automobile companies. They frequently supervise new-vehicle design teams, especially for sporty coupes—a market segment aimed directly at women that includes the Honda Prelude, Mitsubishi Eclipse, Toyota Celica, Acura Integra, and the convertible Volkswagen Cabriolet.

The auto manufacturers have changed their ways to satisfy the needs of this powerful new economic force; they treat women differently from men. As a result, both win. Women get the products they want, and manufacturers sell more new cars and trucks.

The automakers' franchised *dealers,* however, are another story. Most women have always suspected that new-car salesmen treat them differently than men and that, as a result, they end up paying a different price from men—a higher price. That's why many of them drag along their husbands, boyfriends, or fathers when they shop.

Many members of minority groups have suspected they face similar price discrimination.

Now there's irrefutable evidence that substantiates these suspicions.

THE SEARCH FOR THE SMOKING GUN

Ian Ayres, a professor at Stanford Law School and a research fellow of the American Bar Foundation, was interested in testing the ability of competitive market forces to eliminate gender- and race-based price discrimination in markets not covered by civil rights laws. Since a new-car purchase represents a large investment for most consumers, he saw the retail automobile market as "particularly ripe for scrutiny."

Between the summers of 1988 and 1990, when he was an associate professor at the Northwestern University School of Law, he conducted research to examine whether women and minorities were at a disadvantage in the process of negotiating the price of a new car.

He trained several college-educated testers of different genders and races to negotiate in the same way for specific models. They conducted 180 independent negotiations at 90 dealerships in the Chicago area, bargaining to each dealer's "final cash offer." To eliminate other financial considerations, no trade-in vehicles were involved.

THE FACTS OF PRICE DISCRIMINATION

The smoking gun wasn't hard to find. The results were published as the *Harvard Law Review*'s lead article in February 1991. They demonstrated that retail car dealerships systematically offered substantially better prices on identical cars to white men than they did to white women and African Americans.

Specifically, final offers to white women contained about 40 percent more dealer profit than final offers to white men. Offers to African American men contained more than twice the profit, and African American women had to pay more than three times the markup of white male testers.

The tendency to charge African Americans higher prices was echoed in this comment one dealer made to Professor Ayres: "My cousin owns a dealership in a black neighborhood. He doesn't sell nearly as many [cars], but he hits an awful lot of home runs. You know, sometimes it seems like the people that can least afford it have to pay the most."

The study also revealed that testers were systematically steered to salespeople of their own race and gender, who then gave them *worse* deals than others received from salespeople of a different race and gender. Consumers tend to feel more comfortable with someone of their own race and gender; salespeople take advantage of that implied trust and sell them higher-profit deals.

The major conclusions of this initial study were confirmed by a subsequent larger-scale test involving 400 additional negotiations in the Chicago area.

Years have passed since this research was completed, and you might wonder whether the result would be different if the study were conducted today. Based on our personal contacts with thousands of new-car shoppers each year, there is no evidence of significant changes. It would be easier to U-turn a supertanker in the Panama Canal than to change the way car salesmen operate.

GENDER DISCRIMINATION GETS A THEME SONG

On the assumption that our female readers have a sense of humor about this, we'd like to share the lyrics to a little song parody we've written. It's sung to the tune of that old standard "I Found a Million-Dollar Baby in a Five-and-Ten-Cent Store." We call it "I Made a Bundle on the Lady When I Put Her in a New Car." Imagine all those chauvinist car salesmen at their annual convention, hoisting their glasses to toast their male prowess and singing these lyrics:

> She was my lucky April shopper,
> It was my chance to be a star.
> I made a bundle on the lady
> When I put her in a new car.
>
> She thought she'd be here half an hour,
> We kept her here for three or four.
> We made a bundle on that lady
> With the deal she got at our store!
>
> She wanted basic transportation
> But much to her surprise,
> She drove home in a sports car
> With payments twice the size!
>
> So if you're looking for a bargain
> Our showroom isn't very far.
> I'll make a bundle on you, baby,
> When I put you in a new car!

THE ASSUMPTIONS BEHIND THE FACTS

Professor Ayres hypothesizes an explanation for this price discrimination. While there's no way to prove it, we think he's right on the money. Here's the essence of his reasoning.

- The dealer's objective is to maximize profits on each sale. (That's the American way, right?)

- The natural outcome of the bargaining process is that identical vehicles are sold to different buyers at different prices. Dealers make little or no profit on some sales, but a great deal of profit on others.

- The less the competition with other dealers for a given sale, the more profit the dealer is likely to make on the transaction.

- If a dealership can infer that some prospects are less likely to shop at other dealerships—because they aren't well informed about the dynamics of the retail automotive marketplace, or because they can't spend the time required, or because they simply hate the entire bargaining process and just want to get it behind them—that dealership is more likely to view these prospects as potential patsies for high-margin transactions. And that dealership is more likely to conclude that it can safely charge these prospects higher prices.

- Like it or not, our society is still rife with stereotypes about women and minority groups that provide at least a subconscious rationale for sales-people to view them as more likely candidates for high-margin, slam-dunk, sucker deals. Here are the most obvious assumptions they make:

  Women and minorities have less time to shop around for competitive bids. Compared to white men, they are less likely to be able to take time off from work to shop without losing wages. And women are more likely to have family responsibilities that further restrict their shopping time.

  Women and minorities are less sophisticated about the auto-shopping process. They are less likely to seek out information about the realities of the retail market and to understand that the sticker price is negotiable. They will be more passive in the sales situation and less likely to negotiate aggressively. That will make it easier for the salesperson to control the outcome.

  Women, in general, are more averse to the entire bargaining process. Haggling over the price of a new vehicle is a competitive ordeal. Some men relish the battle; for them it's one of the last macho things they can do without a gun. Most women simply hate it. They'll pay a higher cost just to get it behind them.

THE LIGHT AT THE END OF THE TUNNEL

Women and minority readers shouldn't be discouraged by these revelations. The purpose of this exercise is to get into the opponent's brain, to understand what's in there. The good news is, that's just about all that's in there.

And is the salesman going to be surprised when he meets you! Because you're going to shake his faith in the assumptions, confusing him and neutralizing his offense. He'll try all his tricks, but you'll be that knowledgeable, disciplined shopper we promised you'd become, and they won't work.

The road from here to there begins on the next page. It's straight and clearly marked.

3

The

Big

Picture

An IBM sales representative in Milwaukee contracted with a dealer to buy a new Dodge Viper, Chrysler's limited-production sports car, for $2,500 over the suggested retail price. When the vehicle arrived, the dealer sued the customer to get out of the contract. According to the Wall Street Journal, *he thought he could sell it for as much as $20,000 over the sticker price! On learning of this embarrassing incident, Chrysler's executive vice president for sales and marketing lamented, "We have to change the entire culture of our franchise."*

Any deal you make will be influenced by two things that have nothing to do with you: the overall state of the automobile market, and the specific supply and demand conditions for the vehicle you want.

Since the auto sales climate is one of the most overreported subjects in journalism, getting up to speed starts with simply keeping your eyes and ears open. As you think about new cars or trucks, pay attention to those monthly sales reports on the TV news, in your local paper, or in national media like *The Wall Street Journal* or *USA Today.* They'll give you a general feel for how eager dealers are to sell new vehicles.

What you really want to know, however, is how eager some specific manufacturers and dealers might be to sell the vehicles you're interested in buying.

THEIR WEAKNESS IS YOUR OPPORTUNITY

The retail automobile business is driven by momentum, in both the overall market and the fortunes of each specific make. Over a period of years the market runs in cycles, from hot to lukewarm to cold and back again. Within each cycle, there are winners and losers among both manufacturers and specific models. Some automakers watch their sales and market shares wither, while others develop the tough competitor's ability to weather any storm.

The smart shopper understands that these differences create buying opportunities, and that you should be able to negotiate a better deal with those who are most eager to sell.

LEARN HOW THEY'RE DOING

There is real power in knowing how the makes and models you are interested in are doing in the marketplace. Is their sales performance better or worse than their key competitors' and the total market's? Are their inventory levels relatively higher? As a general rule, dealers selling makes that are doing less well, with higher inventories, will be more willing to deal aggressively on price than those selling makes with relatively better sales and lower inventories. Automakers with poor sales are also more likely to offer customer and/or dealer incentives.

For perspective, industrywide inventory levels tend to fluctuate throughout the year in a range from roughly a 55-day supply to about a 75-day supply. For most manufacturers a two-month supply is an ideal target, providing the vast majority of buyers with sufficient color and equipment choices. Inventories higher than that usually increase costs much more than they do sales. Whenever they approach the three-month level, you can bet that the costs of financing that supply are hurting both the manufacturers and their dealers. Those makes should be more vulnerable to smart, informed shoppers.

Here's a comparison of two vehicles to illustrate the point:

• One car's sales are running 38 percent below previous annual levels. The average dealer is selling just one each month. And on the first of the month, there was a whopping 120-day supply in inventory.

• A directly competitive car of another make has sales 5 percent ahead of last year's level. The average dealer sells 15 each month. And there was a 42-day supply in inventory on the first of the month.

Given the relative sales and inventory positions of these two vehicles, which dealers are likely to be more flexible on price? The ones selling the first car, naturally.

Where can you find the information you need to understand the current status of the makes and models you are considering? Visit a large public library and ask to see the most recent issues of *Automotive News,* the industry's weekly newspaper. Many big libraries subscribe to this publication, which prints the most recent sales and inventory data in successive issues each month, by make and model.

It's also helpful to know the number of franchised dealers for each make, shown in this table. These numbers tend to remain relatively constant. In bad times, some dealers go out of business; in good times, manufacturers add a few franchises. (Note, however, that GM, Ford, and Chrysler have a long-term objective of eliminating smaller dealerships and consolidating others. The Korean franchises, Hyundai and Kia, both have a long-term goal of 500 dealerships. Saturn is aiming for 500–525.)

This information enables you to analyze sales figures to determine

Make	Number of Dealers	Make	Number of Dealers
Acura	260	Lexus	180
Audi	260	Lincoln	1,610
BMW	335	Mazda	850
Buick	2,810	Mercedes-Benz	320
Cadillac	1,530	Mercury	2,610
Chevrolet	4,350	Mitsubishi	500
Chrysler	2,960	Nissan	1,085
Dodge	2,925	Oldsmobile	2,885
Ford	4,180	Plymouth	2,950
GMC	2,275	Pontiac	2,850
Honda	995	Porsche	195
Hyundai	465	Saab	210
Infiniti	145	Saturn	385
Isuzu	555	Subaru	610
Jaguar	135	Suzuki	290
Jeep	2,470	Toyota	1,195
Kia	335	Volkswagen	600
Land Rover	115	Volvo	350

how many of each model the average dealer sells each month. That knowledge will often strengthen your confidence by confirming that it's a lot easier for you to find someone who wants to sell one than for them to find someone who wants to buy one.

When you're ready for serious negotiating, you should know that there is an easier way to get the current sales and inventory picture for the makes and models you are considering, along with the data on the current dealer invoice price of the vehicles and an up-to-date listing of manufacturers' incentives for both the customer and the dealer. See chapter 25 for details.

4

Necessity never made a good bargain.

—Benjamin Franklin

Attitude Adjustment

Here are three basic principles of automotive negotiating that you must burn into your brain. Think of them as three legs of the stool that will transform you attitudinally from a potential pushover into a tower of strength.

PSYCHOLOGY 101

This is a serious competition. It may seem relatively civilized, but it's definitely you against them.

One of the primary rules of this competition: Don't give your opponent a psychological advantage. That's exactly what you'll do as soon as you show him that you're emotionally attached to any specific vehicle. As soon as he knows that, he's dealing from a position of greater strength. And you'll end up paying more for the car simply because he knows you have to have it.

Car salesmen are trained to make the purchase process as emotional as possible. Decades of experience have confirmed that they get more money from emotional people than from cool, rational shoppers.

How do you avoid this trap? *By projecting total emotional detachment.*

In the showroom, on the lot, and during the test drive, your behavior should say: A car is a car, something that gets me from point A to point B. Lots of cars will do that, including many that this store doesn't even sell. I'm going to check them all out and make the best deal.

(Ask your friends who shop for antiques about the "Don't-let-'em-know-what-you-really-want-as-soon-as-you-walk-in" rule. They'll tell you it also works well at estate sales, swap meets, and garage sales.)

> HEAVY BREATHING SHOULD BE RESERVED FOR MORE APPROPRIATE OCCASIONS. IN CAR STORES IT LEADS ONLY TO HEAVY PAYMENTS.

That doesn't mean you can't fall in love. Just don't let the salesman know until you've completed the transaction. At your price, not his.

ANATOMY 101

Look down at the floor right now. That's where you'll find the most powerful negotiating tools you'll ever own: your feet.

The only thing a car salesman dreads more than selling you a car too cheaply is watching you walk out of his store, into the arms of another salesman at another store. He's got bags of tricks to keep you there for hours. (Dealers sometimes *require* that their salesmen *not let you leave* without seeing a sales manager!)

> ONE REASON GOD GAVE YOU FEET WAS TO WALK AWAY FROM CAR SALESMAN.

If you think you're being pressured, or he's not listening to you and moving in the direction you want, tell him politely that he's wasting his time . . . and leave. A funny thing happens if you walk: It actually *improves* your leverage when you return later, because he'll know you're someone who'll walk again if things aren't going your way.

REALITY 101

Pick up any buyer's guide to this year's models, and you will find a mind-boggling offering of new cars and trucks. There are many more choices than any civilized society needs to get around town. That's because the people who run car companies are terminal optimists who believe that if they build them we will buy them—all of them. They eventually learn, painfully, that building them is easy, but selling them is hard. Then they are fired and replaced by a new crop of terminal optimists.

Reality is that there will be more car production capacity than car-buying capacity for as long as anyone can see into the future. We'd have to take the minimum driving age down to three years old for all the manufacturers to realize the sales projections they made when they built their production facilities.

> REALITY IS THAT YOU CAN WALK AWAY FROM ANY DEAL, OR ANY CAR,
> AND BE ABSOLUTELY CERTAIN THERE IS ONE JUST LIKE IT, AND
> PROBABLY BETTER, AROUND THE CORNER.

Reality is that it will always be much easier for you to find someone who wants to sell a new car than for a car salesman to find someone who wants to buy one.

Trust this reality.

The time is long overdue for this industry—the largest and most important industry in the world—to erase the popular idea that its No. 1 priority is to pull the wool over everyone's eyes.
—Automotive News editorial

5

The

Juggler

When you're buying a new car, the salesman has three balls in the air, three important areas of opportunity where he can make money on the transaction.

1. He can make money on the front end, on the difference between your purchase price and the dealer's cost on that new vehicle.

2. He can make money on the back end, selling you things like financing (with related life and disability insurance), extended warranty coverage, and dealer add-on options like rustproofing and fabric protection.

3. If the deal includes your trade-in vehicle, he can make money on the difference between what the car store really pays for your car and what they get for it, either by retailing it through their own used-car department or by wholesaling it to a used-car dealer.

If it surprises you to learn that there's more profit potential in the second and third areas than in the first, you are in the group that needs this book the most.

Think of the salesman as a juggler, trained to keep all these balls moving so fast that you can't tell which is which.

He wants to make a good profit on all three if he can. But the total gross is what counts, and there isn't a dealer alive who wouldn't give up profit on one of these balls to swing a deal if he knew he could make a killing on the other two.

The world is full of naive but happy car buyers who think they got a great deal because they bought "below dealer invoice." Or because they got a "fabulous trade-in allowance." Or a "big discount" on an extended warranty policy.

They watched only the ball that they were interested in. But the salesman watched them all.

We'll cover how to watch . . . and even control . . . what happens with each of these balls. But first you need an overall shopping plan.

Ninety-nine percent of the people in the world are fools, and the rest of us are in great danger of contagion.

—Thornton Wilder

6

If You Haven't Got a Plan, You Haven't Got a Prayer

The subject here isn't cars, it's your money, and how a big chunk of it will be divided between you and a car store and a bank or financing company (unless you're among the roughly one in five buyers who pays cash).

THE 80/20 RULE OF LIFE

The 80/20 Rule of Life is one of those maxims that applies to just about any subject you can name. It says that whatever the activity, 80 percent of it is accounted for by 20 percent of the people. Here are some examples:

- 80 percent of the beer is drunk by 20 percent of the drinkers.

- 80 percent of the auto accidents are caused by 20 percent of the drivers.

- 80 percent of the wealth is owned by 20 percent of the people.

- *And 80 percent of a dealer's profits on new-car sales comes from 20 percent of his customers.*

Remember, the salesman's goal is to maximize profit on every deal. He gets paid to determine the highest amount a prospect might be willing to pay and to get that customer's commitment to pay it *before he or she leaves the car store.*

To that salesman, every prospect—including you—who walks into the showroom represents a "slam-dunk"—a potential high-margin sucker deal.

To avoid waking up on the wrong side of Life's 80/20 Rule in this competition, you need a plan. Most people don't have one.

Here's the way most people approach the purchase process:

- They start by visiting car stores and getting excited about specific cars in the presence of car salesmen. *(That's a really bad idea.)*

- Then, still in "new-car heat," they wonder out loud how they'll pay for that pretty thing, and (you guessed it) the salesman tells them how easy it'll be. *(Another bad idea.)*

- Finally, too confused to turn suddenly rational, they wonder out loud what their current car is worth in trade, and they accept the number the salesman gives them without checking it out themselves. *(More bad ideas.)*

They'll repeat this behavior at several car stores and think they're out there dealing. The lucky salesman who gets them at 3:00 P.M. on Sunday will make his weekend quota, and the happy buyers will drive their new cars into the sunset without a clue that they are exactly the kind of prospects that every salesman dreams about.

YES, VIRGINIA, THERE IS A BETTER WAY

Smart buyers don't rely on car salesmen for any important information. They don't give them any either. Smart buyers have a shopping plan that reverses the sequence that most people follow:

• They start by focusing on the car they've got. They know that they're either going to sell it themselves or trade it in, and that the proceeds represent an important part of the new car's down payment. So they begin by finding out how much their vehicle is really worth in their market today, both at retail and at wholesale.

• Then they decide whether they'll sell it themselves at retail or trade it in at wholesale. (They know the difference affects the money available for their down payment.)

• Then they turn to the essential financial questions. They decide on the monthly payment they can handle comfortably, including auto insurance, which costs a lot more for new cars than for old ones. They also determine the down payment they can afford. They know that bigger is better, so they find some loose cash to add to what they'll get for their current car.

• They take all this information and shop for money before they shop seriously for a car or truck. This gives them a good fix on the maximum amount they can pay for a new vehicle, including all the miscellaneous sales taxes and license fees that many salesmen don't mention until you're committed to a price for the car. It also provides a basis for measuring the attractiveness of the financing offered by the dealer or manufacturer.

• They study the advantages and disadvantages of leasing versus buying and decide whether they are candidates to lease. If they are, they do additional homework to understand the key elements of leasing, including exactly how to do the arithmetic to determine the monthly payment.

• Concurrently, they're reading articles on the vehicles they're interested in for information to help narrow their choices, and they're visiting car stores to obtain brochures and take test drives. But they make it clear from the start that they are not going to buy on those visits, and they avoid getting into any salesman's "closing room" because they know they're not ready.

• They decide on at least two or three finalists, including the trim levels and optional equipment they'd like on each. They pick their first-choice vehicle and at least one attractive fallback alternative, based on both emotional appeal and rational analysis.

• Next, they gather all the information they can about what those vehicles actually cost the dealer, including the impact of any current factory-to-dealer incentives, as a basis from which to negotiate a purchase price confidently and aggressively. They also bone up on any direct consumer incentives being offered by the manufacturers.

• They do a little additional homework to determine which dealer finalists they want to approach in the negotiation stage. They recognize that some car stores can be much better places to buy than others, for reasons that have little to do with price.

• With solid knowledge of the real wholesale and retail values of their current cars, the best financing they can arrange independently, and the actual dealer costs of the vehicles they want most, they plan the best way to approach several car stores with an aggressive offer.

• They understand the potential value of proper timing, especially in relation to incentive programs, and they plan their approach accordingly.

• They review the basic tricks salesmen are likely to use to boost their store's profits, including all the high-cost/low-value add-on options they'll try to sell, and they are ready to handle them.

• Then, and only then, are they ready to present themselves to car salesmen as serious prospects.

• Finally, they go into the negotiating process determined to let the guys at the car store do the stewing. They know that those guys need us more than we need them.

For typical buyers, the serious shopping phase takes an average of about five weeks, from the time they start visiting car stores for test drives until the day they drive a new car home.

Following the smart buyers' lead, let's focus now on the car you drive today. We'll start with an illustration of what can happen when you don't keep a close eye on that ball.

Training is everything. The peach was once a bitter almond; cauliflower is nothing but cabbage with a college education.
　　　　　　　—Mark Twain

7

Divide

and

Conquer

Read the next paragraph twice.

Even if you're the world's worst price negotiator when buying a new vehicle, the car store probably will make more profit reselling your clean, well-maintained trade-in to someone else than it will make selling you a new car or truck. *And that profit will come directly out of your pocket.*

It's a fact. Today the average dealer makes more profit selling used than new cars, even though new cars account for 55 to 60 percent of a dealership's gross sales and used cars only about 30 percent. There's typically less than 15 percent gross profit built into manfacturers' suggested retail prices for new cars, and the average negotiated transaction price delivers only a 6 to 7 percent gross profit. But a few years later, dealer asking prices on those same cars as *used* vehicles will include a profit of 20 percent or more, and the average-transaction gross profit will be 11 to 12 percent.

With new-car prices sky-high, there will be continuing strong demand for late-model, low-mileage used cars. If you've got one, you're driving a little gold mine. Car dealers are in the used-car gold-mining business, thanks to the twin factors of simple economics and simple new-car buyers.

THE SIMPLE ECONOMICS

New-car pricing is super-competitive because every dealer has essentially the same merchandise to sell at the same price. A new Chevy Cavalier is the same car, with the same sticker price, at every Chevy store in town. In addition, new cars carry more overhead than used cars, from fancy showrooms to higher inventory financing costs. That makes it even more difficult to sell them for big profits.

By contrast, all used cars are different from one another, even when they're the same year, make, and model. With no standardized sticker prices or dealer invoice costs and no easy way to measure their condition, especially that of the important parts under the hood, it's more difficult for consumers to evaluate their true worth. That makes it relatively easy for car stores to sell every one of them at a profit.

THE SIMPLE NEW-CAR BUYER

The key to a dealer's used-car profit is the new-car buyer. Two out of three deals include a trade-in. And most people literally give away their trade-in without understanding what they are really getting for it.

That's because they don't watch all the balls. Instead, they let the salesman confuse the issue by juggling the new-car sell price and the old-car buy price in a single package deal.

They may think they're getting a great deal because the trade-in allowance is $1,000 over wholesale *Kelley Blue Book* or some other impressive-sounding measurement. They don't realize that the juggler's deal combines that apparently attractive trade-in allowance with a much higher new-car price than they could have negotiated without a trade-in. He's simply taking money out of one of their pockets and putting it in the other. By the time they agree to the package, it's all mumbo-jumbo to them, but at least part of it sounds terrific.

The car store then turns the trade-in into a nice little money machine.

• If it's in relatively good shape and the dealer needs it in his used-car inventory, he'll spend a couple of hundred dollars making it look great and retail it himself for a profit of $1,000 to $1,500 or more. (Two of every three vehicles taken in trade are retailed by the dealership; the average new-car dealer retails over 30 used cars every month.)

• If it's in relatively poor shape, or if he doesn't need it, he'll take a quick $300 to $700 profit by wholesaling it the next day to a used-car dealer. (Each year, new-car dealerships wholesale over five million used cars to used-car dealers.)

Either way he'll probably make more money on that trade-in than on the new car he sold.

The bottom line is that customers with desirable used cars who buy this kind of trade-in allowance deal typically leave between $1,000 and $2,000 on the dealer's table.

If your car is an ugly hulk that barely wheezes onto the dealer's lot, you won't lose much by letting him take it off your hands. But if you have a clean, one-owner, average-miles-for-age vehicle that's mechanically sound, there are two ways to keep most of that money in *your* pocket:

1. The best way is to *sell it yourself* at retail, as described in chapter 9.

2. The second-best way is to sell it to a dealer, but for its *true wholesale value,* as covered in chapter 8. And not just any dealer. . . .

What's the dumbest thing most folks do when they trade in their current car? That's easy. *They trade it to the wrong dealer.*

Here's an example. A Fighting Chance customer in Los Angeles was buying a new Ford Explorer. Her trade-in was a five-year-old Toyota Corolla in great shape with just 24,400 miles on the odometer—a very desirable used car. (Most folks in L.A. drive 24,400 miles in *one* year.) The Ford dealer's first offer was $3,500. She negotiated that up to $5,500, but still felt it was a lowball number. She called us for advice, and we asked her the obvious question: "If you wanted to *buy* that used Corolla, would you look for it first at a Ford dealership?"

"Of course not," she said. "It would look like an orphan there, like maybe there was something wrong with it and the Toyota dealer, who really knows the car, didn't want it."

"It's the Ford dealer who doesn't want it," we told her. "He just wants to steal it from you and wholesale it to the Toyota dealer down the street. So why not eliminate the middleman? Take it down to the Toyota store and sell it yourself." An hour later she had sold it to the Toyota dealer for $6,875—$1,375 more than the Ford dealer's best offer.

As a general rule, a desirable used car will always be worth more to a dealer who sells that make. That doesn't mean you won't see a Toyota on a Ford dealer's used-car lot. You will. But it's a more natural addition to a Toyota dealer's inventory. Used-car shoppers are like new-car shoppers; they know what they want, and they'll go first to a dealer who sells that nameplate. That used Corolla was a more attractive offering on a Toyota lot, and the Toyota dealer's higher price reflected that fact.

This is just plain old common sense, but it's amazing how many adult brains shift into neutral during the new-car purchase process. Most folks trade in their old cars where they buy their new ones, no matter what makes they are.

Note, however, that there are three situations where this general rule may not apply.

1. Many dealers own several different new-car franchises, often located near each other. If the Ford dealer in our example also had a Toyota store, he might have offered more for that used Corolla.

2. A dealer's current inventory mix affects his willingness to pay top wholesale dollar for a used car. If the Toyota dealer in our example had been loaded with Corollas of the same model year and condition, he too might have made a lowball offer, intending to wholesale the car himself to another dealer.

3. New-car dealers usually don't want older, high-mileage cars of the same brand, even those in relatively good condition. If the five-year-old Corolla in our example had had an odometer reading of 100,000 miles instead of 24,400, the Toyota dealer wouldn't have wanted it. Many new-car dealers won't stock used vehicles with over 80,000 miles. They may offer a trade-in value on them, but they'll quickly wholesale them to an independent used-car dealer, moving them down the "automotive food chain" to a buyer who can only afford an older, high-mileage car. Again, if you've got a car like that to trade, our advice is to eliminate the middleman and sell it to the used-car store yourself. At least shop it at one or two used-car stores to get a benchmark against which to judge the new-car dealer's trade-in offer.

One last caveat on this subject: *The way your state calculates the sales tax on new cars will affect your decision on whether to trade in your used car or sell it to another new- or used-car dealer or to an individual.* Most states tax the full purchase price when you buy a new car. But some states allow you to deduct your used car's trade-in value from the purchase price and pay tax only on the difference. Let's assume you live in one of those states and your local sales tax rate is 8 percent. You negotiate a $25,000 price on a new car. The dealer gives you a $10,000 trade-in allowance on your old car, which means you'll save $800 on sales tax (8 percent of $10,000). So you'd have to get more than $10,800 from another buyer to end up with more money in your wallet. (We are not sales tax experts for 50 states, and the tax laws can change over time. So check with your accountant or your state's sales taxing authority before deciding what to do.)

Before you talk trade-in turkey with any car dealer, you must master the next rule. *It's the single most important factor to remember if you're going to succeed in this competition.*

DIVIDE AND CONQUER, COMBINE AND BE CONQUERED

Most new-car shoppers leave a lot of money on the table because they let the salesman combine two elements that should never be combined: the selling price for the new vehicle and the buying price for their used vehicle. When they let him do that, they lose the ability to watch all the balls. As a result, they pay more for the new car than a smart buyer would have and receive less for the old car than a smart seller would have. And they never know what they paid for one or what they got paid for the other.

Write this a hundred times on the blackboard of your mind:

> • **BUYING A NEW CAR IS ONE DEAL.**
>
> • **SELLING AN OLD CAR IS ANOTHER.**
>
> • **KEEP THEM SEPARATE AND YOU'LL WIN.**
>
> • **COMBINE THEM AND YOU'LL LOSE.**

Now let's develop the knowledge you need to keep them separate and thereby keep control of the negotiation.

8

It's powerful pantomime.

The skilled salesman doesn't say a word as he checks out your trade-in. His hands do the talking, lingering over every little scratch or blemish— silently, but effectively reducing the vehicle's value . . . in your mind.

Don't attend his performance. Give him the keys and wait for his return. You'll have a punch line of your own: you know what it's worth.

The Wholesale Truth, and Nothing But

The only right price for your trade-in is its actual wholesale value. Unless you know that number and make the salesman aware that you do, you will get less than true wholesale, and the car store will make an extra profit selling your old car. (You will never get more than true wholesale. If they offer more, the difference is coming from your wallet, not theirs, in the form of a higher price on the new car or a higher interest rate on the financing, or both.)

Knowing your car's true wholesale value also helps you decide whether to trade it in or sell it yourself. Compare that value to the retail price you can expect to get from an individual, a subject covered in chapter 9. The difference will surprise you. If you decide to trade it despite this difference, at least you'll be doing it with your eyes open.

THE TRUTH ABOUT THOSE LITTLE BOOKS

How do you discover your car's true wholesale value? Not by looking in any used-car pricing book—blue, black, or red—because those books don't reflect the current wholesale climate for your car in your market.

Remember, every used car is different, and local conditions always affect values. For example, there's a town in Oregon where almost everyone drives a pickup, so there's always a glut of used trucks on the market there. Take the same truck 40 miles down the road to a larger, more urban market, and it's worth $1,500 to $2,000 more. Yet those little books give us one number for that truck that's supposed to be good for more geography than Marco Polo covered in all his travels. (The western edition of one we subscribe to covers Arizona, California, Colorado, Guam, Hawaii, Nevada, New Mexico, and Utah.) And one of those big-name little books actually admitted to us that the numbers are exactly the same in every regional edition it publishes!

Another problem: the "retail" editions of many of those little 3-by-5-inch books that are typically sold in bookstores and on newsstands give estimates of high and low retail prices, but no wholesale prices. That's because they don't want to offend automakers and dealers, from whom they get much of their information. Check your town's main-branch library, which may subscribe to a more helpful edition—the one that shows both wholesale and suggested retail values. Ask for either the *Kelley Blue Book's Guide to Used Car Values* or *The NADA* (National Automobile Dealers Association) *Official Used Car Guide.*

Despite their limitations, those books are not a bad starting place to get a "big picture" feel for values. They will tell you whether your car is in the $10,000 or $15,000 ballpark, but they won't tell you reliably whether it's worth $9,700 or $11,200. And numbers for the same car can differ widely from book to book. (Be aware that many salesmen will pull out a book that gives lower prices when they're buying a used car and a book with higher prices when they're selling it.) If you have access to the Internet, you'll find that the publishers of those books have web sites where they provide estimates of both trade-in/wholesale and market/retail used-car values. The best-known sites are Kelley Blue Book (www.kbb.com), Edmund's (www.edmunds.com), and Pace Publications (www.carprice.com). Again, don't take these numbers too seriously. They are ballpark estimates at best.

There's an old saying: Nobody has a decision to make until somebody makes them an offer. Well, those little used-car pricing books don't contain any offers, and you shouldn't use them to make any decisions. To get a number you can rely on, you need some real offers.

PLAYING THE GAME

You'll get those offers by playing a little game some morning or afternoon, shopping your used car at a few stores near home or work, including one or two where you'll eventually be negotiating for your new car. (We're assuming that you've got a vehicle that someone might find attractive, not a heap ready for the wrecking yard.)

First, make sure your vehicle is clean and mechanically sound. Then phone a couple of dealerships that sell the make you own. As noted in chapter 7, your car should bring the highest price at stores that sell the same make, where it's a logical addition to the inventory. Ask to speak to the person who buys used cars. (Be sure to write down that person's name, with the correct spelling; a name is the only thing we enter and leave this world with, and most people respond more cordially to strangers who get their name right.) Tell him that you own a very clean, one-owner used car, giving details on the model, model year, and mileage. Say that you want to sell this vehicle because you're buying another one, and ask if he's interested. If he's not, he probably has more cars of that model and year than he needs, and you've saved yourself a useless trip. If he is, tell him you'll be there within the hour to have him check out the car. After you've generated interest at two dealerships for that make, drive to the first one, pull into the used-car side of the business, and ask for the person by name.

As he approaches, remind yourself that the average dealer sells about as many used cars as new cars, that used-car sales account for a much higher percentage of a dealership's net profits, and that a continuous supply of salable used cars is essential for the health of the business, whether new-vehicle sales are up or down. When consumer confidence is high and new-car sales are healthy, folks who would normally buy older used cars from independent dealers are likely to be trading up to the newer ones offered on franchised new-car dealers' lots. When consumer confidence is depressed and new-vehicle sales are down, more people opt for used cars, but there are fewer trade-ins of the late-model, low-mileage cars they'd like to buy. Since only two of three new-car transactions include a trade-in, and many of those are vehicles a dealership won't want for its own used-car department, every used-car manager needs additional sources of good used cars—especially the attractive one-owner cars that are his bread and butter. If you've got one, he is probably more interested in buying it than he wants you to know.

HERE'S THE SCRIPT

Tell him that you're planning to sell your car, you don't want the hassle of selling it yourself, you're visiting a few used-car dealers, and you'd like to know what he'd pay for it. If he asks why you're not trading it for another, say you're buying your sister's year-old Chevy.

He'll take the car, check it out, and come back with a figure. Whatever number he gives, you should say nicely, "That sounds low to me. I got the impression from a couple of other dealers that it was worth more than that to a good used-car operation." *Then bite your tongue and wait for him to say something.*

If he says that's his final offer, you've learned what you came in for. Thank him for his time and drive to another store.

With most used-car managers, however, the first offer is typically a lowball opener to see how easy and uninformed you are. He might increase his initial offer right away. More likely he'll ask what the other guys offered, or what you want for it.

FOLLOW THE BOUNCING BALL . . .

Remember that your objective is to find out how much higher he might go so that you can put a realistic wholesale value on your car. Your answer to his question will depend on the "value ballpark" your car is in. Here are some rough guidelines for answers that will help you get to a realistic number:

• If his offer was under $3,000 but not wildly out of line as an opener for your car, tell him that based on what you've heard elsewhere, you believe the car is worth *at least $500 more.*

• If his offer was between $3,000 and $5,000, tell him that based on other dealers' comments, you believe the car is worth *at least $750 more.*

• If his offer was between $5,000 and $7,000, tell him that based on what you've heard elsewhere, you believe the car is worth *at least $1,000 more.*

You get the idea. If your car's value ballpark is higher than these examples, raise your response accordingly.

Most important, after you respond with a "bump," bite your tongue again! Don't say another word until he says something in return.

If he says your figure is way out of line, ask him if that means his first offer was his best offer. If he says your number is high, ask him how high he thinks it is.

Chances are, he'll counter with a better number than his opener. At this point, tell him (if it's true) that you're the only owner, you've got all the maintenance records, you just had the scheduled service done last month, and all it needed was new brake pads. He's not going to have to invest big bucks in fixing anything.

Then pick a number halfway between your last figure and his, tell him you think it should be worth that much to him, *and bite your tongue again.*

At this point he might say it's not worth that much, that his last offer was his best one. Or he might agree with your new number and ask if you'd sell it to him for that price.

Your answer to either response should be, "I'll certainly consider it seriously. But first I'm going to make a few more stops. How long will your offer be good?" Make a quick note of the answer, tell him you'll get back to him in the next few days, thank him for his time, and head for your next stop.

However the discussion ends, you've learned your car's true wholesale value to that used-car operation. Remember, however, that one used-car department might be fully stocked and the dealer may not want your car unless he can "steal" it from you at a lowball price and wholesale it to a used-car dealer for a quick, easy profit.

To get a reliable estimate, you must repeat the drill at another dealership selling that make. Then, if the new car you plan to buy is that same make, your job is done. If it isn't, you should also get estimates from the used-car departments at the two new-car stores where you're most likely to do business. Be sure to ask each of them how long their offer will be good.

If you've got an older, lower-value car with 80,000 miles or more on the odometer, few new-car dealers will want it for their inventory, no matter what make it is. You should shop it at a couple of big independent used-car-only stores to determine its wholesale value.

You'll spend half a day researching your car's true wholesale value, but it'll pay off—especially a week later when a new-car salesman gives you a lowball trade-in offer for your car and you tell him that Joe Smith, *his used-car manager,* told you last week that he'd pay $1,000 more! And that's the wholesale truth.

Private individuals represent the majority of the used-car market. They've sold over $57 billion in used cars annually without taking trades, providing warranties or service.

Right or wrong, buyers will pay more for a privately owned car. Why? Trust.

—President of a consignment consulting firm that applies the real estate sales concept to the used-car market (quoted in *Automotive News*)

9

Who Needs a Middleman?

The best way to avoid getting used by a new-car dealer is to avoid trading in a good used car. Instead, sell it yourself to an individual. It's more work, but it pays awfully well. The difference between wholesaling it to a car store and retailing it yourself can be $1,000 to $2,000 or more for a mid-priced car in good shape. (Generally, the better the condition, the bigger the spread between wholesale and retail.)

Why give that much money to a middleman when there's bona fide demand for what you've got to sell?

Lots of people would rather buy a clean, well-maintained, one-owner car from an individual than take a chance on something from a used-car dealer. In fact, over 50 percent of used-car sales are between private parties. These folks think they'll get a better car for less money. Also, they typically can get the maintenance records from the owner, and knowing how it's been treated gives them more confidence in its worth.

This preference may be strongest among *nonsmokers,* who now number seven out of ten U.S. adults. Many of them will even pay a premium for a nicotine-free vehicle.

To get a feel for retail prices of cars like yours, it's okay to start by calling your bank or credit union to ask what the used-car book says. *But remember, that book wasn't written about your car in your market this month.* You need to do more homework.

REACHING OUT: LEARNING BY TALKING, NOT WALKING

Fortunately, you can do this homework on the phone. Check the ads in your weekend paper and in those used-car classifieds that seem to be everywhere. Call a few private sellers and ask about their cars—price, mileage, condition, equipment, type of driving done, and whether (a) they're the original owner, (b) they've got the service records, (c) they've permitted smoking in the car, and (d) the car has ever been in an accident. (Tell them you'd plan to have it checked by a mechanic who can tell.)

If they're asking $7,000 or more, find out how low they might really go by picking a number that's between $1,500 and $2,000 less and asking if they'd consider selling it for that price. If they refuse, bump the number in increments, starting with a couple of $500 bumps, followed by one or two $250 bumps, until you find a price they'd consider. Thank them and say you'll think about it.

Then mentally compare your car with theirs to see if you think yours is worth more or less. If the cars are roughly comparable except that they're smokers and you're not, yours should be worth at least $300 more to a nonsmoking buyer, no matter what year or model.

Next, call a few new-car stores that sell your make and ask for the used-car department. Tell them that you're looking for a good, clean used car that's the year, make, and model of the car you own.

If they have one, ask about the mileage, how it's equipped, the asking price, and (lastly) the color. If it's blue, tell them you want red or white and thank them. Don't give them your phone number.

If they don't have one, tell them that you'd prefer to buy from a reputable dealer than from an unknown private party, and ask what would be a fair price. When they quote a price and say they'll find one, say you'll think about it, but you want to talk to a few more dealers. Thank them, but don't give them your phone number.

If you don't get a satisfactory response by phone, visit a few dealers' lots some weekday morning around 8:00 A.M., when there are no sales-people there. Walk around and check the inventory for used cars like yours. Figure that realistic selling prices will be 10 to 15 percent below the retail asking prices on the window stickers.

This exercise will give you a good idea of what your car is worth at retail compared to other cars of the same year, make, and model.

Based on this research among private parties and used-car departments, you should be able to pick your expected price, the price you actually think you can get. Figure that this number is somewhere in the range between realistic dealer selling prices and the prices those private parties would "consider." Then choose a *slightly higher* number for your asking price, keeping it below the used-car department's asking price.

Next, have your car detailed to make it look beautiful inside and out, have the oil changed and all the other fluids brought to the right levels, and fix any obvious engine, brake, or wheel alignment problems that might shake a prospect's confidence during a test drive and kill a sale. Also make sure the radio, air conditioner, heater, defroster, lights, wipers, and turn signals work.

NOW YOU'RE THE CAR SALESMAN

Now you're ready to call your newspaper and those used-car classifieds to place a weekend ad that describes the good things about your car. The hot buttons (if they're true) are one nonsmoking owner, low mileage, very clean, and complete service record. The service record can be particularly reassuring to potential buyers, since many used-car swindlers buy high-mileage cars at auctions, roll back the odometers illegally, and then pose as private parties selling "pampered, one-owner cars."

Don't put a price in the ad. Just say, "MUST SELL," and add the hot buttons just listed, your phone number, and the best weekday and week-end hours to call.

When they call and ask, give them that slightly higher asking price you picked, but make it clear that you've got some flexibility. If they ask for your rock-bottom number, tell them that you haven't established one. Say that some other people are interested in the car, that it's a one-owner car that's been reliable for you, that you're sure somebody is going to like it a lot, and that you're confident you'll be able to work out an agreeable price with that person. Then ask if they'd like directions to your place and about what time you should expect them.

If they like the car when they see it but make an offer that's well below your asking price, assume that's not their final offer. Counteroffer somewhere in between, but still above the price your research said you can expect to get.

To create a greater sense of urgency and value, try the old car salesman's trick: Say you've been offered $450 more by someone who's coming back in the morning. If they really want the car, chances are good they'll raise their offer when they hear that, and your excuse for taking it will be a bird in the hand.

If they like the car but instead of making an offer they ask what your rock-bottom number is, tell them you really don't want to sell the car for much less than your asking price, that you've done a lot of comparison shopping and know it's a fair price for a clean, one-owner vehicle like yours. Then counter by shaving a couple of hundred dollars off your asking price, but stay well above your expected price.

Always bite your tongue and let them react to your counteroffer before you say another word.

If they react negatively, ask them what they'd be willing to pay. If that's ridiculously low, reject it politely and thank them for coming, adding that it's clear they aren't that enthusiastic about the car and you're sure someone else will be. If their willing-to-pay number is not that bad but still below your expected price, counter with that price.

Somewhere in this kind of firm but flexible exchange, you'll get a price you'll find acceptable, one that's a lot better than any car store will give you.

A NOTE OF CAUTION

Unfortunately, we live in a hazardous world. One of the risks you face in selling your car yourself is that it could be *stolen* by a prospective "buyer" during a test drive. The thief may even leave another stolen car with you. (He may be trading up.)

Here are some thoughts on handling this potentially delicate situation:

- Ideally, you shouldn't let anyone test-drive your car unaccompanied.

- But be wary. You wouldn't get into a stranger's car alone, so why would you get into your car alone with a stranger? If you don't have a tall, powerful friend to accompany you, don't go. Most prospective buyers would rather test-drive a car without the owner along anyway.

• It's perfectly proper to ask a stranger for identification before permitting a test drive. Check a driver's license and a credit card and require that he leave one of those items with you until he returns. If he carries no identification or won't cooperate, tell him that you're sorry but you won't allow anyone to test-drive your car without seeing and retaining proper identification.

• Trust your instincts. If you've got any reservations about a person, politely decline the request for a test drive.

• Some serious buyers will want to have your car checked over by a mechanic—an inspection they will pay for. That's a reasonable request, and a sign that you've got an excellent prospect. Again, however, you must be wary. You need a security deposit important enough to guarantee their return—perhaps a wallet full of important identification papers and credit cards, or their current car and keys, after checking the registration information against their other identification data.

Some prospects may be offended by your caution, but if you ask them to put themselves in your place, most will say they'd handle the situation the same way.

TIE UP THE LOOSE ENDS NEATLY

In closing the deal, be sure to do these important things:

• Get a nonrefundable deposit in return for taking the car off the market.

• Ask the buyer to get a certified check made out to you for the full sales price and to meet you at your bank at a mutually convenient time to sign over the title. Don't give possession of the car until this is done.

• Write out a sales receipt, in duplicate, that says you've sold the car "as is" for the agreed amount, and include the buyer's name, address, and driver's license number, plus the date, time of day, and both signatures.

• Call your state's department of motor vehicles to learn how to release your liability for parking and/or traffic violations and civil litigation resulting from operation after the date of sale. Obtain and complete the required form, and mail it promptly.

• Inform your auto insurance agent that you no longer own the car. He will advise you whether to transfer, suspend, or cancel your coverage.

We haven't tried to touch every base in this sell-it-yourself lesson. We've focused primarily on the money issues. If you have questions and need more counsel, you should call the financial institution that has your auto loan, your auto insurance agent, your state's motor vehicle department, or your local auto club for more information.

Now let's look at the issue of financing. (If you're paying cash, you can skip to chapter 11.)

*Let us all be happy and live
within our means, even if we
have to borrow the money to do it.*
—Artemus Ward

10

Auto

Financing

101

Always remember that everything that happens in a car store is designed to make money for that store. There's nothing wrong with that; it's our free enterprise system at work. And that same great system can work for you, too, if you take action at every step to keep it competitive. The first step is shopping for money, and the time to do it is *before* you visit any car stores.

DON'T GET REAR-ENDED

When you get down to negotiating a final deal, the salesman is going to want you to "buy" your financing money through his store. As indicated in chapter 5, that's an important source of his store's profit on the back end of the transaction.

That's when another interested party will get involved—the F&I (finance and insurance) manager. There is a lot of pressure on him to add profit to every deal. He usually gets a commission on anything you buy on the back end, including financing and the life and disability insurance he'll try to include in the transaction. In fact, some F&I managers make more money than any salesman in the store.

The dealership may arrange financing through a bank or finance company, or through the auto manufacturer's own finance subsidiary. These so-called captive companies, such as Ford Motor Credit or General Motors Acceptance Corporation, are very important sources of credit. (GMAC is the largest finance company in the country, with more than $100 billion in assets.) Depending on the automaker, its captive company typically handles between 30 and 60 percent of the consumer financing for its vehicles. It also finances dealer inventories. Nationally, captives provide about 40 percent of all new-car financing, roughly the same percentage accounted for by banks. Credit unions and independent finance companies account for the other 20 percent.

Understand, though, that no matter which company does the actual financing, the car store acts as a middleman and receives a commission or fee for its service. Most often, this income comes from a dealer finance reserve, which is the difference between the contract rate charged to the consumer and the retention rate earned by the bank or finance company.

As a rule of thumb, figure that a car store can *double* its gross profit on a sale if it arranges the financing. No wonder there's pressure there!

Depending on the deal with the lending institution, the car store's participation fee can amount to 5 percent or more of the loan. The longer the term and the higher the rate, the more interest you pay . . . and the more commission the car store receives.

Let's assume the dealer "buys" the money for an auto loan of $14,000 from a lending institution at 8.5 percent interest and "sells" it to you on a 48-month loan at 10.5 percent interest. Over a four-year period that little 2 percent spread will put a $645 profit in the dealer's pocket, nearly 5 percent of the loan amount.

SURPRISE: THE DEALER'S DEAL MAY BE A GOOD ONE

You may find that the financing available through the dealership is quite attractive. To stimulate sales, auto manufacturers frequently offer subsidized, lower-interest loans through their own finance companies—often as an alternative to a customer rebate or dealer cash incentive. (You don't get to "double dip." Customers get either a cash rebate or a below-market interest rate on loans as long as four or five years, but not both. Dealers get either the cash incentive or the cut-rate financing for the customer, but not both.)

Some automakers seldom use conventional incentives such as rebates or dealer cash because they feel they damage the image of their brands. But to boost sales of specific models, those same companies periodically offer 3.9 or 4.9 percent financing on 48-month loans when the going market rate is over 9 percent. Since the consumer doesn't perceive a reduced interest rate as a cut in the price of the car, the brand's image doesn't suffer.

Note, however, that dealers earn no commission on loans with super-low interest rates. If the captive finance company is paying 6 percent for money and loaning it to you for 3.9 or 4.9 percent, there's obviously no financing profit for automakers to share with their dealers. And sometimes, when there's an eye-popping rate as low as 1.9 or 0.9 percent, the dealer actually has to *contribute* money to get that financing for a customer.

Keep in mind, too, that manufacturers usually don't offer incentives *or* below-market interest rates on their hottest-selling models. They don't need to sweeten the deal when they're selling every one they can make, and dealers are stickier on prices when demand exceeds the supply. Conversely, the simple fact that incentives or below-market financing is offered for other models is a strong signal that they are not selling as well as the automakers would like, and that dealers will be more flexible on transaction prices.

Some manufacturers also have "recent college graduate" or "first-time buyer" financing programs to start building brand loyalty with a younger audience. The rates are typically higher than standard bank rates, but these programs are often geared to people who might not qualify for standard bank auto loans simply because they have little or no credit history.

So whether it's your first car or your twenty-first, the car store's current financing options are *always* worth checking out. But doesn't common sense say that you should be able to buy money cheaper if there's no middleman's commission for the financing entity to pay?

The only way to know whether the financing options the dealership presents are attractive is to shop competitively for money before you sit down in a negotiating session at the car store. Then you'll be able to compare the annualized percentage rates (APRs) charged under the different alternatives.

Unfortunately, many new-car buyers don't bother to check out their financing options before entering the F&I manager's den. The Consumer Bankers Association reports that about 80 percent of a bank's new-auto loans are originated indirectly, at dealerships, whereas only 20 percent result from buyers visiting the bank themselves to prequalify for a loan before they purchase a vehicle.

As a result, every year hundreds of thousands of car buyers who could have qualified for direct auto loans at lower rates end up paying a lot more money *to the same banks,* with the difference going to the car stores. Welcome to America, folks—the land where the average consumer is more interested in the convenience of one-stop shopping than in smart money management. Fortunately, you are not going to fall into that trap.

SHOPPING FOR MONEY: A PRIMER

As a first step, you should decide the highest monthly payment you can handle comfortably, *including auto insurance.* Call your insurance agent and tell him what vehicles you're considering. He'll be glad to tell you what your insurance will cost. (He works on commission, too.) He may even influence your final choice if you find that one alternative costs much less to insure than another.

Then decide on a down payment. If part or all of this will come from the sale of your current car, go through the steps in chapters 8 and 9 to learn what it's really worth under each of those scenarios.

CAUTION: DON'T DRIVE "UPSIDE DOWN"

As a general rule, we'd advise putting at least 20 percent down on any new vehicle and financing it over a maximum term of four years. If you can't handle those numbers without changing your lifestyle dramatically, you should buy a less expensive car. This advice may sound conservative, but it will help keep you from getting "upside down" when you want to sell or trade again.

You're upside down when the actual value of the vehicle is less than the principal you still owe on the loan. You've got negative equity in the car, and you'd literally have to pay someone to take it off your hands. Here's why it's easy to get upside down whenever you combine a small down payment with a long financing term (such as 10 percent down and a six-year loan):

• New cars are *terrible* investments. Knowledgeable people will tell you that, depending on the specific vehicle and the timing of your purchase, *most new cars or trucks depreciate from 15–20 percent to as much as 35–40 percent in the first few weeks you own them!* Only the most prestigious high-end luxury cars and full-size sport utility vehicles seem to hold their value significantly longer.

• Add the fact that your monthly payments will include more interest than principal until you get into the latter part of the payment schedule, and you can see how a car's value can go down much faster than your equity in it goes up.

This fact leaves you exposed to significant loss if your car is stolen or destroyed in an accident. Your insurance company will pay you the car's depreciated market value, but you may owe the bank or finance company much more. If you are unwilling to accept this risk, ask the lender about gap insurance, which covers the difference between the car's insured value and the amount you owe. This insurance could cost several hundred dollars over the term of the loan.

After you've decided whether to follow our 20 percent down, four-year rule or some other payment program, you're ready to contact some banks, your credit union, and other new-car financing sources. (If you belong to a credit union, you should start there. Credit union rates on auto loans are typically at least 1 percent lower than bank rates. One reason: Credit unions usually don't provide a participation fee to car stores.)

REACHING OUT AGAIN

Start this process on the telephone by calling a bank loan officer about car loans. Say that you're starting to shop for a new vehicle, that you want to line up financing first, that your credit report is clean, and that you'd like some help in finding the "price ballpark" you should be shopping in. (We'll assume that you're following our 20 percent down, four-year guideline.)

First ask for the bank's annualized percentage rates on car loans. They will typically be higher for lower down payments and, sometimes, for longer payment schedules.

Tell the loan officer that you'd like to learn how large a loan you can afford if you put 20 percent down and finance a car over four years. Then take the total monthly payment you decided on, subtract one-sixth of the semiannual auto insurance premium, and ask how large a four-year loan you could pay off with the remainder.

Add to that loan amount the down payment you decided on previously, and you'll have the *maximum price* you can afford to pay under those terms. (Remember, that total must cover state and local sales taxes, license and title fees, and any other up-front costs. Since license fees can be substantial, you should call your state's licensing agency and ask for an estimate of the fee for a car in your price range.) Then consider whether it's reasonable to expect to buy any one of the vehicles you're interested in for that price or less, given what you'll learn in chapter 15 about what they cost the dealer.

If your maximum affordable price is a lot lower than the dealer's invoice cost, and there's no current consumer rebate offer or factory-to-dealer incentive program, the answer is probably no. That means you've got to lower your sights to a less expensive vehicle, find more down-payment money, or ignore the 20 percent down, four-year rule and risk getting "upside down."

HERE'S SOMETHING THAT MIGHT HELP

Before you make that call, use this amortization table to determine what the monthly payment would be for a three-, four-, or five-year loan.

As you can see, we've chosen annual percentage rates from 2 to 14 percent. This range covers the territory from automakers' highly subsidized below-market rates to sky-high levels that folks with good credit won't pay unless double-digit inflation returns. The dollar amounts in the table are the monthly payments per $1,000 borrowed. For example, assume you're borrowing $13,500 for four years at an annual percentage rate of 10.5. To calculate your monthly payment, go to the 10.5 percent column and find the payment per thousand for a four-year loan—$25.61. Multiplying that number by 13.5 (the number of thousands you're borrowing) gives you the monthly payment—$345.74.

MAKING THEM COMPLETE

You should shop for a money deal as aggressively as you're going to shop for that auto deal. Financial institutions are in a competitive business, too. (They "book" only about two-thirds of the auto loans they approve.) Let them know you're shopping their competitors, and you'll borrow where you get the best terms.

It's worth the extra effort. Assume you borrow $15,000 on a four-year loan. If you can drop the interest rate just 1 percent by shopping competitively, you'll save over $300 in interest payments.

If your local bank quotes a rate higher than what you were quoted by a bank five miles away, tell the loan officer you'd prefer to do business in

MONTHLY PAYMENTS FOR THREE-, FOUR-, AND 5-YEAR LOANS

Payment Factors per $1,000	Annual Percentage Rates				
	2.0	**2.5**	**3.0**	**3.5**	**4.0**
3-year loan	28.65	28.87	29.09	29.31	29.53
4-year loan	21.70	21.92	22.14	22.36	22.58
5-year loan	17.53	17.75	17.97	18.20	18.42
	4.5	**5.0**	**5.5**	**6.0**	**6.5**
3-year loan	29.75	29.98	30.20	30.43	30.65
4-year loan	22.81	23.03	23.26	23.49	23.72
5-year loan	18.65	18.88	19.11	19.33	19.57
	7.0	**7.5**	**8.0**	**8.5**	**9.0**
3-year loan	30.88	31.11	31.34	31.57	31.80
4-year loan	23.95	24.18	24.42	24.65	24.89
5-year loan	19.81	20.04	20.28	20.52	20.76
	9.5	**10.0**	**10.5**	**11.0**	**11.5**
3-year loan	32.04	32.27	32.51	32.74	32.98
4-year loan	25.13	25.37	25.61	25.85	26.09
5-year loan	21.01	21.25	21.50	21.75	22.00
	12.0	**12.5**	**13.0**	**13.5**	**14.0**
3-year loan	33.22	33.46	33.70	33.94	34.18
4-year loan	26.34	26.58	26.83	27.08	27.33
5-year loan	22.25	22.50	22.76	23.01	23.27

your neighborhood but his bank's rate is higher. Ask if that's absolutely the best he can do. He may have to get approval from another manager, but banks are in business to sell money, and you may find there's room to negotiate. It's also common for a bank to give a slightly lower rate if you have an account there and the monthly payment is deducted automatically.

You can do a lot of comparison shopping on the telephone. In many cities you can even arrange your loan by telephone, calling in your application and getting an answer within a day or two.

Frequently, however, in-person meetings are advisable when you get down to two or three loan finalists, especially if you sense anything less than an enthusiastic response on the phone. Financial institutions want to build relationships with successful people, and being well-groomed and well-dressed can help create the right climate for loan approval.

Here are some more tips on financing.

1. Shop the Dealers Against the Financial Institutions

You should bargain aggressively to get the best interest rate from dealers. Usually they have some flexibility. After reviewing your credit application, the automakers' captive finance companies often give dealers a range of interest rates they can charge you, with a low and a high number.

The best tactic is to make the dealer compete with your bank or credit union's best rate, and vice versa. Here's how one Fighting Chance customer reported on his experience:

> I had a preapproved rate of 8.25 percent from a credit union. When the Chevy dealer's finance manager quoted 8.75 percent, I declined, stating the lower rate. He said he would match it. The next morning I called the credit union and told them I was going with GMAC. They said they would match GMAC or do better. I said I was tired of all the options, just give me your best rate. They gave me 7.85 percent, and GMAC could not match it.

Incidentally, you will find *Money* magazine's web site on the Internet (www.money.com/rates) a useful resource for current interest rate information for auto (both new and used) and home-equity loans. It typically lists rates and phone numbers for the major financial institutions in each market, but not for credit unions or automakers' captive finance companies. The site also has a calculator that gives you the monthly payment when you enter the loan term, the annual interest rate, and the loan amount.

2. Explore "the Non-Auto Auto Loan"

You may find, as *Fortune* suggested in one of its investor's guides, that "a home equity credit line is a cheap, tax-smart way to buy a new car." That's because interest is tax-deductible on home equity borrowings up to $100,000, whereas other personal loan interest (including interest on standard auto loans) is not. The Consumer Bankers Association reports that about 10 percent of home equity loans are used to finance autos.

Home equity loans and lines of credit come in many forms, with either fixed or variable interest rates, and with or without "origination points." In most cases, you'll probably pay a lower *effective rate* than you would for a regular car loan, simply because the interest is deductible.

For example, if you're in the 28 percent tax bracket and the loan's annual percentage rate is 9.5, your net effective rate after taxes is only 6.84

percent. That may be significantly lower than any standard car loan rate you're likely to find. (We're not CPAs. You should check with your tax adviser for the best counsel.)

Another side to this that you should keep in mind is that with this type of financing, you'll be pledging *your home* as collateral. If there's any reason to be nervous about your ability to make those payments, you might sleep better with a standard auto loan, knowing that all they can repossess is your car, not your roof.

You should also note that Congress has become alarmed by a decline in the equity held by homeowners, caused in part by a sharp rise in tax-deductible home equity loans used for vacations and auto purchases. The lawmakers have asked the General Accounting Office to investigate equity borrowing. There's a possibility that Congress will move to curb these tax advantages sometime in the future. *This makes it mandatory that you check with the appropriate tax counselor before proceeding.*

3. Beware of the Credit Insurance Rip-off

Don't get pressured into buying credit life insurance as an add-on. You'll often find this item buried in the mouse type in your auto loan documents. These policies are very profitable to both the insurance companies and the sellers—financial institutions and auto dealers, who can earn commissions of 30 to 50 percent.

Money magazine reported that these policies pay out an average of only 38 cents in benefits for every dollar of premium, compared with 83 cents for the typical life insurance policy! And a spokesperson for the National Association of Insurance Commissioners has urged consumers to be particularly cautious of an insurer recommended by a *lender,* who is "going to be looking for the product with the highest commission, and that's usually the company that charges the highest premium."

By law, the purchase of credit life insurance cannot be a precondition for receiving a loan. Yet many people buy it. Ford Motor Credit Corporation reported that of the automobiles financed through a dealership, half of Ford's customers buy credit life insurance and 30 percent buy accident and health (disability) insurance. It's reasonable to project similar numbers for the other major auto manufacturers' captive credit operations.

If you feel you need any type of extra insurance coverage, discuss it with the agents you or your friends and relatives already deal with, and chances are you'll save a lot of money. Standard life and disability insurance policies are generally much better buys.

4. Remember that Finance Terms Are Less Favorable on Used-Car Loans Than on New-Car Loans

Financial institutions will lend a lower percentage of the purchase price for used cars, and they'll charge a somewhat higher interest rate. If you're considering a previously owned vehicle, it's even more important that you shop rates aggressively.

The bottom line: If you follow the steps we've suggested in this brief financing lesson, you'll be in a good position to determine whether the financing available at the car store is an attractive alternative for you or just a good deal for them.

A LITTLE TRAVELING MUSIC

We thought it would be appropriate to end this chapter with a song—one that F&I managers can sing to themselves on coffee breaks. So we've written these parody lyrics to the tune of that old standard, "Pennies from Heaven:"

Every time they finance here
It's pennies from heaven.
It's tough to keep my conscience clear
With all these pennies from heaven.
This really easy money just falls in my cup.
You'd be amazed how quickly
Those little pennies add up.
All those banks and credit unions
Think people are crazy,
But we know one thing they don't:
People are lazy.
We give them one-stop shopping,
They don't know that they pay.
So there's pennies from heaven here every day.

Once harm has been done, even a fool understands it.
　　　　　　—Homer, *The Iliad*

11

Right Brain, Left Brain

After talking with thousands of car shoppers, we are convinced that the purchase of a new car is primarily a right-brain decision.

If your left brain could talk, it would say that no one needs a new car to get from point A to point B, that there are plenty of good used cars that will do the job just as well and save you a bundle, too. In response, your right brain would say that life is to be gulped, not sipped—that our time on earth is too short to drink wine from a box, eat any ice cream but Häagen-Dazs, or drive someone else's problem.

People buy new cars because they feel they deserve them. New cars are about self-esteem and reward for hard work. They are toys that provide gratification for the kid who lives inside every grown-up. They are also accessories that we wear like suits, dresses, or cellular phones—visible statements of who we are, or at least who we'd like others to think we are.

Given the strong emotional tug of the product, our selection criteria tend to be more subjective than we admit. Do I like the way that car looks? Do I look great in it? Has it got an awesome stereo system? Do I like the way it handles? Will the trunk hold four bags of golf clubs? Does it have enough cupholders?

Of course, we all claim to have practical criteria. But, truth be told, often the only controlling one is whether we can afford the monthly payment. If we can, and it's a great-looking car that fits our image of the perfect personal chariot, we'll buy it. We justify that right-brain decision with some left-brain rationale ("It's got four-wheel drive, so it'll go better in the snow"). But mainly we're buying what we want, not what we need.

On one level, there's nothing wrong with that. All the fun stuff happens on the pleasure side of the brain, and what's life without pleasure? It's only natural for someone who spends the equivalent of three or four weeks in a car each year to want a comfortable "home away from home." *But in that decision process, most of us don't give enough consideration to the critical issue of the safety differences between one car and another.*

BE SAFE, NOT SORRY

The time to research the safety question is *before* you form an emotional attachment to a specific vehicle. New cars are very seductive, and once you've committed to one in your mind, it's difficult to view it objectively. The kid in you wants it in your garage *now.* And if safety negatives turn up late in the selection process, it's easy to rationalize that the safety equipment mandated in the last couple of decades has made all cars safe.

True, every new passenger vehicle must meet the federal standards that specify minimum safety levels. Those standards now include the installation of air bags, the highest-profile auto safety devices in history—and a high-tech panacea. We've got front-impact air bags and side-impact air bags and head-impact air bags, and someday we'll probably have roof-impact air bags. Encouraged by the government's PR campaign and the automakers' marketing hype, lots of Americans think they're riding around in a bubble-wrapped cocoon, insulated from harm.

Wrong.

Air bags work, but not nearly as well as originally projected. When the National Highway Traffic Safety Administration (NHTSA), part of the U.S. Department of Transportation, mandated air bags back in 1977, the agency calculated that air bags alone would reduce the fatality risk in all crash modes by 40 percent. As reported in the *Wall Street Journal,* NHTSA's subsequent study of accident experience found that an air bag reduces this risk by 13 percent for unbelted drivers and by just 9 percent for the other two-thirds of drivers who use their seat belts. These reductions are certainly worthwhile, but they're a far cry from the original promise. Some auto safety experts have concluded that the same increase in protection could be obtained simply by driving a car that's 200 pounds heavier. And they worry that air bags encourage a false sense of security among drivers of smaller cars.

Safety Lesson 1 is a no-brainer: *Just as rock beats scissors and match beats paper in that old kids' game, big beats small in a car crash.*

We can't repeal the laws of physics. When a big car and a small car smack into each other at highway speeds, the folks in the big car will probably walk away, but all the king's horses and all the king's air bags might not be able to save those in the small car. In relation to their numbers on the road, small cars experience more than twice as many occupant deaths each year as large cars. So everything else being equal, you should buy the biggest, heaviest car you can afford. If you're considering buying a cute little subcompact for a teenage daughter or son, you'll sleep much better if you spend the same amount on a used Ford Crown Victoria. (Your child won't like it as well, but heck, it's still free wheels.)

GIVE SERIOUS WEIGHT TO RELATIVE CRASHWORTHINESS

Unfortunately, most of us can't afford leviathans-of-the-road like Cadillac Sevilles, Lexus LS 400s, and Chevy Suburbans. So we need to pay close attention to Safety Lesson 2: *All autos are* not *equally safe, even if they're essentially the same type, size, and weight.* Some vehicles are inherently safer than others in a serious crash because they are structurally sounder, and the choice you make could turn out to be a life-or-death decision for you or someone you love.

Fortunately, reliable crash test data are available from two main sources. One is the National Highway Traffic Safety Administration, which has been conducting head-on tests since 1978. In these simulated tests, the entire front of each vehicle hits a rigid barrier at 35 miles per hour. In recent years, NHTSA has also been conducting side-impact crash tests in which a car traveling 17 mph is hit from the side at 34 mph. Tested vehicles receive scores from five stars (highest) to one star (lowest).

The other major source of crash test data is the Insurance Institute for Highway Safety (IIHS), an independent, nonprofit research and communications organization wholly supported by automobile insurers and dedicated to reducing crash deaths, injuries, and property damage losses. Since 1995 the IIHS has been conducting 40-mph "offset" crash tests in which only part of a vehicle's front end hits a formidable barrier, simulating a two-vehicle collision at an angle, driver's side to driver's side. This frontal-offset test provides a good indication of a vehicle's structural performance in serious crashes. Results are scored good, acceptable, marginal, or poor. Many of these tests have been shown on TV in prime time on network news magazine shows.

The NHTSA full-front and IIHS frontal-offset crashes complement each other. Ideally, a vehicle should perform well in both tests. You can find the results in magazines like the *Consumer Reports* annual auto issue, published each April. But these tests are conducted year-round. For the most recent information, we strongly suggest that you visit the web sites of these organizations. You will find the NHTSA data at www.nhtsa.dot.gov/cars/testing. The Insurance Institute for Highway Safety is at www.hwysafety.org.

How much stock should you put in these crash test results?

A great deal, we believe. You will probably be surprised at some of the vehicles that score poorly. Based on the results, there are always several relatively popular automobiles that we would not drive around the block if the automakers gave them away free. Of course, those automakers will claim that the tests are flawed, while the ones whose vehicles score well will use the results in their advertising. But the tests are what they are. One vehicle scores better than another because it's structurally sounder in that crisis situation, period. And if the manufacturer of the low-scoring vehicle has better results from its own crash tests, it can show us the film. (Strangely, manufacturers never do.)

This isn't a money issue; it's about your life and the lives of your loved ones. The purchase of a new car may be mostly a right-brain decision, but this is the one area where you should give your left brain total control early in the selection process. You may not decide to buy the highest-scoring vehicle, but you definitely should avoid any vehicle that gets the worst score on either test (one star on the NHTSA tests or poor on the IIHS test), even if you love everything else about it and have a $2,000 rebate coming on that automaker's affinity VISA or MasterCard.

Your chance of being in a similar crash is relatively small. But you can't control what another driver does on the open road, and if one ever crosses that double yellow line and plows into your family car, you'll be glad it didn't get one star or a poor rating in these tests.

A postal worker took his year-old car to a dealership in Providence, Rhode Island, for an oil change. To kill time while he was waiting, he browsed the showroom, admiring a fancy new sports car. Three salesmen converged on him.

Within minutes he found himself in the credit manager's office, loudly proclaiming that he wasn't in the market for anything new except oil. Before he knew it, he owned that sports car and a five-year payment schedule totaling $40,000.

He sued the dealership for engaging in deceptive trade practices. According to the Associated Press, his lawyer said, "I don't think he actually realized any paperwork had gone through. They made [him] feel empowered and enthusiastic about purchasing a new car. But the fact is [the dealership] took him for a ride and left him financially stranded."

12

The Fine Art of Shopping Without Buying

While you're working on determining what your car is worth, deciding whether to sell it at wholesale or retail, and getting your financial ducks in a row, you should also get to know some new cars well enough to narrow your choices to two or three finalists. You've been salivating over new-car ads for months. You know which models seem most appealing. Maybe you attended the annual automobile show when it came to town. You've devoured the model-year buyer's guides published by

Car and Driver and *Road and Track,* which usually appear on supermarket shelves in late fall. You've studied the annual new-car issues of *Money* magazine, *Kiplinger's Personal Finance Magazine, Consumer Reports,* and other sources for safety, economy, reliability, and insurance cost ratings.

Even with all this information, narrowing your choices may not be easy. Domestic and foreign manufacturers typically offer 500 to 600 passenger car models for sale in the United States each model year!

The real challenge, however, isn't the number of cars; it's the number of car salesmen. You need a safe and secure way to get through the test-driving and information-gathering stage without getting caught up in the juggler's act. Here's how to accomplish that and live to tell about it.

First review Psychology 101 in chapter 4, especially the part about projecting total emotional detachment. Then play the little game outlined next.

MAKE THIS AN AWAY GAME IF YOU CAN

If you live in an area that has several dealers for each major make, gather your information at car stores that are relatively farther from your home or office. That way, when you're ready to start serious negotiations with stores closer to home or work, you'll be an unknown quantity, without the implied commitments of previous visits. (The less a salesman knows about you, the less money he'll get from you.)

That doesn't necessarily mean you should ignore those more distant stores in your final negotiations. Indeed, you may drive a better bargain with them because they'll see you as business they normally wouldn't get. They may agree to a lower gross deal just because you're an out-of-town bird in hand. But, as you'll learn in chapter 20, there are real advantages to buying your new car from a dealer who's more convenient, ideally the one who'll service it regularly.

Plan these trips by checking the dealer association's advertising in your newspaper, where you'll probably find the names and addresses of all the dealers for a given make in your metropolitan area. You may even find a map showing their relative locations. (Dealers love to put maps in their ads!)

Choose the stores you'll visit, grab a pen and a pad to take detailed notes, *leave your checkbook and your credit cards at home,* and jump in your car.

Your objective on this trip is to narrow your choices to a few specific cars that will meet your requirements and make you a happy driver for the next several years. Smile, this is going to be fun!

THE GAME PLAN

As you enter the showroom, walk briskly to one of the younger-looking, less experienced salesmen. Tell him you're just starting to look at new cars, and yes, you do plan to buy one soon. But no, you're not a candidate to buy one today under any circumstances. There are several makes you want to research and test-drive before making a decision.

You have no idea what you'll end up buying. It'll depend on a lot of (unspecified) things. But he's got a couple of cars that are on your list, and you'd like to test-drive them, learn about their features and benefits, and get some literature to review at home.

While you're in this tire-kicking stage, test-drive at least two different cars you like at each dealership. Make those test drives long enough to put the cars through most of the paces you'll require of them everyday. And be sure to drive cars equipped the way you think you'll buy them. Don't test an automatic transmission if you want a stick shift, or the four-door sedan if you want the coupe.

Even if you love both cars, try not to show it. Remember that your behavior should say: A car is a car. I'm going to check them all out and buy the best deal.

When you're around that salesman, act undecided, uncommitted, even a little wishy-washy. For each car, comment on things you like and things you don't like. (If you like everything, invent a few things you don't like.) That will keep him from moving into his aggressive selling posture with the "if" questions designed to get verbal commitments, such as, "If I got you the right price, would you buy this car today?" When he asks that, your correct answer is, "Not today. As I told you, I'm just starting to narrow my choices. I've got more appointments to test-drive cars today and tomorrow, and I plan to keep them."

ANYTHING YOU SAY WILL BE USED AGAINST YOU

Remember, the one who asks the questions controls the conversation. So ask him all the things you need to know, such as, "What rustproofing warranty comes with the car?" and, "What specific direct consumer incentives is the factory offering this month on the cars you sell?" And one he probably won't answer in detail, "What specific factory-to-dealer cash incentives are in effect this month?"

But when he asks you questions, your stock answers should be, "I don't know," "I'm not sure," "I need to discuss it with my spouse," and "I'll have to think about that." When those get tired, answer a question with a question—for example, "How do most people answer that?"

In this little game, you'll get the information you need, but he'll get nothing concrete to move toward his objective of closing you before you leave. Remember, he's in a sell-it-now-or-never business, but you're in a don't-buy-it-now mode.

After test-driving cars you particularly like, write down the key information from the *manufacturer's* window sticker (not the dealer's separate sticker): the vehicle identification number, model number, and suggested retail price for the base car, plus the contents and prices of the optional factory equipment packages and other accessories.

Then thank the salesman for his time. Take his card, but don't give him your phone number or address. If he discovers that you live two gas stops from his store, he'll decide that it's now or never and try to chain you to a chair until you buy.

Above all, don't get roped into his office to talk about anything, including the weather. He's going to want you to sit down for a minute "just to see what it looks like on paper." Tell him politely that you're not ready to do that, and that you've got appointments to test-drive three other makes. Both statements will be true.

If you live in a smaller market without many dealers for the same make, you can't play the game exactly like this. But the essential rule still applies: *You want to get all the information you need while giving him none of the information he needs.*

NARROW THE FIELD, BUT NOT TOO MUCH

After a day or two, you should be able to narrow your choices to a few favorites. Try to keep at least two or three in the running. The big winners in this game will be those who maintain several options right down to the finish line. A single choice isn't an option, it's an obsession—one that's potentially very expensive.

SHAKE THE FAMILY TREE

One good way to open options is to consider "family relations," vehicles that have different brand names but are made by the same manufacturer on the same platform and are quite similar. The key differences are often in trim levels and suspension systems. For example, one might be aimed at older, more traditional buyers who value a cushy ride, another at younger auto enthusiasts who want tighter handling characteristics and more feel of the road. There also can be meaningful price differences.

For example, Chrysler's mid-size sedans, the Dodge Intrepid and Chrysler Concorde, are essentially similar vehicles at different price points. Ditto for the Ford Taurus and Mercury Sable, and the Chevy Blazer and GMC Jimmy.

At any time, there could also be hefty manufacturer incentives offered on some family members but not on others.

If you like one branch of a family tree, you may like another almost as well. And pricing and incentive differences may be meaningful enough to swing your choice to a vehicle you hadn't considered at the start.

Here is a list of "family relations," some of which are the products of joint ventures between automotive manufacturers (for example, GM and Toyota). While these relationships can change over time, with some older models discontinued and new ones added, automakers will always offer different vehicles that share common platforms as a way to produce cars more efficiently.

General Motors (and Partners)

- Buick LeSabre, Oldsmobile Eighty-Eight, and Pontiac Bonneville
- Cadillac Seville (four-door) and Cadillac Eldorado (two-door)
- Chevrolet Astro and GMC Safari vans
- Chevrolet Blazer, GMC Jimmy, GMC Envoy, and Oldsmobile Bravada
- Chevrolet Camaro and Pontiac Firebird
- Chevrolet Cavalier and Pontiac Sunfire
- Chevrolet Express and GMC Savana vans
- Chevrolet Lumina (four-door) and Monte Carlo (two-door)
- Buick Century and Regal
- Oldsmobile Intrigue and Pontiac Grand Prix
- Chevrolet Malibu and Oldsmobile Cutlass
- Chevrolet Metro and Suzuki Swift
- Chevrolet Prizm and Toyota Corolla
- Chevrolet S-Series pickups and GMC Sonoma pickups
- Chevrolet Silverado pickups and GMC Sierra pickups
- Chevrolet Suburban and GMC Suburban
- Chevrolet Tahoe, GMC Yukon, GMC Denali, and Cadillac Escalade
- Chevrolet Venture, Oldsmobile Silhouette, and Pontiac Montana minivans
- Oldsmobile Alero and Pontiac Grand Am

Chrysler

- Chrysler Concorde and Dodge Intrepid
- Chrysler Cirrus, Dodge Stratus, and Plymouth Breeze
- Chrysler LHS and Chrysler 300M
- Chrysler Sebring Coupe and Dodge Avenger
- Dodge Caravan, Plymouth Voyager, and Chrysler Town and Country minivans
- Dodge Neon and Plymouth Neon

Ford (and Partners)

- Ford Contour and Mercury Mystique
- Ford Crown Victoria and Mercury Grand Marquis
- Ford Escort and Mercury Tracer
- Ford Expedition and Lincoln Navigator
- Ford Explorer and Mercury Mountaineer
- Ford Ranger pickups and Mazda B-Series pickups
- Ford Taurus and Mercury Sable
- Mercury Villager and Nissan Quest minivans

Others

- Honda Passport and Isuzu Rodeo
- Nissan Maxima and Infiniti I30
- Toyota Camry V6 XLE and Lexus ES 300

CONSIDER THE BIG HIDDEN COST: DEPRECIATION

As you're assessing alternatives, remember that the most significant cost of car ownership isn't gas or maintenance or repairs or insurance. It's depreciation—the difference between what you pay to acquire it and what you'll get when you sell it as it moves down the automotive feeding chain. Some cars retain their value better than others, and you should factor these differences into your thinking.

Here's an example. Ford's Taurus and Honda's Accord are family sedans in the same general price range. Yet the Automotive Lease Guide's residual value tables consistently show that the wholesale value of a two-year-old Taurus LX sedan will be about 50 percent of its original sticker price (MSRP), whereas a two-year-old Accord LX will command about 60 percent of its sticker. Thus, if you negotiated the same price for each, you'd save about $100 a month over two years by choosing the Honda. To check projected depreciation for the vehicles you're considering, you may purchase the latest bimonthly issue of the Automotive Lease Guide's *Residual Percentage Guide* from Chart Software; call (800) 418–8450.

COMPARE THE WARRANTIES

If several vehicles appeal to your eye, some may look better than others after you compare their basic bumper-to-bumper warranties. The industry standard is 36/36,000, which means that most parts of the car are covered for manufacturers' defects for 36 months or 36,000 miles, whichever comes first. (Typically, the battery and tires are not covered by the basic warranty.)

If you check the warranty table in chapter 19, you'll note that some automakers offer better basic coverage than others. As an example, assume that you like the Honda Passport and its cousin, the Isuzu Rodeo, equally well. Honda's basic warranty is 36/36,000, but Isuzu's is 36/50,000. If you drive substantially more than 12,000 miles a year, that difference may tip the scales in Isuzu's favor.

CHECK THE COST OF REGULAR MAINTENANCE

Every new vehicle comes with a booklet that outlines the maintenance schedule recommended by the manufacturer. The booklet is free, but the service is expensive. (New-car dealers make most of their profits from parts and service, and that little booklet is a major source of their continuing prosperity, whether car sales are up or down.) As with insurance premiums, the cost of regularly scheduled maintenance can differ from one vehicle to another.

To get a handle on this, call the local dealerships for the models you're considering and ask to speak to a service adviser. (This is the person who meets customers as they drive in and writes up each service order.) Make this call in mid-afternoon, when most of his contact and follow-up with that day's customers is behind him. Tell him which car you're considering buying, and say you're interested in learning about the costs of recommended maintenance. Inquire about the mileage intervals for regular service in the first two years, and ask him to tell you the approximate costs for each visit.

IF YOU'VE GOT A QUESTION, CALL HOME

If you can't get all your important questions answered by people at a dealership, try calling the manufacturer. (You'll find a list of their phone numbers in appendix A.)

THE SMART SHOPPER'S TIEBREAKER

If you're having difficulty choosing a favorite, here's an idea that beats flipping a coin: Consider *renting* each finalist for a day or so on weekends, as a way to learn more than you can in those brief test drives. This will set you back a few dollars, but the rental cost pales in comparison to the financial and emotional cost of buying the wrong car.

You may have to make several calls to find what you want, but most popular domestic and import models can be rented. In fact, many dealers rent cars by the day.

However you narrow the field, remember to retain one or two fallback choices. At this stage, throwing away alternatives is throwing away leverage.

Now, they finally have a car do what GM said it would do—compete on a quality basis with small Japanese cars, specifically the Honda Civic—and the most creative thing they can come up with is a no-haggle pricing policy that, while supposedly for the benefit of the consumer, is really just another price hike in disguise.

—A consumer responding to a *Business Week* cover story on Saturn

13

Saturn:

A Different

Kind of Deal

The folksy, down-home ad campaign for GM's Saturn subsidiary carries the tag line "A Different Kind of Company. A Different Kind of Car." They could add, "A Different Kind of Deal."

There's apparently a lot to like in Saturn, General Motors' version of a Japanese subcompact. It's earned high customer satisfaction ratings in the J. D. Power & Associates Initial Quality Studies[sm]. *Car and Driver* called it "the luxury econocar, tightly built and brimming with niceties." It also holds its value relatively well as a used car.

Designed as an import fighter, it's doing its job well: About half of Saturn's customers would have opted for an import instead. And seven out of ten sales have been to people who would not otherwise have bought a GM product.

But the biggest difference between Saturn and the rest of the auto industry isn't in the car, it's in the deal. *There isn't any.* If you want a Saturn, you'll pay the full sticker price, even if the sales manager is your brother-in-law. The reason: *There's no competition between dealers for your business. And there isn't going to be any.*

THE KEY: ELIMINATING COMPETITIVE GEOGRAPHY

In essence, Saturn isn't a car, it's an idea—one designed to extract the maximum amount of money from customers, while simultaneously using a neat bit of psychology to convince them that it's for their own good.

Here's how GM pulled that off. Starting with a clean sheet of paper, Saturn was able to give each dealer a large, exclusive sales territory. Because each market area has only one retail "owner," price competition is effectively eliminated between dealers. This exclusive selling territory could be one part of a huge market, like Los Angeles, or the entire metropolitan area of a smaller market, such as San Diego. In effect, GM has taken one of the most competitive retail businesses and made it noncompetitive for this brand.

With no other Saturn dealers within a reasonable shopping radius, you won't be able to play one dealer off against another to negotiate price. And though no one will admit it, there is clearly a gentlemen's agreement among dealers to follow the company policy and have no price competition between neighboring market areas (such as Los Angeles and San Diego). Although GM says that a dealership may charge what it wishes, the cold, hard fact is that the sticker price is the real price. *Think of it as a legal form of retail price-fixing.*

It's also Saturn's policy not to offer rebates or other incentives—which saves GM anywhere from $500 to $1,500 per vehicle, depending on the competitive climate.

The bottom line for even the well-informed consumer: *You'll pay at least $1,000 more for a Saturn than you would if Saturn had been, say, just another Chevrolet model instead of a separate GM division with an exclusive-territory dealer network.* And the normal market forces of supply and demand will have no impact on transaction pricing.

The bottom line for dealers: They make a lot more money under this exclusive-territory pricing umbrella. With guaranteed front-end gross profits per sale of about $1,600, Saturn is the most profitable small-car franchise by a country mile. Plenty of large-car franchises would gladly trade bottom lines with any Saturn store.

The J. D. Power & Associates Dealer Attitude Study[sm] measures new-vehicle gross profitability per dealership, which is derived by multiplying the average gross profit per vehicle times the average number of new vehicles sold per dealer. In one study, Saturn ranked second only to Lexus on this measurement and was just ahead of Mercedes-Benz, BMW, and Toyota. The average Saturn dealer's new-vehicle profits were four times those of Dodge, five times those of Volvo, seven times those of Lincoln-Mercury, eight times those of Volkswagen, nine times those of Cadillac, and over ten times those of Buick. Wouldn't you like to be a Saturn dealer when you grow up?

The financial picture isn't nearly as rosy for General Motors. The company spent about $5 billion to launch Saturn, and it's not clear whether the stockholders will ever see an adequate return on that investment. (Chrysler's subcompact, the Neon, which sells almost as well as Saturn, was launched with just a $1.3 billion investment.) Small cars don't produce big profits per unit—except, of course, for dealers with exclusive territories who sell them at the full sticker price.

HAVING THEIR CAKE AND EATING IT: A PSYCHOLOGICAL COUP

Fixed pricing doesn't seem to hurt sales: Over the years, Saturn has often sold more new vehicles per dealer than any other auto franchise, including Ford, Chevy, and Toyota (which sell both cars and trucks).

Ironically, Saturn's "no-dicker" sticker is a key ingredient in its success because it eliminates the haggling over price. In the showroom, for a refreshing change, Saturn customers are treated like honored guests. The salespeople simply help them fall in love with the car, tell them that the sticker price is fair, and (most important) assure them no one will get the car for less. No sales pressure is applied.

In grateful response, Saturn buyers pay more than they would for comparable small cars sold by dealers willing to negotiate and factories willing to use incentives. Most of them don't have a clue that the dealer's profit on their purchase is much greater than he could realize with any other small-car franchise. They're so focused on the new-and-improved purchase process that they actually enjoy paying more.

The halo of this more pleasant shopping experience carries over to enhance customers' ratings of the vehicle itself. (Isn't a diner more likely to praise the food when the chef has been a superb host?) These ratings, in turn, enhance Saturn's used-car value as it moves down the automotive feeding chain. Its resale value has been above that of most domestic makes and comparable to the best of the Japanese competitors.

Who are these Saturn buyers? Once, at a research industry gathering, we met one of the most influential automotive consumer researchers and asked him that question over lunch. His answer: "The cream puffs, the people who absolutely can't handle any kind of confrontation, however mild." He added, "Look at the folks they put in their commercials. They're not the most sophisticated shoppers, not people who will typically research dealer cost and incentive information and take a strong stance in a price negotiation. Saturn meets their needs perfectly by taking the anxiety out of the shopping process."

You could almost call it a Saturn cult. To illustrate, think of the mindset you'd have needed to attend that "Saturn Homecoming" several summers ago in Spring Hill, Tennessee. Over 40,000 happy Saturn owners actually drove clear across the country to spend a few fun-filled days in sweltering heat, humidity, rain, and mud to eat GM's hot dogs, tour the Saturn plant, and swat at mosquitoes big enough to have numbers on their sides. Now there's a vacation to savor!

Saturn has a unique market niche. It's a good car, but probably no better than most of the Japanese subcompacts. Making it about as reliable as this formidable competition is a great step forward for GM. But Saturn's major accomplishment was finding and exploiting the "hook" that gets customers to pay the full sticker price—a tribute to American marketing genius.

Saturn's product line will change over the years, as larger "trade-up" vehicles are added to take advantage of Saturn owners' brand loyalty. But the prognosis for prospective customers is "more of the same." More profit for dealers because of exclusive sales territories. Perhaps more aggressive price increases than for other domestic cars. And no deals for anyone.

WHAT'S A SHOPPER TO DO?

You've got two choices. *If your heart's set on a Saturn, your first choice is to relax and enjoy it.* It's a good little car, and you're striking a blow for U.S. economic resurgence. Instead of haggling over price, you'll be treated like visiting royalty. And why shouldn't you be? You're paying the sticker price!

(Think about it for ten seconds. If you called any dealer in the United States and told him you were on your way down to pay the sticker price for one of his cars, he'd probably send a chauffeur-driven limousine to pick you up, if only to keep you from stopping at another car store on the way. At that price, you'd have a wonderful sales experience anywhere.)

The Saturn dealer might make three times the profit on your purchase that he's making selling more expensive cars in his non-Saturn stores. But you'll have the consolation of knowing that the next customer will make a similar contribution to his welfare. No one will walk in and get the car you bought for $1,000 less. It seems almost un-American, doesn't it?

Here's choice number two: *If Saturn is only one of your finalists, you should shop the competition aggressively.* Among subcompacts, that includes the Toyota Corolla and Chevy Prizm, Ford Escort and Mercury Tracer, Nissan Sentra, Mazda Protegé, Honda Civic, and Dodge and Plymouth Neons. Saturn accounts for less than one of every twenty passenger cars sold. You may like some of the other nineteen better, and you shouldn't have to pay the sticker price for any of them.

Facing more flexible dealers and frequent factory incentive programs, you may even discover you can afford a higher trim level in another car for the price of Saturn's lower-level offering. As one reader wrote in response to *Car and Driver*'s comparison of several subcompacts:

> Except for the Saturn, all the cars in your comparison could be purchased for well below the sticker price, including sound system and air conditioning. Only Saturn dealers refuse to dicker. The real competitors in the Saturn's price range are the four-door upscale models of the cars you tested. Saturn offers good value, but in the real world it is not necessarily the best buy.

Warning: Historically, Saturn dealers haven't exactly led the league when it comes to trade-in allowances for your used car. Many customers relax their guard in that no-pressure sales situation and end up accepting lowball offers. Don't let that happen to you. Reread chapters 7 and 8, and be sure you know the true wholesale value of your current car before you enter Saturn's seductive web. And remember, if it's a desirable, late-model car, but not a Saturn, you'll probably get more for it from a dealer who sells that same make.

It's worth noting that the sun doesn't shine on the same dog every day, and the automobile business is no exception. There have been years when Saturn sales were down instead of up—partly because there are only so many people who will buy into the Saturn proposition, but mostly because GM waits too long to make design changes and the car was starting to look really dated.

In that situation, GM and its dealers have found creative ways to be more competitive *and* still get the full sticker price for every car. GM will offer highly subsidized leases through GMAC, with inflated residual values and below-market interest rates providing low monthly payments. (The consumer doesn't perceive an interest-rate cut as a cut in the price of the car, though it has the same effect.) For the dealers' part, they give inflated trade-in values that are more than the cars are worth at wholesale. So you *can* get a deal at the Saturn store if you're shopping when sales are down, but you'll get it on the back end of the transaction.

Saturn *is* a different kind of company. Creating exclusive sales areas is a terrific idea for both the company and its dealers. Most automakers would probably love to "Saturnize" their retail distribution systems, which would mean fewer dealerships, less competition between dealers for our business, and higher prices for their cars. We estimate that Saturn buyers are paying an extra $250 to $300 million yearly, compared to what they would pay if GM had made the car the Chevrolet Saturn or the Pontiac Saturn. Indeed, there is a growing body of evidence that no-dicker sales policies come with significantly higher transaction prices, for both new and used cars. (You'll find more data on this in chapter 14.) If all automotive franchises were set up the Saturn way, U.S. consumers would spend billions of dollars more on basic transportation every year.

Saturn has carefully crafted an image as perhaps the most consumer-oriented company in history, but the bottom line is that consumers are paying a lot more for its products than they would if Saturn dealers faced the retail price competition that all other dealers face. If that's being "consumer-oriented," we're all in trouble.

GM says its research indicates the consumer is unhappy with the traditional new-car purchase process and wants the stress-free shopping experience that comes with no-dicker pricing. Sure, but did GM ask if the consumer was willing to pay an extra $1,000 or more to avoid negotiating the price of a $15,000 car? We doubt it. (If we asked if you wanted to go to heaven, you'd say yes. If we asked if you wanted to die in the process, you might say no. And if you woke up in heaven, wouldn't you want to check the morning paper to see if your name was in the obituary column?)

Does this mean that you shouldn't buy a Saturn, or even that Saturn is a poor value for the dollar? Of course not. Value is in the eye of the beholder. Each individual must decide what it's worth to him or her to avoid the haggling process. There are plenty of good cars in Saturn's price range that don't sell for the sticker price. But if you've got your cap set for a Saturn, go for it. It's a good car.

If our assessment of Saturn seems a little harsh, please remember that our job is to help you keep an eye on your wallet. If there are things going on in the marketplace that the automotive establishment would prefer to hide from consumers, and if the information is public (we have no "inside contacts" in any of these companies), we believe it's our job to share the facts so that you can make the decision that's right for you. The commercial media aren't going to share these facts because they live in daily fear of angering—and losing—their automotive advertisers.

A LITTLE MORE TRAVELING MUSIC

We think Saturn needs a company song, one the dealers can sing to celebrate their good fortune at annual sales conventions. So we've written one called "You Gotta Be a Saturn Dealer," to be sung to the tune of "You Gotta Be a Football Hero," a song you may have heard your father sing.

> You gotta be a Saturn dealer
> To make the max when you sell 'em a car.
> You gotta have exclusive rights to the town
> 'Cause that guarantees the price can't come down.
> To find another Saturn dealer
> They'll have to drive to Timbuktu.
> You gotta be a Saturn dealer
> To see what's really in this business for you.
> You gotta be a Saturn dealer
> To sell this great new American car.
> There's lots of other great little cars,
> There's only one hitch, they can't make you this rich.
> So save your tears for General Motors.
> They're five billion bucks in the tank,
> But they made me a Saturn dealer,
> So I'm cryin' all the way to the bank
> (They pay the sticker),
> I'm cryin' all the way to the bank
> (So will my mother),
> I'm cryin' all the way to the bank.

14

It's a marketing gimmick that dealers use, just like red tag sales, Labor Day sales, you name it. And if you say it's going to sweep the nation and it's going to all one-price dealerships, you're crazy. It's not going to happen. It's simply not going to last.
—Executive vice president of the Greater Los Angeles Motor Car Dealers Association (quoted in the *Long Beach Press-Telegram*)

"No-Dicker" Dealers and the Retail Revolution: Oasis or Mirage?

Before Saturn's initial sales year ended, it had become clear to the automotive establishment that Saturn's greatest achievement was getting American car buyers to pay the sticker price for every car, and that the key to pulling off this startling coup was the elimination of haggling over price. Success in any field breeds imitation.

Other dealers, watching Saturn's apparently magical scenario unfold, decided to play follow-the-leader. They had seen the new religion, and they were converting—dumping their high-pressure sales forces and becoming one-price, "no-dicker" dealers.

That "fair" price would be somewhere between the sticker price and the dealer invoice price. It would be noted on a separate "civilized sticker" placed on each car, and there would be no bargaining. What you see is what you pay. And what everyone else pays.

There are now somewhere between a few hundred and just over a thousand no-dicker dealers—a small fraction of the more than 22,000 franchised dealerships. Some make the switch in desperation, when sales are so poor they have nothing to lose. Others simply want to reap the short-term benefits of doing it first in their markets; they plan to return to their old selling approach if several competitors also adopt a no-dicker policy. And some see it as a long-term strategic move to give their store a unique appeal to the consumer segment that hates to negotiate prices.

Let's examine how this pricing transplant works, from both the consumer's and the dealer's perspective.

FOR THE SHOPPER, THERE'S LESS THERE THAN MEETS THE EYE

As you might expect from the Saturn model, customers at other no-dicker stores pay higher transaction prices than customers at stores where prices are negotiable.

J. D. Power and Associates conducted a study of 24 dealerships that had adopted the system relatively early. The key finding, widely reported by the Associated Press, was that no-dicker dealers make more profit. (Otherwise, why do it?) Nine out of ten dealers reported increased sales since adopting the program. And half the dealers said their average gross profit per car had gone up; the other half split equally between those whose profits were the same and those with lower profits per sale.

A separate study—this one on *used*-car stores—produced similar findings. In recent years, a number of big-money players have launched chains of used-car "superstores," with acres of cars, fixed no-dicker prices, and a no-pressure, no-haggle shopping environment. Perhaps the best known is Republic Industries' AutoNation USA chain.

CNW Marketing Research surveyed 2,900 used-vehicle transactions. They found that customers routinely paid more at dealerships that don't haggle—including those used-car superstores—than at those where there is give-and-take over price. For example, they paid:

- $481 more for a Ford Taurus
- $588 more for a Dodge Caravan
- $646 more for a Toyota Camry
- $694 more for a Ford F-150 pickup
- A whopping $937 more for a used Chevy Suburban

Now imagine yourself driving home smiling in that previously owned Chevy Suburban. You pull into your driveway. Your neighbor pulls into his, behind the wheel of the same sport utility vehicle. You compare notes and learn that he paid $937 less by haggling the price at a Chevy dealership down the street. Wouldn't that wreck your whole day?

From a consumer standpoint, there's another unfortunate consequence of those used-car superstores coming to town: By charging higher, no-haggle prices for used cars, they enable the new-car dealers in town to get higher prices for their used vehicles. According to a separate study conducted by CNW Marketing Research, traditional dealerships are able to charge an average of $500, or 3.4 percent, more than they did before the opening of a superstore in the market. "A superstore sets prices that are reasonable firm," the study said. "That gives competing franchised and independent used-car dealers something simple to aim at. They then lower their asking prices for comparable vehicles, but simultaneously raise the 'take' or transaction price." That narrows the negotiation wiggle room for consumers.

Overall, these studies suggest that the no-dicker system does what it was designed to do: It gets the consumer to pay more, just as Saturn customers do. But Saturn customers at least have the satisfaction of knowing that no one will buy the same car for a lower price tomorrow, or next week.

Is that true for the other no-dicker stores? No. The J. D. Power and Associates study indicated that today's price is just that, and tomorrow's price is anybody's guess.

- The research showed that 33 percent of no-dicker new-car dealers changed their "civilized" prices as factory incentive programs changed.

- Another 29 percent of the dealers changed prices as their inventory conditions changed.

- Fourteen percent of dealers changed prices "when they needed to boost volume," another 14 percent changed them weekly, and 10 percent changed them every two or three days!

So buyers may enjoy the shopping experience, but they'll pay more for the car, and someone else may pay less for the same car tomorrow. And in most cases, they'll still have to dicker over their trade-in allowance and deal with the F&I manager on financing and back-end options.

Does that sound like what you expected, or hoped for, when you heard about one-price, no-dicker dealers? We don't think so.

BEWARE OF CAR SALESMEN BEARING DOUGHNUTS

We decided to do our own research on the subject, and we concluded that one-price stores should be required to post "Buyer Beware" signs, just as cigarette packages carry mandatory warnings. Shopping incognito with a newspaper reporter, we walked into a big no-dicker Ford dealership, where there was coffee and doughnuts and absolutely no pressure. The salesman just walked us around the lot, where the price of every car was on the windshield. He said business was up 42 percent since the store switched to one-price selling—an amazing statistic considering that this had to be one of the highest-priced Ford stores in the state. Its price on a mid-line Taurus was one the village idiot could have beaten by at least $1,000 with one phone call to any other Ford store in the city. Yet business was up 42 percent! Clearly, the store's customers were lulled into lowering their guard by this "we're-on-your-side" selling approach that set them up for the big tumble, which they never even felt. One more triumph for American marketing ingenuity.

To avoid becoming the next victim, remember Bragg's Golden Rule: Whether it's Saturn or one of the Saturn wanna-bes, assume that the more pleasant the purchase experience, the more gold is being lifted from your wallet. Sadly, it's often true that the lower the pressure, the higher the price.

FOR THE DEALER, NO-DICKER IS NO NIRVANA

If car stores make more profit with no-dicker pricing, as both research and empirical evidence suggest, you might logically ask why all dealers don't adopt this selling policy. These are the key reasons:

• In most large markets, there are several dealers for the same make. Chevrolet and Ford, for example, each have over 4,000 dealers nationally. When one adopts a no-dicker policy, he becomes a sitting duck for the others, who can cut prices selectively to steal his customers.

• The 80/20 Rule of Life still applies. Many dealers are reluctant to give up their shot at making a killing on the least knowledgeable 20 percent of buyers, the ones who probably provide 80 percent of the profits.

• In effect, one-price selling says to the customer, "Pay it or go somewhere else." That's not a message most dealers want to deliver. They'd rather make a small profit than lose the sale to a competitor.

• No-dicker is a better strategy for tough times, when sales are hardest to come by. When consumer confidence and sales traffic are strong, no-dicker makes less economic sense to dealers. As a spokesperson for the National Automobile Dealers Association said in response to questions about the no-dicker movement, "Dealers sell the way they do because it works. They are real wizards at local marketing, and they do what works."

• Finally, and most important, the bulk of dealers can't change to no-dicker successfully unless the customer changes, too. But the customer has been trained under the current system, the one dealers use "because it works." What are the chances of most shoppers buying a car at the first price offered? Slim indeed. After decades of 20,000 dealers shouting "shop us last" in their advertising, the cumulative impact has taught consumers that there will always be a better price down the street. As a result, research consistently shows that most new-car buyers prefer to negotiate prices.

As a former mega-dealer in Los Angeles said before he closed his last store, "People will shop you silly, and they should, too. . . . Sooner or later, someone will sell you a car for the price you want."

The lesson for the smart shopper: *The no-dicker dealer is a useful tool. Use him!* If the price is friendly enough, buy from him. If it's not, use it as a place to start negotiating with other dealers. To win your business, they'll have to beat it, maybe by a lot.

Eventually, most no-dicker dealers realize they've got a problem they can't solve: Without a Saturn-like umbrella of exclusive sales territories, they don't have a fail-safe formula. It's like grafting an eagle's wings onto a pigeon: That pigeon can soar, but without talons it can't catch fish.

Some companies, however, are working on the problem.

REASON FOR CONCERN: STORM CLOUDS ARE FORMING AT THE RETAIL LEVEL

As we've noted, to make a no-dicker policy work, the automakers must reinvent their distribution channels. Some of them are moving in that direction. We are in the early stages of a revolution in the retail automobile business, the long-term effects of which may not be consumer-friendly. It's unlikely to change the automotive landscape quickly, but it's something to be concerned about in the future.

General Motors and Ford, who account for over 50 percent of the market, have concluded that they must reduce the number of dealers dramatically to eliminate low-volume stores and reduce distribution costs. They see a future in which cars are sold through fewer, bigger showroom outlets, perhaps at fixed, no-dicker prices, with a greater number of "satellite" service facilities scattered conveniently throughout a market.

This consolidation is happening initially in markets like Tulsa, Salt Lake City, Indianapolis, Rochester, and southern California's San Fernando Valley. There are several possible business models. The automakers could buy all the dealerships of a given make in one area and establish a joint venture with the dealers in another. They could also work with a third party such as Republic Industries, which has been buying many of the largest and most successful new-car dealerships as well as launching its chain of used-car superstores.

Whatever the business model, the net effect in the markets involved will be to reduce the number of car stores and make the business less competitive. This is not good news for consumers, because if Ford controls all the Ford and Lincoln-Mercury stores in Tulsa, it can enforce a no-dicker sales policy.

This revolution, if it continues, is not likely to engulf the entire country overnight, for several reasons:

• First, thousands of car dealers are very successful, very independent entrepreneurs who will be reluctant to sell their businesses while still in their working prime and even more reluctant to work for someone else.

• The plan doesn't work unless all the dealers in the market go along, and it will be next to impossible to get all the dealers in the largest 20 or 30 markets. So consolidation is more likely to happen in the smaller and medium-size markets. But with telephones, fax machines, and the Internet, consumers in the affected markets can easily shop prices in other markets, just as many do today.

• Automakers accounting for almost half the market don't seem to be joining the revolution. The import makes aren't over-dealered like the domestics, so consolidation is not a major issue for them. (If Honda and Toyota dealers will make a deal with you but Ford dealers hold to fixed prices, guess who will win.) And Chrysler seems to be less aggressive than Ford and GM; it's planning to tinker with its dealer network, but without making dramatic changes. So it's reasonable to assume that a major portion of the market will continue to sell cars the traditional way.

We have no crystal ball on the subject, and anything could happen over time. But we believe most new-car pricing will remain negotiable, for the simple reason that most folks prefer it that way and makes and dealers that eliminate that option will lose a lot of business. As one new-car dealer put it, "The no-dicker approach to car selling is not a positive. When competitors adopt that method, it helps us. Most Americans want to negotiate. They have a touch of the horse trader in them, and the only time they can test their trading skills is when they purchase a car."

Consumers are always going to seek out the best deal; if it's not in their city, they'll find it somewhere else. Only Saturn had the benefit of starting from scratch. The other automakers let the retail pricing genie out of the bottle a long time ago, and it will be very tough to put him back.

Over the long term, we believe the competitive market is going to set the price, not the car companies. Supply and demand: It's still the law.

The bottom line from chapters 13 and 14: No-dicker pricing means higher transaction prices, and the Saturn business model is anticompetitive, and therefore anticonsumer. If these policies ever become the norm in the retail automobile business, consumers will suffer, not benefit.

P.S.: DON'T CONFUSE A MANUFACTURER'S "VALUE-PRICING" OFFERINGS WITH NO-DICKER PRICING

There's another, related pricing practice. It's usually called "value pricing," and it's used most often by General Motors (and to a lesser extent by Ford). Typically, the company packages certain models with a standard list of popular options and offers them for an attractively low price as "consumer marketing editions." Often these editions are sold only in certain states, but the dealers there also sell the regular models with standard national pricing.

There are three things you should understand about value pricing:

1. You usually won't find it on the exciting new models. Value-priced cars are almost always models that badly need updating. General Motors' goal is to replace its models every four or five years, as the Japanese do. But that doesn't always happen, and it's hard to get today's prices for yesterday's sheet metal. In that scenario, GM's big idea is value pricing. It's a tactic that can help for a while, but in the new-car business you eventually have to offer the consumer cars that are truly new.

2. Value pricing usually contains a healthy dose of smoke-and-mirrors. That's because the automakers achieve a big part of the retail price "reduction" simply by cutting the dealer's gross profit margin. Recognizing that most buyers don't pay the sticker price, they reduce the MSRP to a number that's closer to a realistic transaction price. As an example, if the old pricing provided a $2,500 spread between the dealer invoice price and the MSRP, value pricing might reduce the built-in profit to $1,000. *Is that a real price reduction?* Of course not, because the MSRP wasn't a real price in the first place. If you subtract thin air from thin air, you don't save any real dollars.

3. Some of the retail price reduction also comes from money the automakers save on incentives, since rebate and factory-to-dealer cash programs usually don't apply to these special editions. (Although you can occasionally find incentives on value-priced cars that are selling very poorly.)

The manufacturers and their dealers would like to sell these cars on a one-price, no-dicker basis. They won't, because most domestic makes are sold by thousands of dealers competing with each other. As Ford's general manager said, "We can suggest a price, but if the market won't bring it, the dealers are going to cut into their gross to make the deal."

These specially equipped and priced vehicles can be great buys. And if you shop around, you're likely to find some price flexibility, too. Our advice: If you live in or near a major market, don't pay the MSRP for any value-priced car, because there is another dealer nearby who will sell the car for less.

15

Learn the Cost or Pay the Price

It happened at a convention of the National Automobile Dealers Association in Dallas. The president of Chevrolet's Dealer Council got up and asked his cohorts to sell one more Chevy a week, even if they made no profit on it.

Why? Because that would mean another 250,000 Chevys sold each year, giving GM billions more for new-product programs over the next few years. (And you thought those guys had no heart.)

O f all the insights we've gained from Fighting Chance customers, this is the most important: *Most dealers agree to several slim-profit deals each month with customers who have done their homework and know how to use it.*

What's a slim-profit deal? For a popular mid-priced family sedan, just a few hundred dollars over the dealer invoice price, not counting incentives (which would reduce the price further). For a high-end luxury import, from $1,500 to $3,000 over invoice.

Why do dealers who make a killing with some customers agree to slim-profit deals with others? For four key reasons:

1. First and foremost, they're in a sales-driven, ego-driven business. At the end of each month, the first question anyone asks is, "How many cars did we sell?" not, "How much profit did we make on each deal?" By definition, almost any sale is a good sale.

2. Frequently, a dealer's future supply is based on his current sales performance. It's called "turn and earn." Most dealers are terminal optimists, and they want to be sure their vehicle allocation will always be sufficient to support their dreams. In this business, an extra sale today means an extra sale tomorrow.

3. Once they understand that you're a knowledgeable shopper who will negotiate a slim-profit deal, they'd rather take the slim profit than give the sale to a competitor. Selling one more car this month and making a modest profit always beats not selling it and making no profit.

4. Finally, since they make the bulk of their profits from parts and service, they want that vehicle out on the road, where it will generate a steady income stream. (Parts and service account for less than 15 percent of the average dealership's gross sales, but more than 50 percent of net profits.)

The centerpiece of your ability to negotiate a slim-profit deal is your knowledge of what the vehicle is going to cost the dealer. With that information, you'll know whether the deal is a good or bad one before you agree to it. That, of course, is the last thing the dealer wants you to know. He wants his salesmen to negotiate based on the sticker price, not the cost.

Frequently, after we make this point on a radio talk show, the first caller is an irate dealer who says, "What right has anyone got to know what I pay for the products I sell? You don't know what a retailer pays for a TV set or anything else you buy." Our response is always the same: "Yes, but you don't get home with your new TV and learn that your neighbor paid $100 less for the same set because he knew something you didn't know. As long as you auto dealers have a selling system geared to take advantage of uninformed people, the public has a right to public information to protect itself." End of debate.

IT'S A THREE-PIECE PUZZLE

Three key elements determine the dealer cost of any vehicle:

1. Dealer invoice price—the actual factory invoice billed to the dealer.

2. Factory-to-dealer incentives—cash paid *only* to dealers for selling specific cars within specific periods, details of which are not widely publicized to consumers.

3. Dealer holdback—a portion of the factory invoice price that is collected and "held back" by the manufacturer, then refunded periodically to the dealer as the vehicles are sold. Holdback has been used for decades by General Motors, Ford, and Chrysler. In recent years, almost all imports have adopted the concept. Today holdback applies to nine of every ten vehicles sold in the United States.

Without learning about all three elements, you can't get a good fix on what the dealer pays for a given vehicle. Let's tackle them one at a time.

THE STARTING POINT: DEALER INVOICE PRICE

The dealer invoice price is the actual price billed by the factory, the "invoice" the dealer must pay when the vehicle is delivered to his lot. (Typically, the dealer pays the manufacturer with money he borrows under his "flooring plan" credit arrangement with a bank or finance company or with the auto manufacturer's finance subsidiary. He pays the lender interest until the car is sold, then repays the loan.)

To determine this figure, you need a printout of dealer invoice prices for the specific vehicles you're considering. To get familiar with the kind of information contained on a printout, turn to appendix B and look at the simplified pricing data we've created for a fictitious car and manufacturer, the All-American Speedster, built by the All-American Motor Corporation.

Our simplified printout for the All-American Speedster contains the following information:

• The dealer invoice price and the manufacturer's suggested retail price (MSRP), which is the price you'll see on the sticker attached to the window of each new car or truck. Note that the list shows pricing for all available body styles and trim levels, from the least expensive low-end Speedster model to the most expensive high-end model.

- Just below the initial price table, a complete listing of all the standard equipment items included in the base price of each trim level.

- Dealer invoice and retail price information for all available factory-installed optional equipment and accessories, including those sold as packages and groups.

- The factory code number, in the column on the far left. This is the manufacturer's computer code, the number by which each model or accessory is ordered or identified, just as it appears on the window sticker of a new car or truck.

It's important to have a printout covering all the configurations a manufacturer offers for a given vehicle. Without the complete picture, you can't make price/value comparisons between different trim levels. For example, a higher trim level frequently represents a better value, because it includes standard equipment in the base price that would be treated as extra-cost options in a lower trim level.

BUILDING YOUR WORKSHEET

Once you have current pricing printouts for the vehicles you're interested in, you can determine the dealer invoice cost for the specific models you want, outfitted with the exact optional accessories and equipment you choose. To illustrate how easy this is, we'll build a simple worksheet using the pricing data we've created for our fictitious car—the All-American Speedster.

- Let's assume you're interested in a Speedster wagon. You don't want the lowest trim level (A), but you can't justify spending more than $3,000 extra for the highest trim level (AAA) because you really don't need things like luxury cloth upholstery and a tachometer. So you settle on the middle trim level (AA, factory code S87), with a sticker (MSRP) price of $15,200 and a dealer invoice price of $13,000. Note that we have entered these numbers on the new-vehicle worksheet on page 82.

- Looking at the preferred equipment packages available for the AA wagon, you're attracted by factory code 444B, which includes air conditioning, rear window defroster, AM/FM stereo radio-with-cassette, power door locks, power windows, and cruise control. The package price is less than the items would cost separately. The retail price is $1,800; the dealer invoice price is $1,500. We have added these numbers to the worksheet.

NEW-VEHICLE WORKSHEET

Factory Code #	Model and Optional Equipment	Dealer Invoice Price	Suggested Retail Price
S87	All-American Speedster AA 4-door wagon	$13,000	$15,200
444B	Preferred equipment package (air conditioner, rear window defroster, power door locks, power driver seat, power windows, cruise control, AM/FM/cassette, P205/65R15 SBR blackwall tires)	1,500	1,800
947	3.8-liter V-6 engine upgrade	470	560
314	Rear-facing third seat	130	160
	Subtotal	15,100	17,720
	Add: Destination Charges	+500	+500
	Subtotal	15,600	18,220
	Subtract: Direct consumer rebate	−750	
	Factory-to-dealer incentives	−200	
	Dealer holdback	−532	
	Grand Total	$14,118	$18,220

• You'd also like to have a more powerful engine than the standard 3.0-liter V-6. Looking at the equipment and accessories list, you see that you can add a 3.8-liter V-6 (factory code 947). Sticker price: $560; invoice: $470. These numbers are also placed on the worksheet.

• The only other item you want is a rear-facing third seat (factory code 314). This adds $130 invoice, $160 retail, to our worksheet.

• We must also add the $500 destination (freight) charge. Note that there is no markup on freight; the dealer simply charges the buyer what the manufacturer charges him. Note also that the sticker price does not include sales taxes or license and title fees.

• Adding the subtotals in the two columns, we find that there's a difference of $2,620 between the suggested retail price ($18,220) and the dealer invoice price ($15,600). This difference is a starting point for understanding the dealer's real cost, but it's not the whole story, as the last few lines of the worksheet imply. We'll return to those lines later in this chapter.

We'll discuss in chapter 21 exactly how to use this dealer invoice cost information in the negotiation process. For now, let's just say that the $2,620 difference between the dealer's cost and the retail price allows significant room for price movement—in your direction.

PRICING CREDENTIALS YOU CAN COUNT ON

At some point in the shopping process, a salesman is likely to tell you that your information on invoice prices is wrong. If you received your pricing data from us, you may confidently invite him to take out the vehicle's actual invoice for a comparison.

The reason you can be confident in the numbers is at the bottom of every page you receive, where the copyright notice cites "Chek-Chart" as the source. Chek-Chart Publications, a division of Macmillan Publishing USA, has been publishing *The New Car Cost Guide* since 1956. This is the *original* pricing guide for new cars, and it has set the standard for timely, accurate, reliable, and complete data.

Chek-Chart's *New Car Cost Guide* is used by loan officers in financial institutions, car rental and leasing companies, fleet administrators, insurance adjusters, purchasing agents, and other automotive professionals. These people must have accurate pricing data to do their jobs. And both the vehicle manufacturers and their franchised dealers have a vested interest in the ability of these people to do their jobs.

We are a Chek-Chart licensee. They keep our pricing data current with regular computer updates.

THE MONRONEY DOCTRINE

That sticker on the window of every new car is known in car-store jargon as "the Monroney," after Oklahoma's Democratic Senator A. S. "Mike" Monroney, the lawmaker who sponsored the 1958 bill that mandated its presence. (Be sure to refer to it as "the Monroney" early in your negotiations, and the salesman will know he's not dealing with someone who just fell off a turnip truck.)

Monroney's federal law requires that label to include the make, model, and identification number of the vehicle; its suggested retail price and the retail price of all factory-installed options not included in the base price; and the amount charged to the dealer for delivery to his store.

It's a federal crime to remove or alter that sticker before the vehicle is ultimately delivered to the purchaser. This effectively prevents car stores from replacing the original with a higher-priced sticker if a manufacturer raises the price on subsequent shipments of the same vehicle.

TRUCK BUYERS, BEWARE

Unfortunately, there's one gaping loophole in the law: It doesn't apply to pickup trucks, which represent about one-fifth of the automobile market. In the vast majority of cases, you will find the Monroney label on pickup trucks. But you may find a few car stores that have replaced the original stickers on some. Manufacturers frequently increase prices during the model year, and some dealers may take advantage of this loophole to change the stickers on their trucks to the latest price, regardless of when they were purchased.

How can you detect this sticker exchange? In a couple of ways. First, look for the EPA label, which contains the federally mandated fuel economy information. This labeling almost always appears on the lower portion of the Monroney sticker, but it may appear legally as a separate label. If a pickup truck's mileage estimates (city MPG and highway MPG) are on a separate label, there's a chance that the other sticker, with the pricing information, has been changed.

If you have doubts, compare the sticker formats on the new cars on the lot with those on the new *trucks*. If they differ considerably, that's another indication the dealer may have replaced the Monroneys with his own stickers.

How should you deal with suspected sticker switchers? *Our advice would be not to deal with such a dealer at all, unless he comes clean.* Ask to see the original Monroney. Check the VIN (vehicle identification number) against the one on the car. It's at the base of the front windshield, on top of the dashboard on the driver's side, where the police can find it easily. If the dealer won't cooperate, find a car store with nothing to hide. There will be plenty of them.

In addition to the invoice price, two other factors influence the dealer's real cost. We'll now look at one of them—factory-to-dealer incentives.

THE INCENTIVES GAME

When Chrysler hired Joe Garagiola in the late 1970s to stand up on TV and say, "Buy a car, get a check," he changed the fundamentals of new-car marketing forever. Enticing buyers with direct cash rebates opened a Pandora's box that no one can close.

You'll read periodically that "manufacturers have decided to raise prices by cutting incentives." The number of incentive dollars spent per vehicle tends to rise and fall somewhat with changing market conditions. But as one industry analyst put it, "Incentive programs are like hard drugs; once you get on, it's hard to get off." The consumer has been trained to expect incentives, and fierce competitive pressure will keep them around as long as there's excess production capacity.

In a strong new-vehicle market, the average incentive offered by U.S. manufacturers per car sold will be close to $500; when times are tougher, that number can shoot to more than $1,000. Even the Japanese, immune to the "incentive disease" for years, now spend similar amounts on incentives, with Nissan and the second- and third-tier companies spending relatively more than Toyota or Honda.

Understand, however, that this $500–$1,000+ range is an average, spread over all the vehicles sold. Some better-selling cars and trucks never need incentives on current models, while other vehicles in a manufacturer's line often carry incentives well above these averages. And some vehicles always seem to have a modest incentive, as a defensive measure against competitors' offers.

Who's paying for this? *You,* the car buyer, of course. *That extra $500 to $1,000+ is simply built into the price of the car.* If the car you're buying has an incentive, that money should end up in your pocket. If it's a customer rebate, that shouldn't be a problem. Dealers will readily share details on rebates, since that money comes from the manufacturer. (You'll sign a paper authorizing the automaker to credit that cash to the dealership.)

But wait, there's more to this incentive game than customer rebates.

The Other Side of the Incentive Coin

Did you ever sit there in front of late-night TV and wonder how so many dealers can shout about "prices below dealer invoice," implying that they're selling them for less than they paid? What they're trying to do, in dealer jargon, is "create a sense of urgency" that will get you off your couch and into their showrooms. The best way to do that, apparently, is to convince you that they're almost giving those things away.

But how can dealers sell cars and trucks for less than they cost? The answer, of course, is that they can't. At least they can't for long and stay in business, and who wants to buy a car from a dealer who's about to go out of business?

So, when they spend all those ad dollars implying that's what they're doing, are they telling us less than the whole truth, or even misleading us? The answer lies somewhere between yes and no. Yes, because a dealer can sell cars all day long for less than he paid for them and still make money. And no, he can't sell cars for less than they cost him without losing money.

What He Paid Is Not What It Costs

Yes, the dealer invoice cost is what he paid for the car. It's the bill he got from the manufacturer, the invoice he had to pay when the auto arrived. But what he paid for the car is not what it ends up costing him because there are several ways manufacturers put money back into his pocket—money that's directly related to the sale of that specific vehicle. One of the ways they do this is through factory-to-dealer incentive programs.

Manufacturers are putting big bucks into these programs. These dollars-to-dealers can range from $200 up to $2,000 or more on mid-priced vehicles, depending on how badly the manufacturers want to move the vehicles. (The incentives can get as high as $10,000 on slow-moving luxury cars.)

There's just one problem: Nobody's telling you, the customer, about most of these dealer incentives, yet you're the one who's ultimately paying for them.

The Mushroom Treatment

Since manufacturers don't publicize the details of these programs, we're kept in the dark, like mushrooms. All we hear are those commercials telling us to "come on down to take advantage of those [unspecified] factory-to-dealer incentives." There's a good business reason for not telling us more. And realistically, if you ran a car store, you wouldn't want consumers to know the details either.

Although the objective of this factory money is to increase sales of a specific vehicle by making dealers more price-competitive, a dealer may use it for any purpose he wishes. He may pass it along to the customer in the form of a lower price. He may also use it to motivate his salesmen, increase his advertising, upgrade his service bays, or even paint the building. Given his choice, he'd like to pocket it as extra profit, just as you would if you owned a car store.

Here's what the president of one of the world's largest automobile companies had to say on the subject: "A dealer typically says, 'Give me the money, I know how best to use it.' In principle, they always say that. In principle, they're right. But let's face it, when we give the money to the customer, it all goes to the customer. Give the money to the dealer, and some of it ends up in the profit of the dealership."

For example, one import manufacturer gave dealers the option of taking incentive money of $1,000 per sale either as dealer cash or as customer rebates. According to the company's national sales manager, only 15 to 20 percent of the dealers opted for the customer rebates. What a surprise!

What you don't know can't hurt the car store. That's the case with factory-to-dealer cash incentives. Why give those factory dollars to people who don't ask for them? And how can you ask if you don't know they exist? According to a *Wall Street Journal* report on one manufacturer's dealer discounts, "As in the past, the money will be paid to dealers instead of consumers, and the factory won't publicize the discounts. So buyers will have to bargain for the money, and many might not know the discounts are available."

Believe it or not, some dealers don't tell their own salesmen about these incentives! That's because they want to retain control over how the money is used. That makes good business sense for them, but car buyers are the ones paying the bill. And knowing the details can help them negotiate better.

CarDeals to the Rescue

Fortunately, there is a way for consumers to learn the details of both the customer rebates and the factory-to-dealer incentive programs in effect. It's a four-page report called *CarDeals,* and it's updated every two weeks. (You'll find an abridged version of a typical *CarDeals* report in appendix C. Note, however, that this is just an illlustration of the kind of information the report contains, not a listing of current incentives.) The information is compiled from "reliable industry sources" by the Center for the Study of Services (CSS), a nonprofit consumer service organization in Washington, D.C. Here's what *CarDeals* covers.

Direct-to-Consumer Offers   Although it's relatively easy to learn about factory-to-customer incentive offers, whether they're cash rebates or below-market financing plans, *CarDeals* includes the current details as part of its one-stop incentive information service. In the listing, these customer offers are the ones followed by a "C."

Direct consumer offers are typically either a specific cash rebate amount or a choice between a cash rebate and a factory-subsidized, reduced-rate financing plan, all of which are detailed in the listing. You're going to have to decide whether the rebate or the financing plan is better for you. (Sorry, you don't get both.) The answer will depend on the size of the rebate, the annual percentage rate (APR) of the factory financing plan, the APRs available from other lenders, the amount you'll be borrowing, and the length of the loan.

Appendix D is a table that will help you compare rebates with financing plans. It was prepared by William Bryan, director of the Bureau of Economic and Business Research at the University of Illinois at Urbana-Champaign. The table lists a range of possible market interest rates down the left side and a range of factory-subsidized rates across the top. It covers loan terms from two to five years. The dollar numbers represent savings per $1,000 of loan amount.

To illustrate how to use this table, let's assume that you were shopping for a Ford Taurus when the issue of *CarDeals* reproduced here (appendix C) was current. According to the information from *CarDeals,* in the mid-size cars section, a Taurus buyer had the choice of either a $750 cash rebate or finance plan 4, a 7.9 percent APR for up to 48 months (see the end of the table for details on finance plans).

Which is more valuable—the rebate or the financing offer? Assume you thought you could buy the Taurus you wanted for about $16,500, including all taxes and title and license fees. You plan to make a 20 percent down payment of $3,300 and borrow the remaining $13,200, paying it off over four years (the maximum term we recommend). Your bank has quoted a 10 percent APR, and the factory plan's rate is 7.9 percent.

The table in appendix D shows that with a factory-subsidized rate of 8 percent (the closest number to 7.9 percent), you'd save $37.44 per $1,000 borrowed, or $494.21 over four years (13.2 × $37.44). Since this is less than the $750 rebate, you'd accept the customer cash alternative. But if the factory-subsidized rate were 6 percent instead of 8 percent, you'd accept the financing alternative, which would save $977.20 in interest charges (13.2 × $74.03).

To help us complete our worksheet on page 82 on the fictitious Speedster wagon, we've assumed that the All-American Motor Corporation is making the same offer and have entered a $750 rebate on the appropriate line.

Important note on sales taxes: Some "how-to-buy-a-car" books advise having any rebate credited as a discount in the selling price, as a way to avoid paying sales tax on the amount covered by the rebate. Unfortunately, that advice usually won't work. Most states tax the full sales price before the rebate (and often before any trade-in allowance is subtracted). Check your state's tax laws.

Before leaving this section, we should add that there are some direct-to-consumer offers that don't appear on the *CarDeals* report. These fall into three categories:

1. Recent college graduate offers—Some automakers offer additional rebates to recent college graduates on the purchase or lease of a new car or truck, typically $400 to $500. These offers are usually from Ford, GM, or Chrysler, though you may occasionally find similar offers from import makes. They make good business sense. If a company can sell you an entry-level vehicle, it probably has a better chance of attracting you to its higher-priced models in later years. (Over 30,000 people take advantage of Ford's program each year.) If you've graduated from college or graduate school in the last year or two, or if you'll graduate within the next year, you should ask about these programs. The money comes from the manufacturer's pocket, not the dealer's.

2. Discounts for commercial users—If you're buying a truck that will be registered to a business, you may be eligible for a commercial discount from the domestic manufacturers, usually around $300 but sometimes more.

3. Customer loyalty discounts—Another kind of offer worth asking about is a discount for people who own or lease a car of the same make, or people who have *ever* owned a car of the same make. Some of the smaller import brands make these offers, since a good percentage of their sales comes from previous customers. As one Fighting Chance customer reported to us, "When I called Saab's 800 number to ask for information, they sent me a coupon good for $750 if I purchased a new Saab by the end of the month." These offers don't happen often, but if you're shopping for a make you've owned before, it's always a good idea to make the phone call and ask the question.

Direct-to-Dealer Offers   Now let's look at the money manufacturers pay dealers to sell cars to you. These harder-to-uncover dealer incentives are followed by a "D" in the *CarDeals* listing. As you review these programs, the Center for the Study of Services suggests that you keep the following points in mind:

• Some of these programs pay dealers more money per car as they sell more cars during the program period. Unless otherwise noted, when you see a range in the listing (for example, the $800 to $1,600 range shown for Isuzu pickup trucks in the appendix C table), this means that a dealer gets more cash per car if he sells more cars.

• In some programs, all dealers have the same volume targets. That means you can expect larger dealers to get bigger cash payments than smaller dealers, simply because they'll sell more cars. Everything else being equal, you should be able to negotiate a better deal with a large dealer during these programs.

• In other programs, large dealers must meet higher volume targets than small dealers to qualify for incentive cash, so there's no reason to expect a better deal at a large dealership.

To help you differentiate these program types, the *CarDeals* listing tells you which ones are based on sales targets set for each dealer, as opposed to targets that are the same for all dealers. As an example, see the generous Nissan Maxima program shown in the mid-size cars section in the appendix C table. Dealers received from $1,000 to $1,500 per car, based on individual sales targets. If a dealer met those targets by September 2, the end of the promotion period, he would get cash for all Maximas sold in the period.

Returning to our pricing worksheet on the fictitious Speedster wagon, let's assume that All-American Motor Corporation's dealers can earn factory cash up to an extra $200 per vehicle, based on individual sales targets. You'll note that we've added that $200 to the factory-to-dealer incentives line on the chart.

We'll discuss in chapter 21 exactly how to use this dealer incentive information to your advantage during the negotiating process, along with the previously outlined dealer invoice cost data. For now, let's just say that since you're the one who ultimately *pays* for it, you're entitled to the benefit, and there's bound to be a dealer or two who'll want to sell you a car badly enough to agree.

Reality Check: The Caveats

After years of studying the biweekly *CarDeals* reports, we've come to some conclusions we must share with you, so that you can gear your expectations to reality.

For openers, CarDeals *is the best source of this kind of information, by far.* The only other significant incentive report is published in *Automotive News,* the industry's weekly newspaper. *CarDeals* usually lists two to three times as many incentive offers.

But CarDeals *isn't perfect.* We believe it picks up 80 to 90 percent of the incentives, including almost all of the national offers, but even the Almighty would have trouble finding the rest. There can be regional offers that you wouldn't learn about or be affected by unless you lived in those markets. The *CarDeals* editor relies on reliable, long-standing sources, including many dealers. But you'd need spies everywhere to ferret out all the regional offers.

For example, one winter BMW dealers in the Northeast couldn't give away convertibles, but Florida dealers couldn't get enough. So in February, BMW gave its snowbelt dealers an extra $2,000 for each convertible sold. This offer didn't show up in any incentive report; we learned about it from Fighting Chance customers.

Reports on dealer incentives frequently aren't detailed enough. Typically, these programs are stair-stepped. For example, a dealer might get $800 per car at the first target sales plateau and $1,200 at the second, with the payment retroactive to the first car sold. If he reaches the third plateau, he gets $1,600 per car for all sales in the promotion period.

In that kind of program, you might occasionally see a dealer's newspaper ad offering cars at prices well below his bottom-line cost. He's willing to lose, say, $1,000 each on the 25 cars he'll sell that weekend because those 25 sales will get him to the highest plateau, where he'll earn an extra $400 each on the 150 cars sold earlier in the promotion period, for a net incremental dealership profit of $35,000.

Unfortunately, the detailed information on these sales plateaus isn't published anywhere, and there's no way to tell where any individual dealer stands in relation to his target. Our advice: Assume a dealer is at the highest plateau, especially if you're within a week or so of the end of the program period, and make more than one dealer tell you you're wrong.

The lesson here: You should *always* check the advertised prices in dealer newpaper ads in your market before you commit to any deal. You might find a dealer with "prices too good to be true" because he's trying to reach the highest target sales plateau. Or because he's got too much inventory and must make a big interest payment next week. Or even because he just got back from Las Vegas and needs to raise some fast cash to cover a gambling debt. You never know.

Another problem with dealer incentives: *The report will give a dollar amount, but indicate that it may vary in some regions.* The regional differences aren't published anywhere. In that case, we're stuck with the published number as the working assumption for our region. *CarDeals* isn't nirvana, but it's as close as we can get.

If you're troubled by the limited detail of the dealer incentive reports, you can take comfort from this fact: *The market itself is so competitive that in most cases, dealers are forced to pass these incentives along to their price-*

conscious customers. It seems there is always one dealer in the market who prices aggressively, forcing the others to follow suit.

All dealer cash offers should end up in your pocket, based on this rationale: The dealer was willing to sell you that car for a certain profit before that extra cash was there. He should be willing to sell you that same car for the same profit after that extra cash is there. The purpose of that cash is to make him more competitive on price.

Don't expect to see incentives on all vehicles. No manufacturer needs to put incentives on vehicles that sell well without them. That doesn't necessarily mean that you can't deal aggressively on price on these vehicles. It just means the automakers don't have sweaty palms over sales. (On the hottest sellers, of course, where demand exceeds supply, you'll frequently pay the full sticker price or more.)

You'll seldom find incentives on all-new models during their first several months on the market. That would be an admission of failure from the start, a signal that the vehicle was overpriced. And some low-volume and specialty vehicles never have incentives. There are many cars whose sales average only one or two per month per dealer. When demand is that low, incentives don't help much. The implicit assumption is that the few customers who want the vehicle are so committed to the product that incentives aren't required, and those that don't want it won't be won over by a $500 or $1,000 rebate.

Some automakers avoid traditional incentives like the plague because they believe they damage the brand image. As an example, we seldom see rebates or dealer cash on current Honda models, though the company has used model-year-end dealer cash offers to move out the previous year's cars. The strategic thinking is that it's crazy to spend $500 million on advertising to convince us to buy Hondas because they're so wonderful, then spend another $300 million to convince us to buy them because they're so cheap. The company believes those actions work at cross-purposes, and it's right.

Does that mean Honda doesn't occasionally spend promotional dollars to boost sales of certain models? Of course not. But the company will put that incentive money into subsidized financing for purchases or leases through its captive finance company, Honda Motor Credit Corporation. For example, Honda might offer four-year financing at a rate that's 5 percent below the market interest rate. If you borrowed $20,000 and had an average loan balance of $10,000 over 48 months, that would save you about $500 a year on interest—a $2,000 savings over the term of the loan. Why will Honda do that but not offer a $1,000 rebate? Because the average consumer doesn't perceive a cut in the interest rate as a cut in the price of the car, so the brand's image doesn't suffer.

Many luxury makes focus their finance deals on leasing, which accounts for the bulk of their sales. In lieu of rebates or dealer cash, these automakers simply transfer the same amounts of money to their captive finance subsidiaries, which use it to increase the vehicle's residual value and/or reduce the lease's interest rate—both of which reduce your monthly payments.

Note that if the *CarDeals* report shows dealer cash incentives on a vehicle, the dealer usually doesn't get that cash if it's a subsidized lease through the automaker's finance subsidiary. But you will get the benefit of that money in the form of lower monthly payments. (In that situation, the automaker is buying the car back from the dealer at the agreed-upon transaction price.)

If, however, the lease is through a third-party financial institution, such as GE Capital or Chase Manhattan Bank, the dealer will get that factory cash, since he's selling the car to someone other than the automaker's captive finance subsidiary. In that instance, the incentive won't be used to subsidize the lease, but you can use that cash to negotiate a lower capitalized cost. From your perspective, it doesn't matter whether the capitalized cost is $1,000 lower or the residual value is $1,000 higher; the effect on your monthly payment is the same. (For more insight on leasing, see chapter 22.)

Unfortunately, the CarDeals *report usually doesn't list details of special financing offers unless they are alternatives to traditional rebate or dealer cash incentives.* These offers come and go like the wind, and no one could maintain an accurate current listing. There are frequently regional differences, and even different financing offers for different models of the same vehicle, depending on inventory status and specific sales objectives.

Automakers typically don't offer both rebates and dealer cash concurrently on the same vehicle, except when desperate times call for desperate measures. As a general rule, Detroit concentrates the bulk of its incentive activity on direct customer rebates, while the Japanese favor factory-to-dealer cash. But it's not uncommon for any manufacturer to have rebates on some cars and dealer cash on others, or rebates in some regions and dealer cash in others. Sometimes the dealers in each market get their choice of a rebate or a dealer cash program.

This isn't all as complicated as it sounds. The car you're shopping for is going to fit into one of these slots. It's just that there are a lot of slots.

Living Proof: Vehicle Options Can Be Valuable

With a current issue of *CarDeals*, you can examine the listing to see whether any of your finalist vehicles are covered by incentive programs. That's when you may discover a very tangible benefit of keeping more than one car on your list. It's not unusual at any time for the maker of one car to be offering a consumer or dealer incentive of $500 to $1,000 or more, while the maker of a similar car offers less, or none at all. That difference may be just what it takes to make one car the best choice for you.

To illustrate, let's assume that you were interested in buying a Toyota Corolla sedan. Turn to the appendix C table. You'll see in the subcompacts section of our sample *CarDeals* report that there was a factory-to-dealer cash offer on the Corolla ranging from $800 to $1,000, based on sales targets set for each dealer. But the virtually identical Chevy Prizm, made in the same plant in Fremont, California, offered a direct customer rebate of $1,500. In addition, the Prizm carried a sticker price several hundred dollars below the comparable Corolla. Knowing that, you might have found the Chevy to be a very appealing alternative.

If you've got your heart set on just one vehicle, and it isn't covered by a current program, you should consider waiting a month or two. New programs start all the time. Remember, though, that incentive programs are almost never applied to many of the better-selling cars and trucks.

As you look over the sample *CarDeals* report, remember that you may obtain the current issue directly from us. It will be part of the information package that contains the up-to-date dealer invoice prices and the current sales and inventory picture for the vehicles you're considering. See chapter 25 for ordering instructions.

Now let's turn to the third factor that determines the real dealer cost.

DEALER HOLDBACK: THE MONEY NO ONE TALKS ABOUT

The third piece of this cost puzzle is called "dealer holdback," and no one talks about it. If the invoice cost is the last thing the salesman wants you to know, holdback is the last thing the dealer wants you to know, right behind factory-to-dealer incentives. Chances are, he doesn't even discuss it with his salesmen because it's the last thing he wants them thinking about. For most makes, both domestics and imports, holdback is one of the most significant ways manufacturers put money back into dealers' pockets.

Holdback is a specific percentage of a vehicle's price that is built into the original factory invoice price the dealer pays, held back by the manufacturer for a while, then credited back to the dealer's account after the vehicles are sold, typically quarterly. General Motors, Ford, and Chrysler each hold back an amount equal to 3 percent of the retail sticker price (MSRP). While this percentage may seem relatively small, the dollars involved can be significant because even a mid-priced new vehicle costs so much today.

For example, a Dodge dealer could take a sedan with a $15,000 sticker, sell it at his invoice price and still make $450 from holdback. A Ford dealer could part with a $30,000 sport utility vehicle at dealer invoice and still realize $900 in holdback on the deal. And a Cadillac dealer could unload a $40,000 luxury car at invoice and receive a holdback credit from GM of $1,200.

In effect, holdback is a discount to the dealer that reduces the cost of the vehicle below an inflated dealer invoice price. Think of it as boomerang bucks: It's money he sends the factory when he pays the original invoice, but it eventually comes back to him.

Because the dealer pays it out up-front, he treats holdback as if it were a cost item, instead of the profit item it really represents when he gets it back from the factory. Since it's a hidden item, it's excluded from the sales transaction. That means he doesn't have to pay a sales commission on it, and it's not on the table for a buyer to negotiate away.

Holdback was instituted in the early 1960s, we understand, as a way to ensure that dealers would have money on hand to pay Uncle Sam at tax time. While that may be one of several benefits to a dealer, holdback clearly benefits manufacturers as well. They've got the use of that money, interest-free, until the next quarterly payment. (In return, they give the dealer an extra couple of weeks to pay for cars received.) And if a dealer owes them money he won't or can't pay, they've always got a chunk of his cash on hand to cover some of that debt.

Few dealers ever share any of this holdback profit with customers. (Over the years, fewer than a dozen Fighting Chance customers have credibly claimed they got a dealer to give up his holdback to make a deal.) Trying to beat them out of this money will make them angry; they count on it to pay basic overhead expenses. But telling them you know about it helps you keep them in their cage, making it more difficult for them to claim they aren't making money on your transaction. In effect, it gives you firmer ground to stand on.

There's an accounting aspect of holdback that you should understand. Frequently, a dealer won't have the exact car you want, but he'll get it from another dealer's inventory. In that situation, the holdback will be credited to the dealer who originally purchased the car, not the selling dealer. But don't let the dealer use this fact as an excuse to go for a higher price. Dealers buy and sell cars with each other all the time, a practice that enables all dealers to operate more efficiently, with lower inventories. Your dealer may lose the holdback on your deal, but next week he'll earn the holdback on a car sold by some other dealer. It tends to even out over time.

The practice of holdback has spread to most import brands. Based on the best inside information available, here are the holdback policies by manufacturer:

• Some automakers hold back a percentage of the MSRP, excluding the destination charge. Like all Ford, General Motors, and Chrysler divisions, Mercedes-Benz, Saab, Subaru, and Rolls Royce hold back 3 percent of the sticker price. For BMW, Hyundai, Jaguar, Nissan, and Volkswagen, holdback is 2 percent of the MSRP.

• Others hold back a percentage of the base sticker price, excluding the destination charge and the price of any additional option packages and accessories. Acura's holdback is 3.5 percent of the base sticker price, Infiniti's 3 percent. For Honda, Lexus, and Mazda, holdback is 2 percent of the base sticker price.

• A few manufacturers hold back a percentage of the base dealer invoice price, excluding the destination charge and the price of any additional option packages and accessories. Porsche holds back 3 percent. Toyota's holdback is also 2 percent of the base dealer invoice, but Toyota gets another 1 percent as a wholesale financial reserve, making Toyota's total hidden profit 3 percent of the base invoice price.

• Volvo's holdback is a standard $300 per vehicle, which is very low for cars in that price range.

• For all of the makes mentioned above, the holdback is built into the dealer invoice price. There are two makes that don't build it in but add it to the invoice price at the point of purchase—which means you'll see it show up as an extra cost item in your transaction. Isuzu adds 4 percent of the total sticker price, excluding the destination charge. Mitsubishi adds 2 percent of the base sticker price, excluding the destination charge and the price of any additional option packages and accessories.

We can't confirm holdback for any makes not mentioned here. Also note that holdback can change over time. (The Fighting Chance information package always gives you the most recent holdback information.)

We'll discuss in chapter 21 exactly how you should use your knowledge of holdback during the negotiating process. Now, though, return to the sample worksheet for our All-American Speedster on page 82. We've assumed that the fictitious All-American Motor Corporation has the same holdback policy as the three actual domestic manufacturers, and we've entered $532 on the holdback line (3 percent of the $17,720 suggested retail price, excluding the destination charge).

Incidentally, we don't recommend making a subtraction for holdback on a worksheet you plan to share with dealers during the negotiation process. Instead, simply note the holdback amount at the bottom of the page to let them know you are aware of it. You'll make your point without making them angry.

THE BIG UNKNOWN: THE UNDER-THE-TABLE STUFF

Every now and then, a puzzled Fighting Chance customer reports a deal that seems too good to be true—a transaction price that's well below the number you'd get after subtracting incentives *and* holdback, when there are no current dealer incentives reported. That sale could have resulted from something that had nothing to do with the car business. Maybe the dealer was a high-roller who just returned from Las Vegas and had to raise some quick cash to cover a gambling debt. Or maybe the bank just increased the dealer's interest rate by a half point, raising the cost to "floor" his inventory and triggering a quick sell-off, which was good news for the lucky folks shopping that week. The next week, with inventory at a lower level, the dealership might have become much less flexible on pricing. Those things can happen. But in many cases, it appears that there's some other money the dealer gets from the manufacturer, under-the-table money that no one learns about. When we suspect that's happened, all we can tell the customer is that sometimes in life you have to take yes for an answer.

Because, yes, there are other ways dealers get additional money from automakers. Probably not from all automakers, and surely not all the time. But it happens. And there's no reliable source of this information.

Occasionally we get lucky and learn about one of those ways. One year, for example, a European import make had a "Partnering for Excellence" program that rewarded exclusive dealerships with bonus money for each car sold. (Exclusive dealerships are those that sell only one make, or where the other brands sold are at least out of sight of that make's customers.) The program offered dealers up to $1,000 per car sold for meeting exclusivity standards. That automaker also offered dealers a separate bonus of up to $1,500 per car for meeting Customer Satisfaction Index (CSI) goals. (Now you know why some dealers are so anxious to get the highest possible scores from you on that follow-up questionnaire you'll receive after you've bought or leased a new car. Many shoppers have even negotiated an additional price concession in return for their promise to give the dealership the highest ratings.)

It is widely suspected that programs like these exist for many makes, but rarely does anyone outside the dealer community get access to the details. We learned about it from a newspaper reporter who had attended that make's dealer meeting at the National Automobile Dealer Association convention that year.

We live in a world where we can never learn everything we'd like to know. In the final analysis, every dealer has to make a profit to stay in business, and that's neither illegal nor immoral. Your objective shouldn't be to beat them out of every last nickel, but to get a deal you can feel good about, based on the best information available in the real world. That information, imperfect as it may be, still provides powerful leverage in your price negotiation. And those who have it will get much better deals than those who don't.

Many that are first shall be last;
and the last shall be first.
                    —Matthew 19:30

16

Timing

Is Money

Success in any serious endeavor can have a lot to do with being in the right place at the right time. For the new-car buyer, timing is money. There are so many timing-related issues in the auto-shopping process that we've prepared a separate chapter to focus your attention on all of them.

In this race, getting there last often beats getting there first. Here are some specific illustrations of how the turtle beats the hare.

DON'T MILK THAT DEALER-INCENTIVE COW TILL JUST BEFORE MIDNIGHT

If one of your finalists is covered by a current factory-to-dealer cash incentive program, turn to the *CarDeals* report and check the program's end date. Then time all your serious price negotiation visits so that you'll be able to sign the sales agreement *on one of the last two or three eligible days.*

Here's why. Every promotion program has a beginning, middle, and end. As the end approaches, there's a lot of pressure to pump out every sale possible. That's because these programs are often structured so that dealers get higher incentive payments as the number of cars sold increases.

You want to buy from a dealer who's at the highest cash incentive plateau. Your purchase might even be the one that pushes a dealer's entire sales organization up to that plateau. In some programs, a dealership that reaches a certain sales target gets extra cash for all cars sold in the promotion period. This could mean hundreds of dollars for each car previously sold. That store might give quite dramatic discounts as it gets close to its target. That store might be ripe for a knowledgeable shopper to negotiate the buy of a lifetime!

As we noted in chapter 15, if one or more of your finalist vehicles isn't covered by a consumer or dealer incentive program today, consider waiting a month or two if you can. New programs start all the time, and you might save an extra thousand dollars or more if you can make these old warriors work for you.

THE END OF THE LINE CAN BE A GOOD PLACE TO STAND

Many people like to buy at the end of the model year, during those year-end cleanout sales. The new models are about to arrive, and dealers have to make space for them. (For the purpose of measuring sales, the industry designates October through September as its model year.)

One reason prices are friendlier then is that most automakers allocate money to help their dealers sell those year-end leftovers. (They won't get heavy orders for new models if dealers are loaded with last year's cars.) This money usually comes in the form of standard incentives, either customer rebates or factory-to-dealer cash. Even vehicles that normally don't get incentives may have them in the July-September quarter.

In the past, two automakers, General Motors and Ford, regularly provided a "carryover allowance" to move out year-end leftovers. That allowance was 5 percent of the sticker price (that's 5 percent of MSRP, not 5 percent of dealer invoice), which they credited to dealers for every previous year's vehicle sold after the new model of the same vehicle arrived in the showroom. On a car or truck with a $20,000 sticker price, that 5 percent represented an additional $1,000 for you to bargain for. The allowance generally covered all vehicles, but sometimes it excluded hot-selling models in relatively short supply, especially if only minor changes had been made to the new models.

In recent years, however, GM and Ford have been tinkering seriously with this policy. As an experiment, GM discontinued holdback, replacing it with extra incentives—factory-to-dealer cash, rebates or subsidized financing and leases—but only on slower-selling vehicles. These incentives were higher in August and September, then tapered off.

In Ford's tinkering, it retained the holdback concept but varied the percentages, paying only 2.5 percent on better-selling vehicles, 5 percent on most others, and as much as 7.5 percent on a few whose inventories were highest. (Again, remember that carryover doesn't come into play on an old model until the new year's model that replaces it arrives on dealer lots. And if there's a rebate or dealer cash offer in effect, carryover typically doesn't start until the incentive expires.)

We have no crystal ball that tells the automotive future, but it appears that holdback may be headed for extinction at GM, and possibly also at Ford. It's reasonable to assume, however, that carryover will be replaced by other incentives, probably of equal value.

Chrysler has traditionally shunned carryover allowances. Several years ago, it offered its dealers the choice of a 5 percent carryover allowance *or* participation in the July–September consumer and dealer incentive programs. As you might expect, the carryover allowance had few takers among dealers, whose basic credo is, "Sell it now and worry about tomorrow later."

Import makes have never used across-the-line carryover allowances, but many of them place hefty factory-to-dealer cash incentives on last year's models of selected vehicles.

A Key Closeout Issue: Slim Pickings

One problem with waiting until August or September or October to shop for your dream car is that you may not be able to find it then. Most automakers stop assembling the current year's models in June and start producing the next year's models in July, to be shipped after Labor Day. As a result, you may have trouble locating the particular color and equipment combination you want, especially if new-car sales have been strong.

Sometimes year-end pickings can be slim in a down market. If sales have been depressed for months, both manufacturers and their dealers may write off a model year when it's only half over. Dealers get very selective with their orders as the current year's production winds down, and the factories structure their buildout plans to allow dealers to maintain lean inventories of only the fastest-moving models. They're both hoping to end the old-model year without a glut of leftovers, so they can focus all their resources on the new-model launch in the fall.

If you plan to shop for an end-of-year bargain, you'll have more to choose from if there are two or three finalists you'd be equally happy to drive home. If you've got your heart set on one model, try to have an open mind on color and equipment.

The Other Side of the Year-End Coin

Don't be blinded by those apparently great year-end clearance deals. Savvy buyers understand that they are a mixed blessing. There's a reason automakers put incentives on last year's cars each summer, in anticipation of the new models' arrival: *They're worth considerably less then.* Indeed, it's proper to question whether those incentives are large enough to make the leftovers a smart buy.

The culprit is depreciation. Any new car—even the new year's model—is worth a lot less the moment the wheels leave the dealer's lot as you drive it home. That's just a fact of life in the new-car business. If you want an asset that appreciates, buy common stock, not common cars.

Similarly, the incentives on year-end closeouts don't begin to cover a vehicle's precipitous drop in value after the new models are introduced. The day the new models arrived, that old model became last year's car. A year later, when next year's models come out, it'll be a two-year-old. If you have to sell it then, you will have taken a two-year depreciation hit in one year, no matter how much TLC you've lavished on it. And if there have been extensive styling changes in the new model, that older, out-of-style car may depreciate even faster than normal because there's a much prettier successor on the highway.

So the first question to ask yourself is how long you plan to keep the car. If you plan to drive it till the wheels fall off, depreciation really isn't an issue; whether you buy the leftover model or the new-year model, it won't have much value when you're done with it. In that scenario, the leftover is probably the smart buy, since anything you save at the time of purchase is a real saving.

But most new-car buyers don't keep cars forever; they trade them on another new car after a few years. If you're shopping for a mid-priced car, you can figure that five years from now this year's new model will be worth at least $1,000 more than last year's leftover, assuming the same mileage and condition for both.

Another issue to consider is the year-to-year inflation in auto prices. Buying last year's leftover makes more sense when prices are increasing 5 percent or more a year ($1,000 or more on a $20,000 car) than when yearly price hikes are just 1 or 2 percent. The dollar-yen relationship plays a major role in this. When the yen is surging against the dollar, as it did in the late 1980s and early 1990s, the Japanese repatriate fewer and fewer yen for each dollar earned here, and they have to raise prices continuously just to stay even. (That's why the sticker price of the Lexus LS 400 went from $35,000 at its introduction to over $50,000 a few years later.) Those Japanese price hikes provide a nice umbrella under which Detroit can raise its prices aggressively. But when the dollar is surging against the yen, as it did in the late 1990s, the reverse is true. The Japanese take home more yen for the same dollar, and there's no pressure on them to raise prices. In some cases, they can even *reduce* them. Which puts a lid on Detroit's ability to raise prices.

In making this decision, your reference point should be the most current model, not the leftover. First determine what you'd have to pay for the new one; then see how much you can save by buying last year's version. Our rough rule of thumb: *On any mid-priced car, if you can't save at least $1,500 buying the leftover, it's usually smarter to buy the newer model—unless you plan to drive it until it's virtually worthless.*

The moral of the story is that year-end is a great time to buy a leftover bargain, as long as you don't have to sell it in a year or two. You should plan to keep that car for several years to ride out the negative effect of the car's lower real value when it was purchased. And when you eventually trade it, you should do it for another year-end closeout model so you don't get stuck selling low and buying high.

GETTING THERE FIRST CAN BE AN EXPENSIVE TRIP

Remember the Mazda MX-5 Miata. (That's a warning, not a question.) The Miata was introduced with rave reviews, with a sticker price of $13,800 and just enough cars to reach from your kitchen to your dining room, end to end. Mazda dealers loved it! Many put their ADM (additional dealer markup) stickers on every one and doubled or tripled their gross profit per car. And the newspapers were still full of consumers' buy-and-sell offers at prices from $20,000. Talk about being in new-car heat!

Today you can buy a Miata for a few hundred dollars over the dealer invoice price and have just as much fun driving it as the folks who paid an extra $5,000 or $10,000 when it was introduced. You just can't be the first on your block to own one.

Supply and Demand: It's the Law

Whatever the item, if more people want it than can get it, those who get it will pay for the privilege. World Series tickets, Super Bowl hotel rooms, the first 2,000 Mazda Miatas . . . you name it.

With most all-new vehicles, there is an initial period of sales excitement, usually three to six months, when dealers are just order-takers, not salesmen, and supply is chasing demand. That's when folks who've been postponing their purchase in anticipation of the new car come in, most of them willing to pay dearly to be among the first to own one. The hotter the car, the longer that period lasts. Eventually the initial excitement dissipates, supply and demand come into their normal long-term relationship, and dealers become more flexible on transaction prices.

You will sometimes find dealers adding "additional dealer markup" or "additional market value" stickers to the windows of cars that are extremely hot and in short supply. When Volkswagen introduced the new Beetle, dealers were getting just two per week but could sell ten. Taking advantage of this situation, they put stickers on every car with an additional markup of $3,000 or more. And some foolish people were actually paying $3,000 over the full sticker price to own the first one on their block.

If you're after a hot car, the ability to postpone gratification can save you a lot of money. Check periodically to see whether dealers have developed any price flexibility. The best way to assess the supply situation in your market is to stop at a few dealerships on your way to work, at 7:30 or 8:00 A.M., when there are no salespeople around to bother you. Check the inventory on their lots. If there are just a few, there's a message there. If there are many, there's a different, more encouraging message. When you begin to see more than a few regularly, and some of the same cars are there from visit to visit, you may assume the leverage is shifting from the seller to the buyer.

The law of supply and demand can also work against the car buyer at the beginning of the model year, though usually less dramatically than in the case of a hot new car like the Miata or the reincarnated Volkswagen Beetle. From October through December, when a new-year model can be in relatively short supply, the dealer may not accept the same price he will later in the year, when the only things standing in line are the cars on his lot.

Bugs Aren't Just on Windshields

There's another reason to avoid a brand-new model in the early months of production: bugs. Even in this era of dramatically improved product quality, it frequently takes auto manufacturers several months or more to get the hang of making glitch-free products.

Look at the vexing little problems that plagued GM's Saturn in its first year. A recall for defective seats. A recall for a corrosive engine coolant. Early buyers' complaints about noisy, vibrating engines.

Saturn was launched with great ballyhoo, following a $5 billion capital investment and seven years of meticulous planning. Yet many say that what Saturn did best in its first year was correct problems with great consumer and public relations sensitivity.

By Saturn's second year, the bugs had been eliminated, and the Saturn buyer could anticipate a glitch-free vehicle. But Saturn's early pratfalls illustrate that even a company determined to get it right can stumble coming out of the blocks. The wise buyer will always count to ten before purchasing a brand-new vehicle.

TALK TURKEY LATE IN THE MONTH, AND LATE IN THE DAY

As it says in the Bible, "There is a time to every purpose under heaven."

• The time to kick tires and take test drives and do research is during the first three weeks of the month.

• The time for serious negotiation is during the last week of the month—ideally the last couple of days.

Every sales organization lives or dies from month to month. Auto manufacturers report sales monthly, and they focus their dealers on the same time frame, using quotas or incentives or just plain fear to motivate them. The dealers pass along the quotas, the incentives, and the fear to their sales managers.

That usually makes the end of the month the best time to buy. Your purchase could be the one that puts them over the top, and you might strike a terrific bargain. (Fighting Chance customers regularly report making a slim-profit offer on the last day or two of the month and having a sales manager accept it immediately, acknowledging that it was a deal he wouldn't have made if he hadn't needed it to close the period on a positive note.)

Some of the smartest shoppers always buy their new cars during the last hour of the last day of December. That way salesmen can't waste their time with their system games. (More on these in chapter 17.) They carry a cashier's check for the maximum amount they're prepared to pay. And they claim they always leave with both the car they want and the dealer's check for the difference between their maximum and the lower price they really paid.

Here's another tactic that works. If it's the last weekend of the month and your price negotiation is stalled on a number that's too high, tell the salesman that you're going home to sleep on it and will be back next weekend. Many times you'll find that the price will drop magically just as you head for the door.

The exception to this end-of-month rule would be if the last days of a relevant factory-to-dealer incentive program come at a different time. Given all the incentive activity in the market, there's probably more buyer leverage in timing those specific factory programs just right. (You'll note, however, that most programs seem to finish at the end of a month, or a few days later.)

AN EMPTY SHOWROOM CAN BE FULL OF OPPORTUNITY

If you're the only one there, your chances of striking a terrific deal may be enhanced dramatically. So don't be afraid to shop "the middles"—the middle of the week, the middle of a blizzard or deluge, even the middle of the Christmas season (as long as you don't tell the salesman it's a Christmas present). And car stores can be particularly accommodating in January and February, when most people are paying off holiday bills and not thinking of buying new cars and trucks.

AT TENT SALES, YOU GET GREAT DEALS ON CAMELS, NOT CARS

The timing elements to ignore are the corny sales events dealers love to advertise. In car salesman lingo, their purpose is always to create a sense of urgency, to get prospects into their showrooms by implying that this gigantic tent sale is the opportunity of a lifetime . . . and when it's over, it's over. Sure it is. Until next month's red tag sale, or the following month's midnight madness sale, or the President's Day sale, or the overstock clearance sale.

The transaction prices at most of these phony events are no lower than they were before the sale. They are probably higher, because those ads attract gullible people who believe that a car dealer's advertised sale is as real as a department store's advertised sale. Unless the ads feature some very specific offer, such as a manufacturer's below-market financing program, the only real opportunities at these events are for salesmen to take advantage of folks who fall for the come-on. So if there's a midsummer heat wave in your town and the "beat-the-heat" sale ads promise free air conditioning with every car sold, you should extend your antennae fully. For a mid-priced vehicle, that air conditioner costs the dealer more than his profit on a typical sale to a knowledgeable buyer. Unless it's supplied free by the manufacturer, assume that you're paying for any "free" equipment. If the dealer giveth, the dealer also taketh away.

TIME IS ALWAYS ON YOUR SIDE, NOT THEIRS

The strongest of warriors are
these two: time and patience.
   —Leo Tolstoi, *War and Peace*

In a waiting game, the loser will be the one who needs the deal the most. The sooner you need to have a new car, the more it's going to cost. If that's today, or this weekend, you'd better have a Brink's truck for a trade-in. A loaded Brink's truck. But if you can wait 'em out, the time will come when they'll want a sale even more than you want a new car. That offer they refused weeks ago has a way of looking much better in the cold, hard glare of the end of another month. Sometimes just one more sale—even a slim-profit sale—can be very important to a dealer.

All it takes is time, a luxury dealers seldom have. If you've got it, use it.

17

We must take a hard look at the way we market our cars . . . and the way we approach customers on the floor and present the deal. Until we address these issues, the image of new-car dealers will remain about the same—awful.

—President of the National Automobile Dealers Association

The Games Salesmen Play

Before you finalize your approach to negotiating price, you should be aware of some of the things car salesmen do to control the sales situation and to get you to do what they want, which is to buy today, at a price that maximizes their profit. Watch for these old favorites.

THE BUDDY SYSTEM

This salesman is on your side; it's you and him against them. He'll do his best to get management to give you a great deal. He leaves the room a lot, only to return to say they wouldn't buy a price that low, they need more. (You're at the blood bank, negotiating with Dracula through a zombie, and the only blood there is yours.)

This is a game, and a transparent one at that. Don't let him play it. Tell him you appreciate his concern for you, but you want to talk to "them," not their messenger. If the game doesn't stop, walk out.

THE SILENT TREATMENT

This is the buddy system's first cousin. The salesman leaves you in the room (they call it "the box") for long periods of time while he's "negotiating for you" with his sales manager.

In reality, that salesman probably knows exactly how low they'll go to sell you that car. While he's away, you can bet he's drinking coffee with the guys, talking about last night's date or next week's fishing trip. He'll eventually come back with a "bump" over your last offer, because "they" didn't buy it.

The game here is to keep you there (so you can't be at any other car store) and to wear you down. They want you so frustrated by the delays that you'll sign anything just to get it finished.

The first time he gets up to leave, tell him nicely but firmly that you've been through this before, that you appreciate the position he's in, but you're not going to sit there for a lot of back-and-forth negotiations with a phantom. Say that if he's not back in five minutes with someone you can negotiate with directly, you've got three other dealers you plan to visit and he can expect to find you gone. Then look him straight in the eye and hit the countdown beeper on your digital wristwatch.

As you're sitting there waiting for the salesman to return, be careful what you say out loud to anyone who's with you. Believe it or not, some car stores have "bugged" their showrooms with listening devices, and anything you say may be used against you. What can they learn with this trick? Some unwary shoppers may mention how high a price they're really willing to pay. Others will talk about how much they love that little teal green sedan and how they haven't seen one like it on any other dealer's lot. Sharing this information electronically over an intercom system will not enhance your negotiating position. Talk in whispers to your companion, or write notes to each other.

Better still, try this little trick to turn the tables on the tricksters. About one minute after the salesman leaves the room, say rather loudly, "If he's not back in four minutes, he's gonna find an empty room because we'll be outta here. Put your coat on." You may find that salesman bounding back through the door in 30 seconds.

THE BUMP-AND-GRIND

This is a more systematic version of the silent treatment. The waiting periods aren't as long, but you're being played up and down like a yo-yo by someone you don't even get to see.

Your buddy, the salesman, leaves the box after introducing you to his sales manager, who'll be "the closer." You've been TO'd (taken over) by a more senior salesman. This guy is usually still a middleman, taking your concessions out to some phantom who scribbles notes you can't read and returning to ask if you can "just help him out" to the tune of another $50 a month so he can close the deal. (Over four years, that $50 a month will cost you $2,400, and the closer will get 10 to 25 percent of that "bump.")

Your response to the bump-and-grind should be the same as to the silent treatment. Either it stops, now, or you walk to another car store, now.

THE LOWBALL OPENER

Some stores will have the salesman quote you an initial price that sounds too good to be true—sometimes over the phone. *You can be sure that it is simply a way to get you into the showroom.* When you agree to that number, he'll return with a "bump," saying they wouldn't go for it. This is just another way to draw you into the game.

If you think he's lowballing, tell him that you've been through this before, that you expect him to return again and say management wouldn't buy it, and that if that's the game they want to play, you've got three other stores to visit and you'll leave as soon as he returns with the predicted news flash. Tell him that you want to talk to someone who can negotiate with you directly, now, or you're leaving.

Note: Another variation is the "lowball send-off." The salesman knows you're going to go out and shop around, so he gives you an unrealistically low quote that no dealership would match, including his. When you leave, he's got you "out on a ball," and he knows you'll be back. When you eventually return to take him up on that lowball offer, you learn that it was too good to be true. By then, he hopes, you'll be so tired of running around trying to beat it that you'll be ready to make any deal he wants.

THE CASTING DIRECTOR

This salesman wants to typecast you as soon as he can. Anything you say will be used against you.

Are you "a payment buyer," someone who cares only that the monthly payment is something you can handle? He can fix you right up, with a deal that maximizes both his profit and the length of your loan. (But the monthly payments will be close to what you said you could handle.)

Don't ever talk to a car salesman about monthly payments. If you've done your homework, you already know what kind of financing and payments you're planning, and it's none of his business.

Are you "an allowance buyer," someone who's focused only on the trade-in allowance they'll offer on your used car? He can fix you right up, with a deal that maximizes both your trade-in allowance and his profit.

Don't ever talk to a car salesman about a trade-in allowance. Go back and review chapters 4 through 9. By now, you're too smart to fall for this one. As you've already learned, the less you tell the salesman, the better off you'll be.

THE CHECK-IN CLERK

In many dealerships, the first thing a salesman will want to do is fill out a data card with your name, address, and phone numbers. He'll add the sticker price information on the car you want, including all the options. Then he'll want to add information about your trade-in, like the vehicle identification number and the mileage.

Then, as long as he's writing, he'll ask your date of birth, driver's license number, and social security number. No deal has been discussed yet, no prices mentioned, but he wants all this personal data. He'll pass the data card to his superior as soon as he leaves the box.

They'll need data like this to run a credit report on you if you end up financing or leasing through the dealer. They'd like to run the report immediately because it can provide valuable information. For starters, they want to be sure they're not wasting their time on a deadbeat or someone who couldn't possibly afford a new car. But in addition, credit reports typically tell retailers who else has requested reports on you recently. If no other car dealers are on that list, they'll assume you aren't making the negotiation competitive and will aim for a higher profit on your deal.

The last thing you want is to have several retailers requesting credit reports on you within a short time period. This will not enhance your credit rating, since the rating bureaus assume that increased activity on an individual's file is a sign there may be a credit problem. Fortunately, there is now a Federal Trade Commission ruling that requires car dealers to get written permission from "tire kickers" before requesting a credit report on them. (Once you move beyond the window-shopping stage and indicate that you are actually purchasing or leasing a vehicle, they don't need your permission. At that point they obviously need that information to begin processing the financing of the transaction.)

So when the salesman presses you for more information than he has a right to have, remind him that this is a car store, not a hotel or a personnel office! And you're not registering for a room or applying for a job. At this stage, you're just starting a dialogue that might or might not lead to a purchase. *Until you've got a deal that you agree to, all you should tell him is your name, and you should make it clear that you are not giving him permission to request a credit report on you.* Even if you end up buying there, they won't need most of that information unless you're financing through the dealer.

THE HOSTAGE TAKER

Many salesmen will ask for a deposit check to accompany your offer when they take it to their superior. They call it evidence that you're a serious buyer. But for them, *that check is a hostage that will keep you at their store and prevent you from shopping around for a better deal.*

Smile nicely, but tell him that you're not writing a deposit check for anything until you and they have agreed on a deal for everything. And that if his store requires a deposit check simply to negotiate a deal, you're sure you can find one that doesn't. The rule will change quickly.

Incidentally, the keys to your current car can also become an effective hostage. Salesmen have been known to "misplace" them, and even to refuse to return them when you ask. At this point, you're not there to talk about a trade-in. *Keep the keys in your pocket or purse.*

If you think you might want them to check out your trade-in on the same visit, take along an extra car key and give them that one, not the ring that has all the other keys to your life. And complete one more important task: Clean out all the papers that might provide a dealership with important information about you. Assume that the person evaluating your car will go through the glove compartment looking for helpful tidbits like payroll stubs, checkbooks, bank statements, and so on. Those papers don't belong in your car.

THE LIMITED-TIME OFFER

You might negotiate to a price that sounds pretty good, but this is only your first store. You plan to go through the same drill at two or three other dealerships. You tell him that it's a big decision for you, that you want to think about it overnight. You thank him and get up to leave. The salesman then says, in a bit of a huff, that if you leave, he can't give you that same price tomorrow. (He's upset; his mission is to close you now.)

Call his bluff (assuming, of course, that there is no manufacturer's incentive that ends today). Smile and say that's too bad, because if it's true, he's going to miss the opportunity to sell you a car. You are leaving, you've got several other dealers you haven't talked with yet, and you're sure one of them will have a different attitude.

Then ask him again if he really meant that he wouldn't sell you that car at that price tomorrow, so you'll be sure not to bother him.

Remember Reality 101: There's another deal that good, and probably better, around the next corner.

Then remember Salesman's Reality 101: If you don't buy, he doesn't sell. And if he doesn't sell, he doesn't eat.

MR. OBNOXIOUS

Chances are, you'll end up with a given salesman just because it's his turn. His number is up when you walk in, and you become his "up."

Chemistry is important. If you quickly find he's someone you'd rather not deal with, excuse yourself to go to the rest room. Then ask someone where you can find the sales manager, walk in, and tell him you've got a problem he's going to have to solve or you're going to have to leave. That salesman is not someone you can work with, and you'd like to talk to someone else. Then go to the rest room.

When you return, you'll meet a new, less obnoxious salesperson— maybe even the sales manager himself.

18

If a Cavalier is advertised for $9,999, you had better load it up with extras or your head is on the chopping block.

—Salesperson quoted in
Automotive News

Back-End Options: Just Say No

The *Random House Webster's College Dictionary* defines "option" as "the power or right of choosing." "Optional" is also defined as meaning "not required."

Car salesmen have a different dictionary. Theirs defines "option" as "any additional equipment or accessories that can be stuck onto a new vehicle to achieve maximum profitability to the car store."

It's bad enough that manufacturers load their vehicles with packages of optional equipment, some of which you may not need or want. At least they typically give you a package price, so that you're not paying that much for the things you don't want.

But then the car stores add their own high-profit dealer options on the back end. You'll find them hung all over the vehicles you're shopping. That doesn't mean you have to buy them.

THE OTHER STICKER

Your first clue that something's up is the other sticker on the window. It's often designed to look just like the Monroney, complete with an illustration of that little gas pump. It's not; *it's the car store's sticker.*

There's often more profit potential for the car store on that sticker than on the basic car itself, but most of the items there won't add a dime's worth of value or utility. Let's replay a few of "the greatest hits."

"The Mop 'n Glow"

This group includes things like "rust-preventive undercoating," "fabric guard protection spray," "paint sealant," "sound shield," decorative striping, mud flaps, and deluxe floor mats. This strange entourage frequently masquerades under important-sounding names like "Optional Environmental Protection Package."

This little protection package can carry a retail price from $300 to as much as $1,000 or more. Its cost to the car store is peanuts—typically under $100. You need this stuff like a moose needs a hat rack!

• Let's start with "rust-preventive undercoating." Today's new vehicles carry very substantial anti-corrosion warranties from just about all manufacturers. The domestics typically cover six or seven years, or 100,000 miles, whichever comes first. The major imports cover five to seven years, usually with unlimited mileage. (Check the coverage for your finalists on page 124.) Probably the best argument against buying dealer rustproofing is that many factories recommend against it! Here's a quote from a General Motors warranty:

> Some after-manufacture rustproofing may create a potential environment which reduces the corrosion resistance designed and built into your vehicle. Depending upon application technique, [it] could result in damage or failure of some electrical or mechanical systems of your vehicle. Repairs to correct damage or malfunctions caused

by after-manufacture rustproofing are not covered under any of your GM new vehicle warranties.

Any questions?

• "Fabric guard protection spray": You call this Scotchgard. A 14-ounce can of 3M's Scotchgard® sells for a few dollars in your supermarket and covers 14 to 21 square feet of fabric. Three cans should do the trick.

• "Paint sealant": Today's automotive paint jobs are technological wonders compared to twenty years ago, when additional protection may have been beneficial. The primary thing it benefits now is the size of the salesmen's bonus pool.

The bottom line: Tell the salesman to leave the Mop 'n Glow in aisle 9, where it belongs. Tell him either he throws in the $79.95 cost of the total package for free or finds you a car without it. If he won't do it, find another dealer who will. (In fact, you'd rather buy a car without it.)

Dealer Preparation

You may see a charge for "dealer preparation." You shouldn't pay it. Virtually all manufacturers include predelivery preparation in the car's base price. (One exception: Automakers don't ship new cars with more than a couple of gallons of gasoline, so it's reasonable for the dealer to charge you for the gas he adds to the tank.)

ADM, ADP, and AMV

Printed boldly on the "other sticker," these abbreviations represent the most arrogant form of customer-fleecing. They stand for "additional dealer markup," "additional dealer profit," and "additional market value." They used to be added to any car in relatively high demand and short supply, particularly imports.

In today's tough sales climate, most car stores have dropped these extra charges, but they're not extinct. You'll find them on virtually all new vehicles at some stores. The added markups can range from $1,000 on a compact pickup truck to $5,000 or more on an expensive sports car. What they provide, of course, is an artificially higher asking price from which to start negotiating.

If you see them, tell the salesman you're going to ignore them. If he won't cooperate, either you've got a dealer who's not living in the real world or you're looking at the rare vehicle whose demand exceeds today's supply (like that Dodge Viper that the dealer thought would sell for $20,000 over the sticker price).

Our advice would be to shop several dealers to find one without "A-words" on his stickers, or to wait a few months for supply to catch up with demand. (It always does.) And remember that a car sold with an "A-word" sticker won't be worth a nickel more at trade-in time than the same car without that initial surcharge.

Some Options Are Hard to Avoid

Some options, both manufacturer- and dealer-installed, just seem to come with the territory. That's most often true on newer models that are in relatively short supply. To maximize profits, manufacturers tend to load those vehicles with every equipment package and accessory, and it can be next to impossible to find a relatively spartan base model—especially one with a manual transmission. Likewise, it might be difficult to find a minivan without an expensive dealer-installed luggage rack. (If you're a minivan prospect, you learn to grin and bear it. What's a minivan without a luggage rack anyway?)

If a dealer doesn't have the exact color and equipment combination you want in his current stock or on order, he can run a computer search of the inventory of all the dealers in the same sales territory, which in some cases can cover several states. If that search turns up your ideal car or one almost like it, he can buy it from the other dealer or trade a similar-cost vehicle for it. He will ask you for a good-faith deposit before getting the car, probably about $500. That's reasonable, considering that you're asking him to add that extra car to his inventory for you.

It's also reasonable for you to demand some assurance that the car will be acceptable to you when it arrives. Ask the dealer for the current mileage on the odometer and a complete list of the equipment shown on the manufacturer's window sticker. Make sure he understands that you don't like unpleasant surprises and you won't buy the car if the equipment turns out to be different or the car isn't in perfect condition. (Put that $500 good-faith deposit on a credit card if you can; then, if there's a last-minute problem, you'll have the option of refusing to pay the charge when your monthly bill arrives.)

If the car has to be trucked in from a dealership a considerable distance away, you should expect to pay that extra cost. To avoid any misunderstanding, be sure to discuss this issue before you instruct the dealer to get the car for you. But be aware that if your heart is set on owning the only teal green Accord coupe left in a four-state area, that's the only way to get it, and the extra delivery charge could amount to several hundred dollars.

Remember, too, that the dealer who purchased the car initially is the one who gets the factory holdback dollars on the vehicle. (See chapter 15.)

Here's one option you should avoid: the car store's logo, either drilled into or glued onto the back end of your new car. Make sure you tell the salesman you won't accept delivery of any vehicle with his store's advertising attached to it. (The exception to this rule is a license plate frame bearing the dealer's name, which you can remove easily. As you'll learn in chapter 20, this can be a useful long-term ally.)

INDIVIDUAL FACTORY ORDERS: THE SOLUTION TO THE OPTION GAME?

As you may know, domestic cars can be special-ordered from the manufacturers. This is an excellent way to get a vehicle equipped exactly to your specifications. And perhaps there is something special about having one built just for you.

Special orders are placed most often by buyers of full-size pickup trucks. These vehicles come in a mind-boggling array of configurations: half-ton, three-quarter-ton, and one-ton models; regular cab, extended cab/club cab, quad cab, and crew cab; two-wheel drive and four-wheel drive; short bed and long bed; V-6, V-8, V-10, and diesel engines; and a long list of trim levels, equipment groups, and optional accessories. A dealer would need hundreds of trucks in inventory to stock just one of each possible configuration.

Any dealer would be happy to take your factory order for a car or a truck. It's an easy sale, and unlike his regular inventory, he doesn't have to invest anything in your car because you'll own it the day it arrives. He may even accept a lower-profit deal just because it'll help his "turn and earn" record. Many dealers are allotted cars based on past sales performance. Moving a lot of cars, especially in a poor sales year, will help ensure that he'll get all he needs in better years, when the most popular cars are scarcer and markups are higher.

In most cases, a dealer will want a deposit from you as "earnest money," probably about $1,000. That's a reasonable request. You've asked him to commit for a vehicle he wouldn't necessarily purchase for his regular inventory, and he wants some assurance that you're going to fulfill your end of the bargain. Mostly he wants to be sure you don't go down the street and try to beat the deal at another dealership.

In addition to getting exactly the car you want, without equipment that you don't want, we have learned from Fighting Chance customers that a fac-

tory order often can save you a lot of money if you're shopping for a hot-selling vehicle that's in short supply.

New cars are nothing but high-priced commodities, and pricing flexibility is determined by supply and demand. Because there are many more makers and models and dealers than we really need, supply always exceeds demand for most vehicles. But almost always, there are a few "hot" models for which supply trails demand.

Ours is a fad-driven culture, in part, and public interest in a given product can increase dramatically overnight. If that product is a lipstick color or a clothing style, manufacturers can turn on a dime to meet the demand. But the lead time required to react to changes in demand for automobiles is seldom measured in weeks or months. And whenever a dealer gets fewer units of a vehicle than he can sell, he will demand—and get—higher prices.

There are two ways to beat a sticky price situation. One is to postpone your purchase for a few months. Supply always exceeds demand eventually. The alternative is to order one from the factory. Many customers report buying vehicles in short supply for a few hundred dollars over the dealer's invoice by placing a special order. It's a quick, no-brainer sale, so he's often willing to settle for a more modest profit . . . plus holdback, of course. Most important, he doesn't have to burn his slim inventory on someone who's done his homework; he can save it for the idiot who'll walk in after you and pay him the sticker price or more to buy a scarce vehicle. The downside, of course, is that you'll wait two or three months for your new toy to arrive.

If you decide to place a factory order for a hot vehicle, there's a candid up-front discussion you should have with the dealer. We have heard from a few people who placed a similar order that, about the time the car was to arrive, they got a call saying it had fallen off the truck as it was being delivered and was a total loss. This is not a believable tale. More likely, another customer saw the car coming off the truck and offered the dealer $2,000 more than your price to drive it home. This can happen. Make the dealer assure you it won't happen to you. And contact the dealership periodically throughout the waiting period to ask for progress reports. Dealers can probably learn when the vehicle has been produced.

The Caveats

Special ordering has many advantages, but there are some potential downside issues you should consider as well.

- For openers, it'll take six to eight weeks or more to get delivery, if you're lucky. A lot of things can happen to your current car in that time—none of them good—that may cause the dealer to lower his offer for your trade-in.

- You usually have to place your order before the first of May if you want the current year's model. Detroit's automakers need at least two months' lead time, and they switch over to the next year's model in July.

- You may not be able to predict a realistic delivery date, especially if you order in the second half of the model year. When sales are slower, manufacturers periodically shut down selected factories for a week or more to avoid excess inventory buildup. The plants selected may include the one that makes your car.

- In the worst-case scenario, the United Auto Workers might go on strike, which would add two weeks or two months to the timetable, and you'd be thumbing a ride to work.

- Only the domestic automakers will actually build a vehicle to your individual specifications. You can "order" an import make, but that just means the dealer adds your car to the normal order he places periodically for his own inventory. In general, your ability to customize a vehicle is more limited because import models don't offer as many different configurations, trim levels, and options as GM, Ford, and Chrysler products. And you face a longer lead time if the model is made in Europe or Japan.

- Even with a domestic factory order, it's not as easy as it used to be to get the exact configuration you want. Manufacturers don't really customize orders the way they did decades ago. Many of them sell certain popular options only in packages, which may contain things you don't want.

- You may not be able to take advantage of either consumer or dealer incentive offers with a factory-ordered car. Both the consumer rebate and low-cost financing programs and the factory-to-dealer cash programs require that you take delivery by a certain date. A program may be in effect when you order a vehicle, but not when it's delivered. If that happens, you'll pay the $500 to $1,000+ built into the price of the car to cover these programs, but you'll receive no benefit. (Unfortunately, the automakers never announce new incentive programs until the current ones have expired.)

- Finally, you've probably got a better shot at negotiating an attractive price on a car that's in a dealer's stock than on a special-ordered car. He's paying floor-plan interest to keep that car in inventory, so he's highly motivated to get it off his lot and into your garage.

Here's how to estimate how long a car has been in a dealer's inventory. Look for the federally mandated manufacturer's sticker or plate, which shows the month and year of manufacture. It also carries these words: "This vehicle conforms to all applicable federal motor vehicle safety, bumper, and theft prevention standards in effect on the date of manufacture shown above." It's usually placed inside the jamb of the driver's door but may also be under the hood—on the firewall between the engine and passenger compartments—or on one of the wheel wells.

If the date of manufacture is more than four months earlier, you may assume the dealer is particularly anxious to sell that vehicle and might accept a lower offer than for a car that just arrived on his lot.

19

Ethically, we should quote payments on a stripped vehicle to customers. But that cuts out the finance and insurance manager, so we are told at the meetings to quote loaded payments. You can always come down, but you can't go up.

—Salesperson quoted in
Automotive News

Are Extended Warranties Warranted?

The sale of an extended warranty contract, which pays for repairs that occur after the initial factory warranty runs out, is a big back-end profit item for every car store. These contracts typically cost $700 to $1,200 and can exceed $2,000, depending on what they cover and what the traffic (you) will bear.

You can expect to get a strong recommendation to buy one, frequently from the store's F&I (finance and insurance) manager. Watch out for this guy. You've escaped from the "closing box," but you're in the clutches of another commissioned salesman. He's a low-pressure operator who wants you to trust his advice as you would your father's. He's not your father; he's interested in your wallet, not your welfare.

BE PREPARED FOR THIS ONE

You should determine beforehand whether this purchase makes sense for you. The decision hinges on your answers to these two questions:

1. What's the basic bumper-to-bumper warranty on the car you're buying?

2. How long do you plan to keep the car, and about how many miles will you drive it?

BASIC WARRANTIES ARE NOW CLOSE TO PARITY

The old standard bumper-to-bumper warranty of one year or 12,000 miles (whichever comes first) is a thing of the past, thanks to Toyota, Honda, and Nissan. The Japanese Big Three provide a basic warranty of 3 years or 36,000 miles, and starting with the 1992 models, Detroit's Big Three finally matched their key competitors. (Ford and Chrysler maintained the ancient 12-month/12,000-mile warranty on most vehicles through the 1991 model year.)

The basic bumper-to-bumper warranty covers most parts of the car. An additional powertrain warranty covers the things that make the car go (the engine, transmission, and drivetrain), frequently for a longer period than the basic warranty. And a longer corrosion warranty covers actual holes in the body caused by rust. Separate warranties cover the battery, tires, emission control system, and accessory items you may add to the vehicle. There are no warranties covering parts that must be replaced owing to normal wear, such as brake pads, clutch linings, lightbulbs and fuses, wiper blades, filters, and so on.

Of course, to keep that warranty in effect you must maintain your car according to the guidelines in the owner's manual. Be sure to retain copies of all the paperwork detailing the regularly scheduled maintenance performed on your car.

You should be aware that some dealer-added options can void a manufacturer's warranty. The main one to avoid is dealer-installed cruise control. Check with the manufacturer before you authorize the installation of any option that might jeopardize your vehicle's warranty status; if they say there's no problem, ask them to confirm the answer in writing.

The warranties in effect as we're writing this are shown in the following table, stated in terms of years and miles. For example, "3/36,000" means the warranty is good for 3 years or 36,000 miles, whichever comes first. Since warranty policies can change, you should check the current specifics for the makes you're considering.

AUTO WARRANTIES

Manufacturer	Basic Warranty	Powertrain Warranty	Rust-through Warranty
Acura	4/50,000	4/50,000	5/unlimited
Audi	3/50,000	3/50,000	10/unlimited
BMW	4/50,000	4/50,000	6/unlimited
Buick	3/36,000	3/36,000	6/100,000
Cadillac	4/50,000	4/50,000	6/100,000
Chevrolet	3/36,000	3/36,000	6/100,000
Chrysler	3/36,000	3/36,000	5/100,000
Dodge	3/36,000	3/36,000	5/100,000
Ford	3/36,000	3/36,000	5/unlimited
GMC	3/36,000	3/36,000	6/100,000
Honda	3/36,000	3/36,000	5/unlimited
Hyundai	5/60,000	10/100,000	5/100,000
Infiniti	4/60,000	6/70,000	7/unlimited
Isuzu	3/50,000	5/60,000	6/100,000
Jaguar	4/50,000	4/50,000	6/unlimited
Jeep	3/36,000	3/36,000	5/100,000
Kia	3/36,000	5/60,000	5/100,000
Land Rover	4/50,000	4/50,000	6/unlimited
Lexus	4/50,000	6/70,000	6/unlimited
Lincoln	4/50,000	4/50,000	5/unlimited
Mazda	3/50,000	3/50,000	5/unlimited
Mercedes-Benz	4/50,000	4/50,000	4/50,000
Mercury	3/36,000	3/36,000	5/unlimited
Mitsubishi	3/36,000	5/60,000	7/100,000
Nissan	3/36,000	5/60,000	5/unlimited
Oldsmobile	3/36,000	3/36,000	6/100,000
Plymouth	3/36,000	3/36,000	5/100,000
Pontiac	3/36,000	3/36,000	6/100,000
Porsche	4/50,000	4/50,000	10/unlimited
Saab	4/50,000	4/50,000	6/unlimited
Saturn	3/36,000	3/36,000	6/100,000
Subaru	3/36,000	5/60,000	5/unlimited
Suzuki	3/36,000	3/36,000	3/unlimited
Toyota	3/36,000	5/60,000	5/unlimited
Volkswagen	2/24,000	10/100,000	12/unlimited
Volvo	4/50,000	4/50,000	8/unlimited

The most important warranty, by far, is the basic bumper-to-bumper coverage. For most people, it doesn't make sense to accept below-average basic coverage from an automaker, even in return for superior powertrain coverage.

In the past, powertrain warranties covered most of the major problems you might encounter after the original warranty expired because the only really expensive repair bills came from powertrain problems.

Today's automobiles, however, are loaded with complicated new systems that have nothing to do with the things that make the car go. Electronic instrument panels with all kinds of gadgets. Power equipment options. Anti-lock braking systems. Cruise control. Air bags. Sophisticated steering and suspension systems. Diagnosing and fixing problems with these systems is more difficult and expensive than it was with their predecessors. And when they need fixing after the basic warranty period, it's your money that's on the line.

Worth noting: Several import makes have competitive basic warranties and separate powertrain warranties extending beyond the bumper-to-bumper coverage. This makes their warranties somewhat better, overall, than any domestic company's.

THEY'VE GOT SECRETS

If a vehicle problem is serious enough for the federal government to require a recall, all owners are notified by mail. But with less serious but persistent problems, sometimes automakers decide to pay the repair cost on their own, even after the original bumper-to-bumper warranty expires. Trouble is, they don't publicize the availability of these "secret warranties." Some owners learn of them only after repeated complaints for the same problem; most don't know they exist. And only a few states have passed laws requiring their disclosure.

The automakers say that secret warranties don't exist. They call this practice "goodwill service" or "policy adjustments" instead. Dealers learn the specifics of each program from the manufacturer's regular technical service bulletins, which tell them how to fix the problem.

You can learn about the service bulletins for your car from the National Highway Traffic Safety Administration (NHTSA). The best way to do this is to visit NHTSA's web site on the Internet at www.nhtsa.dot.gov/cars/problems. You can get copies of bulletins on file by writing to NHTSA, Technical Reference Library, Room 5108, Washington, D.C. 20590. Ask for "service bulletins" and state the make, model, and year of the car and the year you think the service bulletin was issued. You may also call NHTSA at (800) 424–9393.

With most major manufacturers now at or near parity on basic warranty coverage, your decision on whether to buy an extended warranty contract will depend more on how long you'll keep the vehicle and how far you'll drive it.

THIS CAN BE EXPENSIVE OVERINSURANCE

Remember, these extended warranties don't kick in until the basic coverage kicks out. If you buy a car with an initial factory warranty of 36 months or 36,000 miles, your extension coverage doesn't begin until either mile number 36,001 or the first day of month 37.

Will you keep the car that long and/or drive it that far? If you will, how much longer and farther do you think you'll own and drive it? If you plan to keep the car only about one year or 12,000 to 15,000 miles beyond the initial warranty period, don't buy an extended warranty. Instead, put $500 to $1,000 into a rainy-day account and pray for sunshine. (This alternative may be very attractive if you're buying a Toyota or Nissan product that comes with an extended powertrain warranty.) But if you're planning to drive the car until the wheels fall off, an extended warranty can be a wise investment. Inevitably, something expensive happens between 50,000 and 100,000 miles.

If you're leasing the car, don't even think about buying an extended warranty. One of the major advantages of a lease is that the car is covered by the original bumper-to-bumper warranty for most, if not all, of the lease term. Ideally, you shouldn't lease a car for longer than the warranty period. If you have to stretch the lease one year beyond that period to keep the payments affordable, set up the rainy-day account recommended in the previous paragraph, but don't buy an extended warranty contract.

Note that you don't have to make this purchase decision when you buy the car. In most cases, you may buy this contract anytime within the first 12 months or 12,000 miles. And here's the best part: You can buy the factory-backed policy from any dealer who sells the same make.

NEGOTIATING WARRANTIES

"You Better Shop Around"
—Smokey Robinson and the Miracles,
number-two song in January 1961

Salesmen will tell you that an expensive postwarranty repair could cost you over $2,000, making this $1,000+ "insurance policy" a good investment. What they won't tell you is that this $1,000+ extended coverage contract costs them only about 50 cents on the asking-price dollar. This is one of the highest-margin items a car store sells. And most car stores would rather sell it and make a $100 or $200 profit than not sell it and make nothing.

To get the best price, you have to make the negotiation as competitive as that for the car itself. The place to start is with the dealer who sells you the car. First, you need to determine which contract you want; they come in many flavors—"premium care" versus "extra care," deductible versus no deductible, 6-year/75,000 miles versus 6-year/100,000 miles, and so on. Ask for the selling dealer's best price on the one you want. Tell him you're going to shop other dealers and you'll buy from them if their price is the lowest. Then call the F&I managers at several other dealerships for that same make and ask for their best prices. Your target will be somewhere between half and two-thirds of the asking price (MSRP).

Buying a factory-backed warranty is a safe choice. Over the years, some third-party underwriters have gone bankrupt, leaving unwary consumers holding worthless contracts that neither the factories nor the dealers would honor. But there are other safe choices. Here are three alternatives to consider.

1. Ryan Warranty Services—Ryan is a big outfit that has been around for decades and administers several factory-sponsored service contracts. Ryan also sells its own extended warranties for all makes and models through new-car dealers. Its MSRPs are typically somewhat lower than comparable factory-sponsored plans. If your selling dealer doesn't offer Ryan contracts, talk to others. Dealers that represent Ryan can usually sell contracts for any car, not just for their own makes.

2. MBI Policies—Mechanical breakdown insurance (MBI) policies are sold by credit unions and independent insurance agents. Backed by a large, top-rated insurance company, they offer direct payment to any licensed repair shop. Coverage is essentially the same as a typical manufacturer's service contract: bumper-to-bumper except for routine maintenance and normal wear items, with a choice of different time/mileage limits, deductibles, and so on. Unlike most automakers' extended warranties, MBI policies are priced according to a vehicle's repair history. Ratings go from 1 (the best) to 8 (the worst). (Automakers' warranties don't do this; they don't want you to know which vehicles will spend most of their life in the shop.)

Since mechanical breakdown insurance is an insurance policy sold by licensed property/casualty agents, with coverage and rates regulated by each state's department of insurance, the prices are non-negotiable. But they are generally significantly lower than the cost of similar coverage in standard extended warranty plans.

Unfortunately, MBI policies aren't sold in all states. An independent insurance agency, Mechanical Warranty Agency, in Elyria, Ohio, sells the policies by mail in 16 states: Arizona, California, Florida, Illinois, Iowa, Maryland, Massachusetts, Michigan, Minnesota, Missouri, North Dakota, Ohio, Oregon, Tennessee, Utah, and Wisconsin. For specifics, call (800) 874–7863 (800–334–7476 in Ohio). If you live in one of these states, you may also find that your credit union sells them. If your state's not listed, it will be difficult to find a source.

3. GEICO Multi-risk insurance—If you have GEICO auto insurance, check out its excellent mechanical breakdown policy. Key advantages: You purchase coverage for only 6 months at a time but can renew it continuously, up to 100,000 miles.

TWO IMPORTANT LAST-MINUTE SUGGESTIONS

1. Read the fine print before you sign the contract. Understand which parts are not covered, whether there's a deductible charge per repair, whether the contract is transferable to the next owner if you sell the car, and whether you'll get any money back if you cancel.

2. **"Use it or lose it."** With both the initial bumper-to-bumper factory coverage and the extended protection, why have it if you don't use it?

This question is especially relevant as you approach the end of the coverage periods.

During the last month or the last 1,000 miles of coverage, ask your dealer's service department to go over the car thoroughly to determine whether any major problems are on the horizon. Request that they do something now about these problems, while your car is still under warranty. A good service operation will be glad to do this for a regular customer.

Two roads diverge in a wood, and I—
I took the one less traveled by,
And that has made all the difference.
—Robert Frost, "The Road
Not Taken"

20

Picking

Your Dealer

Finalists

Now it's time to choose the dealers with whom you'll have serious price negotiations on your finalist vehicles. *The ideal dealer to buy from will not necessarily be the one who'll give you the best price, but the one who'll give you the best service.*

Given what we've told you so far, we may seem to now be throwing you a curveball. We're not; this is simply one more aspect of smart buying.

Your dealer finalists should be those that satisfy two key requirements:

1. They're geographically desirable, reasonably close to either your home or your workplace.

2. They've got service departments with above-average track records.

The convenience factor is obvious. The last thing you need is a 40-mile round trip to have your car serviced regularly. The "service-over-price" factor is less obvious. We are not suggesting that you pay a hefty premium to buy from the dealer who will service your vehicle; if his price is a lot higher, buy somewhere else. (You might even say to him, "I plan to have the car serviced here, and I'd like to buy it here, but I'm not going to pay a big penalty to do that.") But there are advantages to buying where you'll have an ongoing relationship, and they may justify paying a modest premium in the price of the car.

You need a good ongoing relationship with a dealer's service department if you're going to get your money's worth from the second-most expensive purchase of your life, the machine you count on daily to take you where you need to go. With the right dealer and the right service department, you can get so much more than your money's worth that the $100 to $200 you might save buying the car somewhere else will look like very small change—especially when you need warranty work.

According to the National Automobile Dealers Association (NADA), parts and service represent roughly 15 percent of the average dealership's total sales but account for over two-thirds of total profits! (Less than 10 percent of the average dealership's profits come from new-car sales.) If parts and service is the golden goose, you can bet that dealers are going to protect that goose any way they can to maximize its profits.

As you probably know, any franchised dealer will perform repairs on your car that are covered by warranty. But most people don't know that dealers make less profit on factory-paid warranty repairs than on regular, customer-paid work. Here's how dealers typically are compensated for warranty work.

• First, while the factories might pay dealers the same hourly wage rate for warranty work that you pay for nonwarranty work, they typically set specific time limits for almost every type of repair and won't compensate dealers for additional time spent. For many legitimate reasons, including difficulty in pinpointing problems quickly, the time spent can exceed the time allowed, and dealers frequently end up "eating" a lot of that unreimbursed time.

• Second, and probably more important, the manufacturers control the dealer's markup on warranty parts, thus limiting a major profit opportunity.

You may assume that the retail markup on parts that you pay for ranges from 60 to 100 percent, depending on the part and the dealer. But the domestic and import automakers, which profit substantially by selling the dealer those same parts, pay him a much smaller wholesale markup on those used in warranty work—typically 40 to 45 percent. (It used to be only 30 percent.)

But wait, there's more!

• The paperwork blizzard required of dealers to document and claim reimbursement for warranty repairs is a costly nightmare. (If you've ever signed off on warranty work, you know.) And, of course, the speed of factory reimbursement doesn't compare with the instant payment received from customers for nonwarranty work.

• Finally, to add insult to injury, many manufacturers require that dealers save the replaced parts so that they can check them later, if they wish, to ensure that those parts did indeed warrant replacing.

You don't need to be a rocket scientist to understand why no service manager in his right mind would want to load his shop on any given day with warranty work.

ARE THERE TWO CLASSES OF OWNERSHIP?

Whenever one dealer has a better service operation than others selling the same make, the word gets around. People start using the better service facility more, especially when their factory warranties have expired and they're spending their own money. That's why there are a dozen cars in line at 7:00 A.M. at some dealerships and only two or three customers at the same-make dealership three miles down the road.

So what does the manager of that busy first-class service operation do when you call to schedule warranty work on a car you bought somewhere else?

• First, he checks his schedule. If it's crowded, he may put you off to a slow day later in the week, when he'd rather have warranty work than no work. (But he'd probably find a way to squeeze in a regular customer.)

• If he takes you, he might tell you he's not sure he can get it out today. (You could end up at the end of the line if enough regular customers come in.) And you may get one of those phone calls saying, "We can't finish the job today because we needed to send out for a part."

But more important over the long term is what he doesn't do, which is go out of his way to do anything special for you. He'll follow the letter of the law, but he probably won't bend it in your favor, as he might for regulars.

To illustrate, let's look at some things a good service operation can do to keep its regular customers happy.

CREATIVE RULE-BENDING

Has this ever happened to you? You take your car in for regular service and learn when you pick it up that they've fixed something important, something that you didn't even know was broken. Since this expensive work is covered by your warranty, you're pleased that the service department was so thorough.

You'll probably be surprised to learn that there's a reasonable chance that they didn't make that repair to your car, they made it to the car of another good customer whose warranty perhaps had recently expired. They simply charged the factory paperwork to your (in-warranty) car. Neither you nor the other customer knew this, but you both drove home happy.

The manufacturers' service people will never admit that they condone this action, but they want happy customers, too. A few bad dealer service operations can affect their company's overall consumer satisfaction ratings, which, in turn, can affect sales. Common sense says they're likely to look the other way when the rules get bent occasionally by a dealer who keeps his customers happy.

Here's another example of how a good service operation can make life simpler for a valued customer. Have you ever had a car perform badly all day, but when you took it to the dealer it ran beautifully, and his computer analyzer said all the parts were fine?

You had "an intermittent problem," which is often the lead-in to a terminal problem, but because the computer said the part was okay, the dealer couldn't replace it under warranty. (Remember, the factories want dealers to save the replaced parts so they can check their condition and refuse payment if they still work.)

First-class service departments may handle this more creatively. They don't want customers' problems to reappear after they've declared their vehicles fixed. They've seen this complaint before, and they know which part is causing the problem. They decide to replace it now, despite what the computer says. To eliminate any potential reimbursement problem, they'll hook up that used part to their Godzilla Electric Chair to guarantee that it'll be a dead soldier if and when the manufacturer tests it.

We're not saying these things are done routinely every day. But they are done, and they're more likely to be done for the most valued customers. And that's why, if you have your car serviced where you bought it, it's a good idea to leave the dealer's license-plate frame on the car as a reminder to his service people that you're one of them.

Eventually, of course, you will become a valued customer simply by having your car serviced at a dealership repeatedly, whether or not you purchased it there. And there will always be new people moving to town with cars that need be serviced, customers the dealership will be glad to get. But there is something nice about dealing with just one store from the start, even making a point of meeting the service manager or one of the senior service advisers the day you pick up the new car. Ask for his business card, and seek him out when you take the car in for its first regular service. The next time you're there, he'll call you by your first name, and you will have made a potentially valuable ally.

Incidentally, a good service department doesn't necessarily have to bend the rules to accomplish small miracles for you. Many times they'll simply call the manufacturer's regional service manager and ask for special favors for good customers. And the factory people are more likely to grant favors to a service operation that causes them fewer problems.

THE PERVASIVE POWER OF THE CSI

As everyone with a TV set must know by now, CSI stands for Customer Satisfaction Index. In the competitive market they face today, both the manufacturers and their dealers are in the CSI business, not the automobile business. CSI scores are important on several levels.

• On one level, J. D. Power and Associates' CSI data are publicized nationally, providing an important halo for the auto makes that score well. The leaders celebrate their performance in advertising, and consumers are influenced positively.

• On another level, recognizing the critical importance of satisfied customers, the manufacturers are conducting regular in-depth research among their own buyers to establish CSI ratings for each individual dealership. This helps them identify rotten apples that might spoil the whole crop. It also gives them a basis for rewarding top performers. Many automakers base dealer bonus payments on customer satisfaction, not just sales. For example, Chrysler has a dealer cash incentive system in which the payments are based on a combination of sales performance and consumer satisfaction ratings. (This is what prompted the former chairman Lee Iacocca to quip, "It seems a helluva note in life that we must pay a dealer to be nice to his customers.")

• Individual dealer CSI scores also provide a rationale for allocating scarce product. For example, in order to qualify to sell certain limited-volume "image vehicles," dealers are typically required to have a minimum CSI score on an automaker's internal rating scale.

• Finally, a dealer's CSI in his current stores is a key factor in determining whether he'll be granted a franchise by another manufacturer when it's expanding its dealer base.

Many dealers today are mega-dealers who own several different franchises. For example, of the 500 Mitsubishi dealers, about 20 percent also have Chevrolet franchises, 15 percent Toyota, 15 percent Nissan, 14 percent Hyundai, 14 percent Oldsmobile, 14 percent Honda, and 13 percent Ford. The average Mitsubishi dealer owns 2.7 franchises. And only the ones with above-average CSI scores are likely to get additional makes to sell.

Great CSI Scores Are Built on Service, Not Sales

Once you drive that car home, your long-term satisfaction with the selling dealer will be based on how well that dealer's service operation treats you and your expensive baby. Smart dealers understand that "price may bring 'em in, but service brings 'em back." These dealers work harder than others to keep customers happy, and that extra effort helps keep their overall CSI scores among the leaders. These are the kinds of dealers you want.

Assuming you're sold on this point of view, it's time to narrow your choices.

CHOOSING YOUR FINALISTS

You can learn something useful from the dealership experiences of friends and neighbors driving the same make. But you'll gain the most insight by doing your own research, relatively painlessly, over the phone.

Reaching Out Again

Start by making a list of geographically acceptable dealers. Call each and ask for the name of the service manager.

Then call those managers, one by one, and have a little truth session. Tell him your name. Say you're planning to buy that make of car or truck in the next couple of weeks, and that you're trying to pick the right dealer. Tell him you think that several dealers are going to be pretty close to each other on price. But even if they're not, in the final analysis, the quality of the service department will be more important to you in the long run than saving a few dollars up front, and you'd like to talk to him for a couple of minutes about his service operation.

He will like this attitude, because it places the focus where he thinks it should be. It also affirms his importance in the dealership. While he runs his own show (reporting to the dealer's general manager) and produces the bulk of the dealership's profit, he probably doesn't get the respect he deserves. Most dealer principals are sales types, as are their general managers. Sales is, after all, the catalyst for the entire business; a car must be sold before it can be serviced.

Specific Areas to Probe

First ask how long he's been there, and where else he's worked. If he has recently arrived, how long was the previous manager there? (Revolving-door management is not a good sign.)

Then, acknowledging his significant experience, ask him what he thinks may be better about his service operation than some of his same-make competitors. This will give him an open field, so to speak, and he should have some substantive things to say. If he's got a good story to tell, you may hear about how well equipped his shop is, the factory training his people get regularly, his attitude toward customers, and even the dealership's overall CSI.

If you don't hear these things, either he's shy and inarticulate or he's got no great story to tell. Give him the benefit of the doubt, and ask a few more detailed questions.

- **Ask about the dealership's overall CSI score, and specifically, how it stacks up against other same-make dealers in the same factory sales zone.** This is something he has to know about, given its importance to the dealer and his department's key role in making sure it's favorable. If his CSI is above-average, he should be glad to tell you about it. If he hedges or says he's not sure, it's probably below-average. Ask if he'd show you the report if you came in to see him. You want to have your car serviced where the CSI is at least average or better compared to other stores in the same factory sales area.

• **Ask how well equipped his shop is.** Does he have to send cars out for many operations? For example, does he have wheel alignment and wheel-balancing equipment? A brake lathe to turn drums (for drum brakes) and rotors (for disc brakes)?

• **Has the dealership won any recent factory awards for service excellence?** Do his people regularly go to factory training sessions? (Or is the boss too tight to send them?)

• **Does the dealer offer a courtesy shuttle service to take customers to work or home after they drop off a car?** (Many do, but few will also pick you up to return later.) Are loaner cars or low-cost rentals available? And are the service department's hours convenient for you?

Obviously, what you want to hear is that the CSI is above-average for the sales zone, the service manager's job there is not a revolving door, the shop is well equipped, it wins factory excellence awards frequently, the mechanics attend factory training courses regularly, and he'd be glad to give you a shop tour, if you'd like.

After two unsuccessful attempts, beware of service managers who don't return your calls. If you have trouble getting them for a five-minute phone conversation, you may assume their customers have the same problem.

THE ENVELOPE, PLEASE . . .

Not all service departments are created equal, and you'll learn a lot from this relatively painless exercise. You should be able to pick two or three finalist dealerships near home or work. You may even come away with a sense of which dealer you'd like to buy from.

None of this means you're going to be any less disciplined in negotiating price! You're still going to work those sales operations for a minimum-profit deal. You will even use price quotes from car stores you'd never consider buying from to get concessions from your finalists. Whatever deal you strike, you'll be happier buying from the right dealer because your ongoing relationship is more likely to be a good one.

People who have no weakness are
terrible; there is no way of taking
advantage of them.
                         —Anatole France

21

Showtime!

You've done all your homework. You've decided either to sell your
old car yourself at retail or to sell it to a dealer at wholesale, and
you've learned its true wholesale value. You've decided how
much you can spend, and you've researched financing alternatives. You've
taken your test drives and chosen your vehicle and dealer finalists. You've
got your worksheets showing suggested retail prices and dealer invoice
prices, current consumer and/or dealer incentives, dealer holdback, and
carryover allowance for a model-year leftover—assuming that carryover
hasn't been discontinued by General Motors and Ford, the only companies
that ever employed the concept (see chapter 15).

Most important, you've got at least one other vehicle that's an acceptable alternative to your first choice, and you've settled on a couple of colors you'd be happy with for each.

You're ready for the games salesmen play and the back-end add-ons they'll try to sell you. You've decided whether you're a candidate for an extended warranty contract. And you've timed your "talk turkey" visits for either the end of the month or the end of a juicy dealer incentive program.

You've reviewed chapter 4 (Psychology 101, Anatomy 101, and Reality 101) and chapter 7 (Divide and Conquer). You've got the knowledge and the right attitude, and you're going to be a very disciplined shopper. You're just about ready.

THE GAME PLAN

Let's review what you're going to accomplish.

1. You'll visit at least three dealer finalists to negotiate a slim-profit price, using your knowledge to get a better deal than the 99.9 percent of buyers who don't have this knowledge. The car stores will understand they're competing against each other for your money, not against you. And you'll keep the price negotiation completely separate from any discussion of selling your old car or financing the new one.

However you plan to finance the vehicle, it's a good idea at the outset to give the impression that you've got an open mind about financing through the dealership, if the terms are attractive. Chances are, you'll negotiate a better purchase price if they think they have a shot at the financing profit; if they know in advance that you'll finance somewhere else or pay cash, they may hold out for a higher-profit deal. (The same thinking applies to your potential trade-in. Even if you've decided to sell it yourself to an individual or another dealer, let them think initially that you'd consider selling it to them.)

2. After establishing the new-car price, you may open the discussion of financing, telling the salesman you'd like to know what the dealer or the factory has to offer so that you can compare it with other options.

3. At that time you may also open the discussion of your old car, saying that you might want to sell it to a dealer, depending on the price, and asking how much they'd pay you for it. You'll also make it clear that you know what your vehicle is worth at wholesale, and that you don't plan to leave any money on the table.

WHAT TARGET PRICE SHOULD YOU SET?

In a word, a *low* one. The automobile market is the most competitive environment in retailing, mainly because there are twice as many makes, models, and dealers as any civilized society needs. Use that fact to your advantage by playing those makes, models, and dealers off against each other to get what you want—the lowest price.

Remember the key insight we've gained from the thousands of customers who have used the Fighting Chance information service: *Most dealers agree to several slim-profit deals each month with customers who have done their homework and know how to use it.*

Dealers are eager to move their inventory. They've got acres of vehicles, each costing them from $75 to over $150 a month in floor plan interest. They want those autos in your garage and in their service bays, where they make the real profits. Selling one more car this month and making a modest profit always beats not selling it and making those interest payments again.

Think of yourself as the incremental sale, from the dealer's perspective. Assume that they are always dealing—either because sales are down and they want to move them up, or because sales are up and they want to keep them up. And don't be bashful about presenting relatively low offers. Remember that you can always go back and offer more, but you can't go back and offer less.

Having said this, we should add that we are not "anti-dealer." We believe it is appropriate for a dealer to make a profit when he sells a product worth six months' wages for the average household. You just don't want the profit on your deal to finance his next round-the-world cruise.

Remember that negotiation is a two-way process, and you can't drive that new car home until it's yours. Your objective is to arrive at a price you both can agree to. By definition, that price will be a compromise between the dealer's fantasy (getting more than anyone has ever paid for that car) and yours (paying less than anyone has ever paid for that car). Creating the initial impression that your objective is to beat the dealer out of every last nickel will not establish a favorable negotiating climate.

True, some people consider this an enjoyable sport and are willing to spend two or three additional weekends squeezing another $100 or $200 out of a dealer or two. And they may eventually find a dealer desperate enough to accommodate them. We'd say to those folks, "Get a life!" Life is too short to waste even one extra weekend that way. Every other retail store we patronize makes a profit on our purchases; why shouldn't a car store?

The prices knowledgeable shoppers pay for a given vehicle don't differ much from market to market. But average transaction prices can differ substantially from one dealer to another in the same market. Every market has some dealers who want to sell cars in quantity and others who want to maximize the profit on each sale. The first group understands that it's the profit *dollars* they put in the bank, not the profit *percentage*. Both groups will make high-profit deals with customers who don't know what they're doing, but the aggressive dealers will bank more profits because they'll also make several lower-margin deals with better-informed negotiators like you.

The deal will always proceed more smoothly if you're really willing to give the dealer a fair but modest profit, in addition to the holdback. Of course, his definition of "fair" may differ substantially from yours. Here are some general target price guidelines for cars in good supply, based on the feedback we've received on actual transaction prices from thousands of Fighting Chance customers.

• For cars with suggested retail prices up to about $25,000, you can feel good about prices in the range of $300 to $700 over the dealer invoice price. It doesn't seem to matter whether the car is priced at $12,500 or $25,000; transaction prices for people who have done their homework and are willing to walk out of the showroom once or twice seem to fall in this general range. Some tough negotiators will beat this range on the low end, depending on how desperate the dealer is to sell. Others may pay a little more on the high end, depending on how anxious they are to buy.

• For vehicles with suggested retail prices from $25,000 to $40,000, the range of transaction prices among knowledgeable customers is $500 to $900 over dealer invoice on the lower end of the price spectrum and $1,000 to $1,500 over invoice on the higher end. Again, some may do a little better and others a little worse, but you can feel that you've done pretty well anywhere in these ranges.

• For cars with sticker prices from $40,000 to $60,000, the target range is $1,500 to $3,000 over the dealer invoice price. We regularly get reports of customers paying $2,000 to $3,000 over invoice for cars with MSRPs of more than $50,000, which have about a $10,000 profit built into the sticker price.

• The most expensive high-end luxury cars, with sticker prices above $60,000, can be relatively easy to deal on. Dealers don't want to inventory many of them, but they like to have one or two in the showroom as image builders for the dealership. Most dealers want to move those cars regularly. Often a few thousand dollars' profit will motivate them to sell, even if there's a $15,000 to $20,000 profit built into the sticker price. Selling the same car several times a year, so to speak, gives the dealer more overall profit than waiting for the occasional rare deal that delivers the maximum profit for a single sale. He knows he's in a competitive business, even at the highest end. He also knows that he puts profit *dollars* in the bank, not profit percentages.

In all cases, we've assumed the dealer will earn his factory holdback dollars in addition to the profit ranges outlined here. A dealer will almost never share his holdback with you; he counts on it to pay some basic overhead expenses, like the heat and light bills. But you will strengthen your bargaining position by reminding him that you know about it and mentioning the dollar amount, making it more difficult for him to plead poverty when you offer him a slim-profit deal.

As we noted in chapter 15, when one dealer has to obtain the car you want from another dealer, the holdback profit typically remains with the original dealer. But don't let them use this fact as an excuse to negotiate a higher selling price. Dealers regularly trade cars back and forth; it helps all of them operate with lower inventories. Each dealer wins some and loses some, but the trades tend to even out over time.

The price range guidelines above apply to all cars, domestics and imports. Import franchises used to be much tougher to deal with, but times have changed. Today even Honda dealers run ads about prices "$100 over invoice." The Honda Accord is one of the best-selling cars in the United States, and the best-selling cars in any country are usually not in short supply. Anyone who isn't buying a Honda or any other import make for well under MSRP isn't negotiating a realistic price in today's market. If an import dealer won't talk price, move down the road to one who will. He's waiting for you, with a lot full of unsold cars.

If there's a factory-to-dealer incentive program on the car you want, you should end up with all of it because you're paying for all of it. If he'd sell you the car for, say, $500 over invoice if there were no incentive, he would settle for the same profit with customers who know about the factory-to-dealer cash. Make him an offer that starts with the invoice price, subtracts the entire incentive, then adds back an appropriate profit. If one dealer won't cooperate, take your business to another who will. In a market with several competing dealers, they shouldn't be hard to find.

Direct customer rebates should be kept out of the price negotiation. They are your entitlement, almost always paid entirely by the factory. You'll use them as part of your payment after the price is settled. (Typically, you'll sign a document that authorizes the automaker to credit your rebate to the dealer's account.)

ARE THERE VEHICLES ON WHICH YOU CAN'T DEAL?

Yes. You won't get much of a price break on any car when the demand exceeds the supply. The most common example is a hot-selling new model in the first few months after its introduction. And if you must have the only teal green Accord coupe within 500 square miles, it'll cost a lot more than those blue ones lined up on every dealer's lot.

As we noted in chapter 18, frequently there are a few vehicles in short supply because they have become popular almost overnight and automakers can't add production capacity quickly enough to meet demand. In that situation, you may have to take a number, get in line, and pay a lot more than you'd like. You should consider postponing your purchase or placing a factory order. If you can't do either, try calling around in neighboring markets to find a high-volume dealer. Remember, product allocations are based primarily on past sales performance. A dealer who sells just one or two a month gets only one or two a month, and he's going to hold out for the maximum profit on a scarce vehicle. But other dealers who sell and receive 20 or 30 a month may be much more flexible on pricing, if only to move more units and ensure their future supply.

Several makes used to be noted for holding firm on price, but they have become a vanishing breed. The European luxury car dealers would have liked to play the game by the old rules indefinitely, but the Japanese invasion of their high-end turf has changed their attitude, and they are dealing.

The bottom line is that you should make aggressively low offers to just about any dealer today. If it's the end of the month and the cars are sitting there, he just might bite. Remember, you can always decide to pay more later.

THE OTHER CAVEAT: COMPETITIVE GEOGRAPHY

There's another factor that can severely restrict your ability to negotiate a favorable price: the number of dealers for a given make within your area. If you live in a smaller market and there's only one dealer for the car you want within a reasonable driving radius, he's got real pricing leverage. Our advice: Shop by phone or fax with the sales managers at dealerships in the nearest major market, then ask the local dealer if he's really going to force you to leave town to buy the car for a reasonable price. Chances are, you'll reach a compromise price that will keep the business in your town, where you'd both like it to be.

GM's Saturn is a special case: Price competition doesn't exist because each dealer has been given an exclusive sales territory. Eventually, there may be several Saturn stores in your town, but they're likely to all be owned by the same person. And he's not going to compete with himself on price. In our view, Saturn has traded a selling system that takes advantage of some people for one that takes advantage of everyone (see chapter 13).

CREATIVE SNOOPING FOR THE CAR YOU WANT

Before you begin serious price negotiations, it would be helpful to know whether any dealers in town already have the vehicle you want, outfitted to your specifications. Everything else being equal, you'll have more leverage if they already own it, are paying inventory carrying charges on it, and will get the holdback profit when it's sold. You can then call or walk in and say that they've got a car you're prepared to drive home today if the price is right.

To gather this intelligence without being pounced on by a car salesman, get up early some morning—early enough to be walking around the lots between 7:00 and 8:00 A.M. The service department may be open, but you're unlikely to see salesmen before 9:00 A.M. (On a Sunday you won't see anyone except perhaps the security guard at that hour.) If anyone asks what you're doing, tell them you're just fantasizing about your next birthday present.

CURTAIN TIME!

Now we're going to take you through a hypothetical, in-person negotiating session. Of course, we can't script a single approach to apply to all situations, but this example illustrates how you can use your strong base of knowledge in a very disciplined way to achieve the result you want. Think of it as a cat-and-mouse game, with you as the cat. You've got all the tools you need to win, and dealing from strength can actually be fun.

Round One: "The Hammer Wrapped in Velvet"

Start by visiting the dealer you'd most like to buy from, so that you can avoid wasting time with others if you get the price you want. Walk into the showroom with your worksheet pad under your arm. A salesman will greet you. (You're his "up.") He will not be happy to see your pad. If he comments on it, tell him you've got a terrible memory and might want to refer to some notes.

A note of caution: If you are female and are greeted by a saleswoman, don't assume that's a stroke of good fortune. In the research discussed in chapter 2, dealerships seemed to steer testers to salespeople of their own gender and race, who proceeded to offer them worse deals than other testers received from people of a different gender and race. Would a nice saleswoman try to take advantage of you? You can bet on it. No matter how nice she may seem, she is assuming that you will trust her, and that your trust will lead to a higher-profit deal.

From the start, your projection should be friendly but quite confident, disciplined, and firm. You are definitely someone who knows what you want, and knows a lot about what you want. (He'll quickly learn that you know more than 99.9 percent of the people who walk through the door.)

You're knowledgeable, but you're not going to be cocky about it. What you are going to be is very straightforward. And you are always going to act like someone who is going to buy a car.

Smile and introduce yourself. Then tell him that you're definitely going to buy a car in the next week or so, you've taken test drives and know exactly what you want, you're shopping several dealers, and you're going to buy where you get the best price. Then add that a friend wants to buy your old car, but you're not sure that's a good idea. Tell him you've checked out some financing alternatives but haven't made a decision. And say that you'll be happy to discuss selling your old car to him, and to consider his dealership's financing options, but not until you've settled on the price of the new vehicle.

As an overall tactical objective, you want to be the one asking the questions, defining the key issues that need to be resolved, and moving the discussion in a straight line toward a resolution. That way the pressure will be on the salesman to respond to your moves, making it difficult for him to get and keep control of the sales situation.

For example, when he begins asking personal questions about your job or marital status, it's perfectly appropriate to say, "Please don't take this the wrong way, but I know your time is valuable, and if it's okay with you, I'd rather get into a discussion about the car. I already know I can qualify for financing; the question is whether we can agree on a price." If he hasn't invited you to sit in an office by this time, suggest that you go to one to discuss a possible deal in more detail.

When you get there, tell him nicely (perhaps with a little self-conscious smile, but maintaining good eye contact) that you know the auto business is super-competitive today, and that although that makes it tougher for him, you plan to take advantage of that competition, just as he would if he were you.

Then tell him the things he will least like to hear: that you know the dealer invoice price, you're aware of any consumer rebates or factory-to-dealer cash offers in effect, and you've got a feel for realistic transaction prices among knowledgeable buyers. Add that you're not going to try to beat him out of every dollar—you expect him to make a profit on the sale—but that he's not going to finance his next Hawaiian vacation on your deal. Say that if he wants to sell you a car and make a reasonable profit, you'll be an easy customer to close quickly. But that if he and his colleagues want to play their good cop/bad cop, back-and-forth game, you're not going to let them waste your time, and you won't waste theirs. *Then bite your tongue and wait for a response.* The pressure will be on him, not on you.

Remember, you're saying this very calmly, as a really nice person who is also a very knowledgeable shopper he isn't going to be able to fool.

What You've Already Accomplished

You've won the first skirmish with this straight-ahead, no-baloney approach, and you've neutralized his major weapon. He can't do what he does with most prospects at this stage—find their hot button (whether they're payment buyers or trade-in allowance buyers) and move to exploit it.

You've defined the turf on which the battle will be fought: simple cash price. You've also put all the key issues on the table early in the game, making it difficult for him to waste your time bobbing and weaving around them. You are going to learn, reasonably quickly, whether these people want to sell you a car and get on to the next customer or work hard to make you a victim of Life's 80/20 Rule—the one that says 80 percent of the profits come from 20 percent of the buyers.

TAKING CONTROL

At this point the salesman may continue to work with you himself, or he may have been told to pass the most knowledgeable customers along to his sales manager. They may even spirit you away to another part of the office, behind a closed door, so that you won't contaminate their other customers.

Whether you're dealing with the original salesman or with someone new, your next move should be to take out your worksheet, telling him that the best place to start is with the dealer invoice price. By now he's probably classified you as a tough customer, which is fine. (It's wrapped in velvet, but your hammer is there.) *Remember that it's much easier for you to find another dealer than for him to find another real prospect.* As long as you act like someone who's going to buy somewhere soon, he'll keep the discussion alive. To shorten the agony for both of you, you should be prepared to make an opening offer, one that's somewhat below what you're really willing to pay for the car. Here's an approach to moving the dialogue along.

Let's assume there's a current $400 to $800 factory-to-dealer incentive program on your vehicle. For openers, you should start with the total dealer invoice price (including the cost of all optional equipment and the destination charge), subtract the entire $800 factory-to-dealer cash payment, then add back a reasonable profit number. For example, if the vehicle's sticker price is $25,000 or less and you're willing to give them a profit of $500, leave yourself some negotiating room by offering them, say, $250 in your opening bid. Remind him that any direct consumer rebate doesn't figure into this offer, that it will simply be part of your cash payment after you settle on a price.

Here's where you'll use your knowledge of holdback. While holdback isn't something most folks can extract from even the most desperate dealer, it can be used artfully in this game. Just before you end your opening-offer speech, you'll tell him you know they'll get another $400 in holdback profit from your deal, making a total profit of $650. *Then bite your tongue and wait for a response.* (In this cat-and-mouse game, the next one who talks loses. Make sure it's the mouse.)

According to our feedback from Fighting Chance customers, most dealers are going to treat you in a straightforward manner from this point onward. They may not be delighted to hear what you know, but they do want to sell you a car. A very small number may actually kick you out of the store, but that's fine; you'll have uncovered their true colors without wasting half a day enduring their good cop/bad cop selling system. (Remember, you don't know where the bone is until you hit it. You can always call later and offer them more.)

Usually the salesman won't accept your opening offer, whatever it is. If he did, he'd worry that you'd have buyer's remorse, wondering if you'd offered too much. You might even get cold feet, refuse to sign the deal, and go down the street to another car store to see if it would take less. So always expect him to "bump" your offer. Here are some of the responses you can expect to encounter:

• He might say first that there's no way they can sell that car for anything like the price you offered. Your response should be that if that's the case, all he has to do is give you a firm no, and you'll go somewhere else. (Be gathering your things, getting ready to walk out as you're saying this. He will not tell you to go.)

• Since he knows you've been shopping elsewhere, he might ask what price the other guys have quoted, or what price he has to beat. Your response, with a smile: "The only price you need to match if you want to sell me a car is the one in my offer." (It's never a good idea to tell any salesman the prices other salesmen quote.)

• He also might tell you to go out and shop around for the best price, then come back and he'll beat it. You'll say, "I'm sorry, I'm not going to spend a month playing games with car dealers. I am going to buy a car from some dealer within the next week. But if we can't move the discussion along to a final price on this visit, I won't be back to do it later." If he refuses, you should leave.

• He may say that your invoice price numbers are wrong. Your response will be to call his bluff, nicely, by asking him to take out his factory invoice so you can compare the numbers and see where they differ. Tell him you'd be glad to go out to the lot to compare your suggested retail prices with those on the Monroney sticker on the car, and that you expect the MSRP numbers to match exactly. Add that when they do, you'll both know that your invoice numbers are right on the money. Say that if he's going to tell you that the automaker raised the price to the dealer without passing any of the increase along to the consumer, you're going to have a problem believing anything he says. (Note, however, that most dealers add a group advertising charge to their version of the invoice price, though it is not included on the manufacturer's sticker. This is a legitimate expense, discussed later in the chapter.)

If you're still with the original salesman, he probably doesn't have the authority to finalize a deal. Which means he's got to take your offer to his boss. As he leaves—without the hostage deposit check you refuse to write—tell him nicely that you don't know how his store operates, but you're not going to wait there long for him to return. If he's not back in about five minutes, you'll leave. Also say, with due respect for his position, that if he's not someone with whom you can bargain directly to a final purchase price, without passing a lot of messages back and forth, he should bring the decision-maker with him when he comes back.

Don't just sit there while he's gone. To strengthen your psychological advantage, wander around the lot, so that he'll have to look for you when he returns. That'll make him worry that you might leave, and it'll ensure that he won't be gone long, "negotiating for you." (Remember, if he doesn't sell cars, he doesn't eat. He needs you.)

His boss is likely to say that they can't sell a car at that price without losing money; they've got more invested in floor-plan interest payments than your offer allows in profit; they're not going to earn the maximum dealer incentive of $800 anyway; and the bottom line is that they need an additional $700 to even consider a deal.

Your response should be that you hope that's not his best price, because if it is, he's not going to sell you a car. Take out your worksheet and let him look at it. Tell him that you're surprised that a big sales operation like his isn't at or near the maximum incentive payout two days from the end of the program, that dealers that seem to have less volume and inventory have said they were getting the full $800, and that you guess you ought to buy from one of them. Say that you'd expect him to be even more eager to sell you a car if he's below the target with only two days to go.

This would be a good time to inject this new thought, if it's true: Tell him his store is convenient to your home or workplace, and that if you bought the car there, you'd plan to have it serviced there. Since parts and service account for the lion's share of every dealership's net profits, that should give him another reason to be flexible on the transaction price.

Then move the discussion along by adding $100 to your bid, offering him $350 plus the $400 holdback, for a total profit of $750. You already know what you should do next: *Bite your tongue and wait for a response.* If he comes down substantially and it's clear you can make a deal for your target price of $500 over invoice or less, then move to conclude the negotiation quickly and get on with your life. But if he moves by only $100 or so, he's probably expecting to start a series of concessions to see how much higher you'll go. When you refuse to budge, he'll ask, "Why don't we split the difference?"

Never, ever fall for this "generous" split-the-difference offer. Instead, this is where you'll get up and say very politely that it looks as if you aren't going to agree on a price today, that you've got some other stops to make, and that your phone number is 345–6789 if he has a change of heart later—99 percent of car salesmen do, 99 percent of the time. Then ask for his business card, thank him for his time, and leave. You do have other stops to make. And he will be there later if you want him.

PREPARE FOR THE MATINEE

If that was a morning show and your emotional favorite didn't make an offer you couldn't refuse, plan a couple of afternoon performances at other dealer finalists. You'll be more comfortable in these shows, and better prepared for the curveballs they'll throw because you've seen a few. By the end of the day, you'll have a good feel for the parameters of a possible deal and for the probable differences in price flexibility between dealers. Depending on the number of finalist dealers on your list, you may spend a second day completing these round-one visits.

As you review the bidding at the end of this round, factor in your feelings about where you really would like to buy. Where does that store stand on price? Whether it's on the high end or close to the leader, you'll have further discussions with the people there tomorrow.

ROUND TWO:

The next step can be handled best on the telephone. Call all of the players, the last ones you talked to in each store. Thank them again for their time, remind them that you're still planning to buy a new car in the next few days, and tell them that you're calling to see whether they've had a chance to think about your last offer. Your objective here is to get them down as low as they'll go for a live prospect, one they thought had got away.

They might ask, "What's the best price you've been offered?" Just say that it's well below their last offer. Whatever number they give you, tell them it's not your best offer but that you aren't going to make a decision until tomorrow, and they've got your phone number. Thank them again for their time and hang up.

Call your emotional favorite last. Start the conversation the same way. After his response, tell him that you'd really like to buy the car there, for reasons that go beyond price, but that you don't want to pay too dearly for the privilege. You live (or work) right nearby, and you hope he's not going to make you buy a car somewhere else.

Tell him he doesn't necessarily have to be the low bidder, but he's got to be in the ballpark, and he's not quite there now. Emphasize again that you're ready to come down today and finalize the deal. *Then bite your tongue until he says something.*

If you've got two vehicles you'd be equally happy with, it's in your interest to take them both down to the wire. You might be surprised by one dealer's eleventh-hour concessions, especially near the end of a major factory-to-dealer incentive program.

Somewhere in this back-and-forth process, you'll find a deal and a dealer you can live with.

FINALIZING THE DEAL

Before leaving home, review chapter 18 on back-end options. When you get to the dealership, make sure the car isn't loaded with dealer sticker items you don't want. If it is, demand that they throw them in free or find you a car without them.

Be alert at this stage for a host of little surprises, things salesmen "forget" to tell you about until they've got you so committed it would be a real hassle to walk away.

For example, they may charge a fee to process the documents. Of course, they can't sell anyone a car without processing some documents. You could argue that's their cost of doing business, not yours. But frankly, it's not worth much of an argument unless the fee is unreasonably high. We wouldn't dig in our heels over $25 or $30, but if it's $200, we'd apply for a job processing documents there.

Dealer Association Advertising Charge

There's one surprise that dealers spring on customers these days—the local dealer association advertising charge. All manufacturers require their dealers to participate in the group advertising effort in their markets. (These are the commercials inviting you to "Visit Your Southern California Toyota Dealers," not the ones promoting an individual dealer's store.) The dealers form an advertising committee, and they assess every dealer a certain dollar amount for each vehicle sold. This is typically 1 to 3 percent of the invoice price, depending on the media costs in the market and how often the dealers need to run advertising. The charge is usually several hundred dollars per car, and dealers include it in their version of the invoice price. (On a Toyota dealer's invoice, for example, it might appear as "TDA," or Toyota Dealer Association.) The manufacturers don't include this in their dealer invoice prices because the amounts will differ from market to market, and there are hundreds of TV markets. When the dealer claims that your invoice price information is too low, this advertising charge will usually be the main reason.

Is this a legitimate charge to the buyer? We believe it is. Don't we pay for the advertising of everything we buy? When other retailers run ads to attract us, aren't we paying for those ads when we respond by visiting their stores? Of course we are; the cost of the advertising is built into the price of the products we buy there. The only difference is that the car store treats the advertising as a separate charge that's added to the final bill.

Some books on this subject tell you to refuse this charge. And every few months a Fighting Chance customer tells us he did just that and walked away, and the dealer waived the charge because he needed to make the sale. But those reports are rare, and in most cases that customer had to walk away from several dealers before finding one so accommodating. In our view, those other books are giving dated advice. Today virtually all dealers are demanding that customers pay this group advertising expense. Occasionally a dealer may not want to risk losing a sale over it, but most dealers will let you walk if you refuse to pay it—especially if you've already negotiated a slim-profit price on the new vehicle. If a dealer doesn't mention an advertising fee, that may be a sign that you're paying much more than you should for the car. (Some luxury-car dealers don't discuss this cost as a separate charge, but you'll be paying it; it's just built into the hefty gross profit in the deal.)

Wrapping Up the Deal: The Final Checklist

• If you want an extended warranty contract, remember that you don't have to buy it from the dealer who sells you the car. Review the advice in chapter 19, especially the part about soliciting competitive price quotes from other dealers. Wherever you decide to buy the contract, read all the fine print before you sign it. Make sure you understand what it covers and what the deductibles are.

• Read every word of the sales agreement before you sign it. Make sure all the blanks are filled in. And be sure someone with proper authority signs it for the dealership before you do. (If the salesman's signature isn't binding, you don't have a firm deal.)

• Make it clear that you will inspect the car when they tell you it's ready; if you find any significant problems, you have the right to cancel the sale.

Put this in writing, and get them to sign it. When they balk, tell them this true story and say that you won't let this happen to you:

> A Fighting Chance customer arrived to inspect his new vehicle and found a deep scratch that could not be buffed out. When they told him the door would have to be repainted, he said he would not accept that vehicle because it's virtually impossible to match the original factory finish. He was paying for a new car in perfect condition, and he wouldn't accept less. The dealership was uncooperative and argued with him and his lawyer for over two weeks, but finally got him another car.

• If they require a deposit, use a credit card if possible. That way, if there's any last-minute problem, such as this one with the scratched finish, they won't really have any of your money. You can simply refuse to pay that charge when the monthly statement arrives.

• This is the time to explore the potential appeal of the financing plans offered by the dealer. You've done your homework, so you've got a basis for comparison.

• This is also the time to say you're not sure it's smart to sell a used car to a friend. If the price were fair, you'd consider selling it to them. (Don't give them an asking price; make them give you a price first. And don't accompany them for the inspection show pantomime.) They'll take your car and come back with an offer, which you can counter based on the homework you've done on the car's true wholesale value. If they won't pay you that number, or something close to it, take it to one of those places that will.

End of negotiations!

Unfortunately, buyers are not really wise on leasing right now. . . . If you are willing to pay $250 a month, I can make a lot of money on you. If you haven't compared me with other dealers on the details, I can probably really take advantage of you . . . if I were that kind of guy.

—General manager
of a large import-make
dealership, quoted in *Kiplinger's Personal Finance* magazine

The Leasing Alternative: Breaking the Language Barrier

Retail auto leasing is here to stay, and it's big. Pick up any paper. Half the car ads are pushing leases, and not just at the luxury end of the spectrum, where leased vehicles have traditionally accounted for over half of new-car sales. What's happened?

What's happened is that the prices of new cars have skyrocketed, and the automakers and their dealers have found leasing to be an effective way to combat monthly-payment creep. Leasing enables consumers to drive more car for the same monthly payment, or the same car for a lower payment. Addressing the Consumer Bankers Association's Automobile Finance Conference, the chairman of Ford Motor Credit said, "Leasing will become as big as the auto industry wants it to be." Some analysts predict that it will eventually account for 40 to 50 percent of new-car and -truck sales. That would make over 20,000 auto dealers very happy.

WHY DEALERS LOVE LEASING

Leasing is popular among dealers for several reasons, all of which have to do with profit.

• First, it generates quicker customer returns to the dealership, since the average lease term of two to three years is shorter than the average new-car loan of four to five years.

• Second, because dealers know exactly when a lessee will need another new car, they have a tremendous advantage over other dealers in the market. They can start contacting the prospect months before the end of the lease.

• Leasing also provides dealers with a predictable supply of relatively low-mileage, one-owner cars—the bread and butter of a profitable used-car operation.

• *Most important, leasing frequently gives dealers an opportunity to make more profit than they'd earn on a straight sale of the same vehicle.* That's because most consumers don't understand leasing well enough to negotiate the terms effectively.

Here are two examples that illustrate the last point.

A friend faxed us the figures for his three-year lease. It was a done deal, but he wanted our opinion anyway. The details, presented in full on the dealer's summary sheet, showed a capitalized cost of $18,457. Terrific, except for one thing: The full sticker price of the car was $18,302. This friend had "negotiated" a lease in which the price he paid for the car was above the manufacturer's suggested retail price! We told him it was okay, that if he was comfortable with the monthly payment, he should relax and enjoy his new car. But what we were thinking was, "If he were *buying* that car, and he paid the sticker price, would he fax a copy of the sticker and ask what we thought of the deal?"

A student at one of our smart car buyers' seminars came up after the class with two contracts in hand—one for a purchase that didn't happen, the other for a lease of the same car. She had first agreed to buy the car for a net price of $9,500, after subtracting the value of her trade-in. When she arrived the next day with a $9,500 cashier's check, she mentioned to the salesman that she was a real estate salesperson who would use the car for business. Learning this, he said, "You shouldn't buy this car, you should lease it. That way, you'll get more favorable tax treatment." (Why would anyone take tax advice from a car salesman?) She agreed and quickly signed a five-year lease on the car. The lease contract showed the capitalized cost: $13,500! They had added $4,000 to the price of the car and made it a five-year term to keep the payments down. Is it just a coincidence that *leasing* rhymes with *fleecing?*

Unfortunately, we hear stories like these regularly. Many people are paying the full sticker price or more for leased cars. They don't realize what's been done to them because they don't understand leasing. They only understand monthly payments, and the monthly payment on the worst lease deal can be a lot friendlier than the monthly payment on the best purchase deal.

As these two instances illustrate, simply disclosing capitalized costs in leasing contracts doesn't protect the uninformed consumer. In both cases, the paperwork clearly spelled out the size of the rip-off by stating the capitalized cost. But those numbers meant nothing to people who didn't know that the capitalized cost was the price they were paying for the car. And the dealers laughed all the way to the bank.

Many car salesmen will say to you, "What do you care what the price of the car is? You're not buying it, you're leasing it." Nice try, guys, but no cigar. The lion's share of every lease payment you make will pay for depreciation, which is the difference between the price you pay for the car and its value at the end of the lease. And whether you pay the full sticker price or $2,000 less, the value at the end will be the same.

We'll give you all the information you need to avoid a leasing rip-off. But the first question to address is whether leasing represents a viable option for you. Let's examine the issues you should consider.

THE PLACE TO LOOK IS IN THE MIRROR

Leasing can make a lot of sense for some people and be a poor choice for others. Start by asking yourself these questions:

• Do you like to trade cars with reasonable frequency, at least every three or four years?

- Do you value the image you project by always driving a late-model vehicle?

- Would you like to drive a more expensive car than you can afford to buy? Or would you like to drive the same car for a lower monthly payment?

- Do you drive an average of less than 15,000 miles a year?

- Would you rather take the cash you'd use for a down payment and put it into an investment that appreciates?

- Conversely, are you someone who can afford to make the monthly payments but doesn't have enough cash for a significant down payment?

- Are you in the early part of your career and needing the reliability of a new car, but not yet able to afford the monthly payment required for a purchase?

- Do you like the idea of taking a two-year "extended test drive" before committing to the purchase of a new vehicle?

- Do you need one kind of vehicle now but know you'll need another kind in two or three years?

- Are you more intrigued with the concept of paying only for vehicle usage than with the psychic rewards some people get from vehicle ownership?

- Would you like to always be driving a car that's covered by the automaker's initial bumper-to-bumper warranty?

- Are you willing to make monthly car payments indefinitely?

- Do you own a business that will be making those payments?

If you answered yes to many or most of these, you're a candidate for leasing. Leasing is a viable option for people who trade often and drive a moderate number of miles each year, especially if they can write off most of the payments as a business expense. It also makes sense for folks who want to minimize their monthly car payments.

If you answered no to most of these initial questions, ask yourself a few more:

- Do you hate making car payments?

- Do you look forward to Car Payment Freedom Day, when you've made your last payment and you get the title certificate from the lender?

- Do you buy new cars infrequently, typically keeping them five years or more?

- Are you someone who likes to squeeze the last drop of value from every dollar you spend?

- Is keeping up with the Joneses relatively unimportant to you?

- Are you someone for whom pride of ownership of a car or truck is important?

- Do you drive significantly more than 15,000 miles a year?

- Do you have enough cash to make a down payment of 20 percent or more on the vehicle you want, and can you afford the monthly payments on a four-year auto loan?

If you answered yes to most of these and no to most of the previous group, you're not a good candidate for leasing.

If you're a candidate for leasing, you'll be pleased to know that you can almost always lease a better car than you could buy with the same monthly payment, and do it with little or no down payment. And frequently, automakers' subsidies reduce lease payments further by offering below-market interest rates and inflated residual values that reduce the depreciation you'll pay for.

If you're not a candidate for leasing, you'll take comfort in the flip side of this fact: The average car loses 65 to 70 percent of its value in the first five years. As depressing as that is, it does say that the average car retains 30 to 35 percent of its value after five years . . . which is 30 to 35 percent more value than you'll ever retain if you always lease your cars.

Although monthly lease payments are almost always lower than the monthly payments for a purchase with conventional financing, leasing is always more expensive than buying in the long run because lessees never own their vehicle. The only way to squeeze every drop of value from the money you spend on a car is to drive it until the wheels fall off. If you pay for a car in four years and use it for eight years, you'll be driving relatively cheap transportation during the last half of its life. And you'll spend much less for the use of a car than someone who leases several vehicles sequentially over the same period. On the downside, you'll pay the psychic cost of driving a somewhat older car than your less frugal neighbors, the Joneses.

Here's another aspect worth considering: In a sense, people who lease a car for two or three years have a much wider range of vehicle choices because their time frame is so short.

If you're planning to buy a car and own it five years or longer, your analysis has to be fairly pragmatic because your objective is a successful long-term ownership experience. You'll be projecting your automotive needs over a lengthy time span and narrowing your choices based on those needs. You'll probably carefully weigh ratings of initial quality and long-term reliability. And the emotional component in the decision will take on additional meaning, because this is going to be *your car* for a long time. In a small way, this is like marriage, and most of us are going to be very picky in deciding which car to buy.

By contrast, choosing a car to lease is more like picking a partner for a brief fling. Long-term needs aren't an issue; you get to shuffle the new-car deck and deal again in two or three years. Long-term reliability isn't an issue; it's covered by a bumper-to-bumper warranty for virtually the entire period. If there's a problem, it's their problem, not yours. And the emotional component has less meaning because *it's not your car,* it's really just a Hertz car that you're renting for a while. All of which leaves you open to almost any vehicle, because there's no serious penalty for making a mistake.

If you've already decided that leasing is not for you, you should skip to the next chapter. But anyone considering leasing should pay close attention to this next point.

AUTO LEASE ADS ARE FINE-PRINT HEAVEN

Let the buyer beware: Mouse type was invented for car leases. You'll need a magnifying glass to read the ads, and you'd better use one. Here are some actual fine-print examples (the italics are ours):

- "Lease based on total MSRP including destination charge."

- "Optional equipment not included in monthly payment."

- "Mileage charge of $.15 per mile over 15,000 miles/year."

- "Monthly payment based on *10% down payment.*"

- "Customer responsible at signing for first monthly payment, insurance, taxes, title and registration fees, *plus $450 documentation fee.*"

- "Prices may vary based on dealer contribution."

- "$7,079 *dealer/customer* capitalized cost reduction due at lease signing."

- "$350 disposition fee due at lease end *if vehicle is returned.*"

- "Non-refundable prepaid rental reduction of $1,350 (cap reduction) required."

If leases seem more complex than standard auto loans, it's primarily because the language of leasing is so different from that of buying. And both new-car dealers and independent leasing companies can use that extra layer of "boomfog" to take advantage of leasing prospects.

LEASING BASICS DEMYSTIFIED

If you like the idea of leasing but are put off by the language barrier, relax. Although leasing has more aspects to consider than conventional financing, it is neither mysterious nor hard to understand. A straightforward walk through the basics should convince you that it's a relatively simple concept that gets tangled in its own underwear by the terminology.

The Simple Concept

Think of leasing as long-term car rental. When you sign a lease, you agree to make a specific monthly payment for a specific number of months in return for use of the car during that period.

In lease language, you are the **lessee,** and the company that leases you the car is the **lessor.** The lessor is typically not a dealer but a separate financing company that buys the car from a dealer and then leases it to you. This could be one of hundreds of independent leasing companies, a national, regional, or local bank, or an auto manufacturer's captive finance subsidiary, such as GMAC or Toyota Motor Credit Corporation.

What You Pay For

The monthly payments you make to the leasing company cover two basic elements:

1. You're paying for the estimated depreciation in the vehicle's value over the term of your lease. You're not paying for the whole car; you're paying only for the part of its value that you use. That's why the monthly payment will be lower than a standard auto loan payment.

2. You're paying an interest charge. Often called a lease fee or a lease rate, it's the equivalent of a bank's interest charges on an auto loan. You're paying interest on the depreciation, which you are financing and paying off over the term of the lease, just as you would pay off the principal of a conventional car loan. You're also paying interest on the balance of the car's value—what it will be worth at the end of the lease term. That's because the leasing company has to pay the dealer for the whole car, not just the depreciation. Otherwise, you couldn't drive it home. In effect, you're borrowing that lease-end value and driving it around for a few years.

In the language of leasing, the amount of depreciation that you pay for is determined by the difference between two components: the capitalized cost and the residual value. Here's the simple equation:

Depreciation = Capitalized Cost – Residual Value

The **capitalized cost** is the equivalent of the purchase price paid when you buy a car. It is the price the leasing company pays the dealer for the vehicle. *That amount should be the transaction price that you've negotiated.* It can also include other miscellaneous start-up charges, title and registration fees, and sales taxes (depending on your state) if you choose to finance them by folding them into the lease and paying for them monthly instead of up front.

The **residual value** is an estimate of the car's value at the end of the lease period, usually stated as a percentage of the vehicle's original sticker price (MSRP). That percentage typically is established by the leasing company, the financing entity that will own the vehicle, and it is not negotiable.

If you think about this for more than five seconds, you'll recognize that the higher the capitalized cost and the lower the residual value, the more depreciation you'll pay for and the higher your payments will be. And, of course, vice versa.

The **lease rate** or **lease fee** is the interest rate the leasing company charges you to finance the lease. It is also typically not negotiable, and it's stated as a **money factor,** a decimal number used to calculate the interest part of the monthly lease payment. (To convert a money factor to an approximate interest rate, multiply by 24. For example, a money factor of .003125 times 24 equals .075, or 7.5 percent. We'll discuss this in more detail later in the chapter.) The higher the lease rate, the higher the payment. And, of course, vice versa.

Keep It Closed

Virtually all leases today are closed-end agreements, which is the only kind you should consider. That means you'll know all the financial requirements from the start. At the end of the lease term, you'll return the car and walk away with no additional obligation. The residual value of the vehicle is predetermined; if the car is worth less, that's the lessor's problem, not yours, as long as you've taken reasonably good care of it.

Keep It Repaired

Because the residual value estimate assumes you'll return the car in good shape, you'll pay the cost of fixing anything beyond normal wear and tear. The better leases contain guidelines for acceptable damage, but some definitions can be fuzzy. Ford does a pretty good job of defining what's acceptable and what is not. For example, Ford tells customers these items are normal wear and tear:

- Dings
- Minor dents
- Small scratches
- Stone chips in the paint finish
- Reduced tread on tires

By Ford's definition, these items represent excess wear and tear:

- Broken or missing parts
- Dented body panels or trim
- Damaged fabric
- Cracked or broken glass
- Poor-quality repairs
- Unsightly alterations
- Tire/wheel damage or less than one-eighth of an inch of tire tread remaining
- Mechanical and electrical malfunctions

As you can see, there is room for subjective interpretation on several items in each category. To be safe, assume that you should take better care of a leased car than you would of your own, and that "unacceptable damage" means anything you'd repair or replace if it were yours. A dented fender. A broken antenna. An automatic window that won't go up and down. If anything needs fixing, have the work done before you return the car at the end of the lease term. It will cost you much more if the lessor has it done.

Down Payments

One of the selling points of a lease is that you don't need to come up with a down payment. You will, however, have to write a **drive-off check** in order to get the car keys. This typically covers the first month's payment, a lease acquisition fee, the first year's vehicle registration fee, sales taxes depending on your state, and a refundable security deposit equal to about one monthly payment. (The security deposit is usually waived the second time you lease from the same lessor.) For most cars this drive-off check will be $1,000 to $1,500.

But there are lots of exceptions, especially in the most attractive leases. You'll note that the ads for many of those low-payment lease deals have fine print that says something like: "Estimated monthly payment is based on suggested retail price, with a nonrefundable prepaid 10 percent capital cost reduction"—otherwise known as a *down payment*. This **cap reduction** pays part of the depreciation charge in advance. Even when no cap reduction is required, some folks might decide to make one to reduce their monthly payments, perhaps by using the proceeds from selling or trading in their old car.

Advance Payment Leases

Some leases offer the option of a single large payment up front that covers all costs for the term of the lease, with no monthly payments thereafter. Such a payment avoids the interest charge for depreciation and prepays the interest on the residual value. These leases tend to be for luxury cars, probably because only luxury-car buyers can write a check that large.

The Purchase Option

You'll have the option to purchase the vehicle for its residual value at the end of the lease term. Going in, you want the highest possible residual value. The higher the residual, the lower the depreciation and the lower your monthly payment. (As we'll discuss shortly, the automakers often subsidize leases by using incentive dollars to establish artificially high residuals.)

Of course, an inflated residual value works against you if you plan to buy the car at the end of the lease. But you can't have it both ways; it's "pay me now, or pay me later." If that **buyout price** is above the street value of the car, you're not going to pay it . . . and neither is the dealer. In that situation, the leasing company's alternative is to send the car to a wholesale auction, where some dealer will buy it for a price well below the residual value. So if you want the car, make the leasing company a realistic offer, as you would for any used car. In theory, everything is negotiable in this business, and they may take less if the residual is out of line with reality.

There is a way to get a low residual/buyout price. Simply have the company write the lease for 25,000 or 30,000 miles/year instead of the standard 12,000 or 15,000. The residual will be artificially lowered to a much friendlier buyout price, but your monthly lease payments will be sky-high. That will make sense only for people who can write off those payments as a business expense. Before doing this, talk to your accountant to make sure you won't be waving a red flag at the IRS.

Always check a leased car's street value before you turn it in. Occasionally a vehicle can be worth substantially *more* than its residual value at lease-end. If it is, and if your next car will be the same make, the dealer may convert some or all of that extra value into a price concession on your new car. Alternatively, you may want to buy your leased vehicle and resell it yourself for a quick profit. Note, however, that your state may allow only a brief time period before requiring that you pay the sales tax on the purchase. That means you'll want to have the next buyer lined up before you buy the car.

Excess Mileage Charges

The lease contract will specify a **mileage allowance,** and a penalty for exceeding it. Typical terms: 12,000 or 15,000 miles a year over the term of the lease, and a penalty of 10 to 15 cents per excess mile. If you know you'll exceed the limits, some lessors will sell you extra miles at the beginning of the term for a somewhat lower rate, and you'll pay for them with a somewhat higher monthly payment. (But you may not get your money back if you don't use those extra miles.)

Since the terms of most leases are negotiable, you may find you can get the lessor to waive the mileage restriction, reduce the penalty charge, or increase the yearly mileage allowance. This is generally not easy to accomplish, but it's worth trying.

There's a happy flip side to this issue. If you drive only 5,000 to 10,000 miles a year, you may qualify for a low-mileage discount from some leasing companies, since your car will have a higher value at the end of the lease.

The Lease Term

Most automakers are pushing short-term leases of two or three years so that you'll be back soon for another new car. What's the best lease term for most people? One that's no longer than the length of the original bumper-to-bumper factory warranty, so you'll never have to face a big repair bill. If you opt for a longer term to lower the monthly payments, you should consider purchasing an extended warranty policy to avoid that risk (see chapter 19). We'd self-insure for a lease term that's only one year longer than the initial warranty but purchase the extended warranty for anything beyond that.

Early Termination

Don't sign a lease for a term that's longer than you're sure you'll keep the car. Every lease has an **early termination clause,** and it's a painful end to consider. You'll usually have to make all of the remaining payments. No leasing company will let itself get stuck with a year-old car from a three-year lease contract. That's because you're making level monthly payments over the lease term, but the car doesn't depreciate at a level rate. The biggest depreciation hit occurs in that first year, and one year of payments doesn't begin to cover the actual loss in value.

Before you sign any lease agreement, be sure you understand your liabilities in the event of early termination.

Closing the Gap

What happens if your leased car is stolen or damaged beyond repair (totaled) in a wreck? All lessors treat a stolen or wrecked car as a form of early termination. Your insurance company pays them the car's market value, but that number can be a lot lower than the amount you still owe on the lease. It's not smart to leave yourself open to this financial risk.

Many auto manufacturers' captive finance companies—such as GMAC, Ford Motor Credit Corporation, and Nissan Motors Acceptance Corporation—shield their customers from losses if a leased vehicle is stolen or wrecked, paying any difference between the insurance payoff and the lease balance and allowing the customer to get a new car. To cover potential losses, they provide their own **gap insurance,** either by self-insuring or by paying a modest premium for each vehicle leased (probably under $50 per vehicle). They build this cost into your monthly payment.

Whether you're leasing from one of the captive companies or from an independent leasing outfit, you should ask about *and get* gap insurance. If it's not built into the lease agreement, treat it as a bargaining point and ask the company to provide it at no cost. (They may not agree, but it's worth a try.) Gap insurance shouldn't add more than a few dollars to your monthly lease payment. For example, a credit union in California charges only $102 for a policy covering a three-year lease term. But beware of rip-offs. One large independent leasing company quoted a $100 per month premium on a five-year lease of a luxury car! Clearly, the dealer was an accomplice in this larceny, and the biggest gap was between the price and the value of that insurance. If anyone tries to pull this on you, walk out and lease somewhere else.

Basic Auto Insurance Costs

You may have to pay more to insure your leased car. Leasing companies tend to require higher limits than many people normally carry. Check this out early and factor it into your cost projection.

Credit Requirements

Most financing companies have higher standards of creditworthiness for leases than for conventional auto loans. If your credit history is spotty, you may not be approved for a lease, or the company may require a significant down payment and charge you a higher interest rate.

Sales Taxes

Most states treat leasing like any other purchase and tax the total amount of your payments, including the interest portion. But there are exceptions. A few states make you pay tax on the entire capitalized cost up front, as if you were purchasing the vehicle. (Typically, you may pay it then or finance it and include it in your monthly payment, amortized over the term of the lease.) If your state has a personal property tax, expect the leasing company to add that in. And if there's an automaker's rebate or "loyalty discount" that reduces your capitalized cost, most states treat it as if it were a down-payment check you had written and require that you pay tax on it, too. To determine how leasing is taxed where you live, call your state's taxing authority or ask your accountant.

These Lemons Don't Make Lemonade

All states have lemon laws, which protect consumers from getting stuck with chronically ill cars. And most of these laws give the lessee (you) the same rights as the lessor.

But why should you have to go through that hassle, when it's the leasing company's lemon? They buy all those cars, so they've got the leverage with dealers and manufacturers. Ask how they'd handle a lemon situation. If you like their answer, get it in writing. If you don't, lease from someone else.

Miscellaneous Fees

The leasing company gets much of its income from fees, which are typically not negotiable. The most common one: a *lease acquisition fee,* sometimes called a *bank fee,* of $300 to $700. Then, when you turn in the car, there's a *disposition fee* of $100 to $300 if you don't exercise your option to purchase the vehicle. These extra charges may seem like rip-offs, but they really aren't. Here's why.

When a financial institution or finance company makes a typical four-year auto loan, it earns a profit by buying money at one interest rate and loaning it at a higher rate. After checking the customer's credit and approving the loan, there are virtually no additional expenses unless the borrower defaults on the loan and the car has to be repossesed. The financing entity receives 48 monthly payments, then mails the ownership document to the borrower.

A lessor's world is more complicated because the financing entity actually owns the leased car. It must inspect the vehicle at the end of the lease term, determine whether the lessee must pay for excess wear and tear, and have any needed repairs made. If the lessee doesn't purchase the car, the leasing company must sell it to a dealer or send it to a wholesale auction. To do this, it needs extra people and a place to put them—costly overhead expenses that wouldn't be required if it weren't in the leasing business. Yet the leasing company can't necessarily charge a higher interest rate for a lease than for a purchase. So how does it cover these extra expenses? With the lease acquisition fee on the front end and the disposition fee on the back end.

Occasionally an automaker is so desperate to move cars that its captive finance company waives one or both of these fees. But with most leases, you will have to pay them.

FACTORY-SUBSIDIZED LEASES

As we noted earlier, people who lease come back for a new vehicle more often than people who buy. That's the main reason automakers funnel big incentive money into leases—even those that shun customer rebates and factory-to-dealer cash incentives because they think those things cheapen the perceived value of their brands. Using incentive dollars to reduce monthly lease payments allows automakers to cut the price under the table, so to speak, without the stigma of open price-cutting.

Instead of offering you a $1,000 rebate, or giving dealers a $2,000 cash incentive, the manufacturers take the same sales promotion dollars and shift them over to their captive finance companies. The finance companies use that money in two ways to lower your monthly lease payments. They can inflate the residual value to an artificially high level, reducing the depreciation charge. They can also "buy down" the interest rate to a level below the market rate, reducing the finance charge. The net result can be a very attractive deal.

It's not unusual for different vehicles of the same make to have very different residual value percentages and interest rates, depending on how aggressively automakers are pushing certain models in specific time periods. They usually don't need lease subsidies to sell the most popular products, but when the market is soft you might find special lease deals on almost any vehicle. Manufacturers' different lease incentive programs can come and go like the wind, and tracking them all would be impossible. We know of no reliable source of information on current offerings, but many of them are advertised in newspapers. (*Note:* The factory-subsidized lease deals are available only through the manufacturer's financing arm, not through independent banks and leasing companies.)

Do You Get the Incentive If You Lease?

You might logically ask whether the purchase incentives offered to buyers by automakers are also given to customers who lease. They are, but not necessarily in the same way.

A lessee usually won't qualify for a rebate because he's not buying the car, though sometimes manufacturers apply a rebate to either a purchase or a lease. From your perspective, it doesn't matter whether they do or not. If you don't get the rebate on the front end to lower the capitalized cost, you'll see an equivalent value on the back end, in the form of a higher residual value and/or a lower lease interest rate from the automaker's captive finance company. You won't care whether the capitalized cost is $1,000 lower or the residual value is $1,000 higher, because your monthly payment will be the same either way.

Similarly, the benefit of a factory-to-dealer cash incentive shows up either on the front end or the back end, depending on whether the lease is with the captive finance company or another financial entity. If it's a third-party lease, the dealer gets that cash and you can use it to negotiate a lower capitalized cost. But if it's a factory-subsidized lease, the captive finance company usually gets the cash, not the dealer, and you see it in the form of a higher residual and/or a lower interest rate.

Occasionally, when the lease subsidies are particularly heavy, the dealer may even be required to pay part of the cost. For example, when there's a super-low interest rate, such as 0.9 percent or 1.9 percent, the automaker is selling money at a rate well below the rate it must pay for the same money. In that instance, a dealer may have to contribute several hundred dollars to help defray the extra expense, and you may find dealers less flexible on transaction prices.

NEGOTIATING A LEASE WITH CONFIDENCE

Because the key elements of a lease sound like a foreign language to many people, car salesmen can use that language barrier as a smoke screen while they make some of the most profitable deals in the business. As soon as a prospect mentions leasing, the only thing a salesman wants to talk about is the monthly payment. Indeed, the dumbest opening question anyone can ask a car salesman is, "How much per month to lease this car?" That's like walking in with a big sign that reads, "I Just Fell off the Turnip Truck." The payment quoted will be based on the full sticker price or more. As we noted earlier, showing the purchase price under the heading of "capitalized cost" may not alert the uninformed. And because the monthly payment on a terrible leasing deal can be a lot lower than one on a good purchase deal, it's relatively easy for consumers to get fleeced if they haven't done their leasing homework.

THE INFORMATION YOU NEED

The first part of that homework is the language of leasing; the other is the arithmetic. You need to do that arithmetic yourself to be sure the leasing company hasn't added an extra $30 or $40 a month. Fortunately, it's easy to do if you have the information on these four key elements that determine the size of the payment:

1. The **term of the lease,** typically three years or less.

2. The **capitalized cost,** which should be the purchase price you negotiate, plus any additional elements that you agree to include (such as a lease acquisition fee, if you'd rather not pay it up front).

3. The leasing company's **finance charge,** expressed as either an interest rate or a money factor. If they give you the interest rate, divide it by 24 (a constant factor unrelated to the length of the lease) to get the money factor. (For example, 7.5 percent or .075, divided by 24 equals a money factor of .003125.) If they give you the money factor, multiply it by 24 to get the approximate equivalent of the annual percentage rate (APR) for a loan. (A money factor of .003125 times 24 equals .075, or 7.5 percent.) If the rate is above the current APR on conventional auto loans at your local bank, you should ask the dealer to shop for a better rate from another leasing company.

4. The **residual value** of the car, or its estimated value at the end of the lease. This is stated in the lease agreement; it's the price at which you may buy the vehicle at lease-end. It is shown as a dollar value but figured as a percentage of the gross sticker price (MSRP), before any equipment package discounts. Different vehicles depreciate at different rates, depending on the demand for them as used vehicles. Your monthly lease payment could be lower for a more expensive car that holds its value well than for a less expensive car that depreciates more rapidly.

The industry's "bible" for residual values is the Automotive Lease Guide's *Residual Percentage Guide.* Published bimonthly, this guide lists each vehicle's estimated wholesale value, as a percentage of the original sticker price, after two, three, four, and five years. These estimates assume that you won't buy the car when the lease ends, and that the leasing company will sell it to dealers at an auction.

In our experience, the residual values in lease agreements almost always exceed those in the *Residual Percentage Guide* by anywhere from a few percentage points to ten or more points, depending on how aggressively manufacturers are subsidizing leases. The exception: If a vehicle is hot and in short supply, and you have to take a number and get in line to buy one, the manufacturer can easily move every car without subsidizing leases. For all other cars, you should view the values in the *Residual Percentage Guide* as low-end, red-flag numbers. If a dealer quotes you a number that low, you should ask him to shop other leasing companies; if he quotes a lower number, they are trying to charge you for "phantom depreciation," and you should walk away and lease from someone else. To check projected depreciation for the vehicles you're considering, purchase the latest issue of the *Residual Percentage Guide* from Chart Software (800–418–8450). The cost should be about the same as the price of this book.

It's common for different leasing companies to assign different residual values to the same vehicle. When leasing began to grow dramatically, many banks and finance companies lost a lot of money guessing wrong on residuals. As a result, some lessors estimate more conservatively than others. For example, assume you're considering a three-year lease of a sedan with a sticker price of $22,000. One leasing company estimates a 55 percent residual value of $12,100; another uses 48 percent in its calculation, or $10,560. You will pay that $1,540 difference—an extra $42.78 per month, plus interest.

Tell the salesman that you are aware of these potential differences. You know that the residual percentage may not be negotiable at any specific leasing company, but you expect him to check several sources to determine which is the most favorable. Understand, however, that your objective is to get the best overall deal, and that a higher residual frequently comes with a higher interest rate and won't necessarily net you a lower payment. (As noted earlier, the highest residuals and lowest interest rates often come from the automaker's captive finance company when incentive money is allocated to subsidize the lease deal.)

Here's a helpful shopping tip: Call finance managers in advance at several dealerships to ask about current residual values and money factors for the car you want. Tell them you're considering two different cars, one of which their store sells, and this information will help you choose one over the other. Some of them may share that information when you're in this "competitive browsing" phase, especially if you tell them you'll shop their store if you decide to lease the car they sell.

RUNNING THE NUMBERS

Now let's assume you've negotiated a transaction price of $20,000 on a car with a $22,000 sticker price, and that the car's residual value after three years will be $10,000. If you were to *buy* it and finance the whole purchase, part of each payment would pay off the $20,000 principal, and the rest would pay interest on the loan. You'd owe $20,000 at the beginning and nothing at the end. On average, over the life of the loan, you'd have an outstanding principal of $10,000—half of the original balance.

When you *lease,* you still pay interest on the whole amount because the financing entity (the leasing company) has put up $20,000 to buy the car from the dealer. But unlike a conventional auto loan, the only "principal" you pay off is the $10,000 of depreciation—the difference between the capitalized cost of $20,000 (your negotiated price) and the residual value of $10,000. You don't "pay off" that residual value, but you pay interest on it because you're borrowing it and driving it around for the term of the lease.

Now let's do the arithmetic, assuming a 36-month lease with a 7.5 percent interest rate. We'll do it using the **constant yield method,** which is used by all major leasing companies except Ford Motor Credit. This isn't brain surgery, but it's different, so stay awake.

1. Figure the monthly depreciation charge. Divide the $10,000 depreciation by 36 months to get $277.78.

2. Determine the monthly finance charge. Add the $20,000 capitalized cost to the $10,000 residual value. Multiply that $30,000 by .003125 (the money factor, figured by dividing .075 by 24) to get $93.75. It appears that we're double-counting the residual value, but we're not. The money factor has a built-in assumption that everything gets paid off, like the principal of a conventional car loan, so it cuts everything in half—assuming that on average, the outstanding "principal" is half of the total. That works for the depreciation, since you pay it off over the term of the lease. But you don't pay off any of the residual value. So you must double it before you apply the money factor, which brings it back to its original value.

3. Add the $277.78 depreciation and the $93.75 interest, for a total monthly lease payment of $371.53. Plus tax.

To calculate the effect of making a down payment, or "cap reduction," just reduce the capitalized cost by the amount of the payment and do the arithmetic again.

That's it. Knowing this relatively simple calculation can be very empowering. With it, you can easily "solve" for any of the three factors if you know the other two. Since you negotiate the capitalized cost, and the residual value is stated in the lease agreement, the only missing factor is usually the interest rate. Dealers are not required to disclose this rate, or the money factor, though many will do so when they understand that you can perform this simple calculation.

To solve for an interest rate, start with the monthly lease payment (before sales tax) and subtract the monthly depreciation charge. The difference is the monthly finance charge—$93.75 in the example here. Then divide that finance charge by the sum of the cap cost and the residual value ($30,000 in our example), and you get a money factor of .003125. Multiply that money factor by 24, and *voilà,* there's the interest rate—7.5 percent.

With just a few minutes' practice and an inexpensive calculator, you can figure hypothetical lease payments based on different assumptions of cap costs, residual values, and money factors. Take your calculator with you and run the numbers at the salesman's desk. You will thrill and amaze him. Chances are, he doesn't know how to do it—not because he couldn't perform these simple calculations, but because the dealer wants him to think that only a computer can do anything that complicated. You'll be in complete control, which is the way it should be.

If there's an exception to every rule, Ford Motor Credit Corporation is the exception on leasing arithmetic. Ford uses an antiquated method to determine lease payments, applying one mysterious money factor to the capitalized cost and another to the residual value. Ford's money factors include a built-in administrative fee that makes the effective APR of the lease 1.5 to 2 percent higher than the "internal" interest rate quoted to you by Ford dealers—a discrepancy that you'll discover when you run the numbers.

There's an alternative method that Ford dealers sometimes use to calculate lease payments. They figure the monthly depreciation charge in the standard way, as we have done here. But they perform two nonstandard calculations to figure the finance charge. First, they develop a money factor by dividing Ford's internal interest rate by 12. Then they multiply this money factor by the capitalized cost to get the finance charge. This method also generates a higher effective APR than the more commonly used constant yield method.

Of course, you can easily determine the real rate Ford and its dealers are charging by using the arithmetic outlined here. While it appears that they'd like to hide that rate from you, Ford isn't necessarily padding the interest rate. If a dealer quoted Ford's internal rate at 7.5 percent, but the current bank rate on conventional auto loans were 9 to 9.5 percent, the company's calculation shenanigans wouldn't really be costing you anything. But if the market rate were also 7.5 percent, you'd draw the opposite conclusion.

Back in chapter 10, you learned that car stores earn a commission or fee from lenders when they arrange the purchase financing. That's also true with leasing. Whenever the lease rate is at or near the going market rate for auto loans, the dealer is probably getting a few basis points. (A basis point is one-tenth of a percentage point.) That's neither illegal nor immoral; it's an important income source for auto dealerships. Unfortunately, there's no way to determine the dealer's cut. Your protection against getting ripped off on lease financing will come from (a) knowing the current rate in your market for standard auto loans, and (b) doing the arithmetic yourself to uncover the real interest rate on a proposed lease deal.

Dealers probably get less financing income from leases than from purchases. Based on several years' experience going through lease deals with Fighting Chance customers, we've concluded that the typical lease rate is about 1 to 1.5 percent below the going rate for car loans. That's because the marketing battles are fought in lease ads featuring low monthly payments; to keep those payments low, automakers must hold down interest rates. In this competitive climate, there's less financing profit for leasing companies to share with dealers, and sometimes none at all when the rates are highly subsidized and well below market.

Most people will find the simple arithmetic of the constant yield method more than sufficient to help them negotiate a lease effectively. However, if you have computer skills and would like to own software that performs all the calculations forward and backward, you should check out the "Expert Lease" programs published by Chart Software. They enable you to analyze lease terms, perform lease-versus-buy analysis, compare leases, and print payment tables for use during negotiations. One version even contains the Automotive Lease Guide's residual value tables. For current information on specs and prices, call Chart Software at (800) 418–8450.

THE ONE-PAYMENT LEASE

If you don't want the hassle of writing a check every month and can afford to write one very large check, you might consider the alternative of a single-payment lease. This will save you some interest expense, maybe a lot.

When you write that one big check, you'll avoid paying interest on the depreciation, since you'll be paying the entire depreciation charge up front, instead of paying it month by month. You'll still pay interest on the residual value, since you're borrowing it and driving it around for the lease term. But you might negotiate a somewhat lower interest rate because you'll pay all the interest on day one, instead of in monthly installments.

Let's assume you're leasing the same vehicle we used in the earlier example—a 36-month term, a $20,000 capitalized cost, a $10,000 residual value, and a 7.5 percent lease rate. The monthly payment was $371.53, for a 36-month total of $13,375. With a one-payment lease, you'd write a check for $12,250—$10,000 for depreciation plus $2,250 for interest (7.5 percent time $10,000 residual value times 3 years). Your net interest savings: $1,125. You'd save another $150 if they cut the rate to 7 percent.

SHOWTIME!

Now it's time to use your leasing knowledge to negotiate the deal. You're going to do it with essentially the same direct, no-baloney approach you'd use to buy the vehicle, outlined in chapter 21. Your price target should be the same, whether buying or leasing.

First, you'll say that you're going to lease either an Accord or a Camry, you don't really care which, in the next ten days. (Never let them know they've got the only model that makes your heart beat faster.) And you're going to base your decision on price.

Then tell the salesman that you aren't going to talk about monthly payments until you've established the price of the car. And that price will become the capitalized cost of the lease, unless you decide to add other charges to it. Add that you expect him to make a profit, but you're not going to finance his next Hawaiian vacation.

Tell him you've done your homework. You know the dealer invoice price. You know about the dealer's holdback. (If there is any, be specific). You know how sales of that model have been going. (If sales are down or sluggish, or if the average dealer sells only a few each month, be very specific.) And you've got a good feel for transaction prices among knowledgeable customers. Most important, you know how to do the leasing arithmetic, including how to determine the interest rate or money factor, and you aren't going to sign a lease with any dealership until you can run the numbers and come to the same monthly payment they're quoting.

Say that if he wants to make a fair but modest profit and will deal with you in a straightforward, cards-up way, you're going to be the quickest, easiest lease deal of the month. But you're not going to let him waste your time, and you surely won't waste his.

Then make him an offer, using the same basic approach you'd use to buy the car. Start with the dealer invoice price and add an appropriate number for profit—smaller at first than you're really willing to agree to. Remind him of the specific amount he'll receive in holdback. Then bite your tongue and wait for a response. As we've said before, the person who talks next will lose. If he really wants to lease you a car, you should be able to strike a deal with a minimum number of counteroffers. When you reach your target, stand firm.

If he tells you he could sell you the car for that price but can't possibly lease it for the same price, get up and walk out. Many dealers try to get a higher front-end profit on a leased car because they have fewer opportunities to make back-end profits by selling extended warranties, extra rustproofing, and additional accessories, which people are less likely to buy for leased cars. But if the dealer is willing to sell the car to you for a certain price, he should be as willing to sell it to a leasing company for the same price. If he's not, tell him you're sure you can find a more cooperative dealership. Just as with a straight purchase, you must be ready to end any lease negotiation abruptly if the salesman's being unreasonable. (Remember Reality 101: You can walk away from any deal and be absolutely certain there is one just like it, and probably better, around the next corner.)

Once you've settled on price, get the other details of the lease—the lease term, the mileage allowed, the residual value, and the interest rate or money factor—so that you can do your calculation. The lease acquisition fee, if any. The security deposit. Gap insurance. The early termination penalty. The excess mileage charge. Everything you need to know. If the salesman doesn't know the answers, ask to speak to the dealer's F&I manager. If he's reticent about sharing all the details, remember that one reason God gave you feet was to walk away from car salesmen. Chances are, he won't let you walk. You're a live sale for him!

Here are a few more suggestions that will help you negotiate the most favorable lease.

Rule 1: Lease Early in the Model Year

Timing can be as important in leasing as in buying, and the right time to lease in some instances is early in the model year. You usually get a better lease deal then, for two key reasons:

1. Most auto manufacturers have at least one price increase during the model year. Some have several. If you lease after an increase, you'll have a higher capitalized cost, which means a higher monthly payment.

2. The later it gets in the model year, the closer you'll come to leasing a car that will be four years old in only 36 months. The numbers go down a little with each bimonthly issue of the Automotive Lease Guide's *Residual Percentage Guide.* Unless the automaker is subsidizing the lease to offset this shrinking value, the leasing company will establish a lower residual value as the model year progresses, which will require a higher monthly payment. This can become a very significant issue if you're considering leasing last year's model after this year's model has arrived. Without big manufacturer subsidies, it will actually cost you more to lease the older model. So if it's July, August, or September, it may pay to wait until October, November, or December and lease next year's model.

The caveat: If the manufacturer is aggressively subsidizing the lease, it doesn't matter where you are in the model year, and this rule doesn't apply.

Rule 2: Don't Gild the Lily

Don't overaccessorize a leased car. If you're a music nut, spring for the 6-disc CD changer if you must, but forget the $1,200 aluminum wheels and the $400 decorative "gold package" and the $100 pinstriping job and the $300 walnut-trimmed dashboard. They add little value, and you'll just be buying them for the next owner. Even think twice about whether you really need 4-wheel drive or a moonroof or an 8-cylinder engine. This isn't your car, it's a rental car, and it's silly to spend another $50 or more a month for unessential equipment or unnecessary ornamentation. (Would you buy a diamond engagement ring for someone if you knew you wouldn't be together two years later?)

It's also silly to put a fancy security system in a leased car. Think about it: You've got your regular car insurance, plus gap insurance, so if the car is stolen, you'll come out whole financially. Aren't the insurance companies the only ones you're protecting with that $500 security system?

Rule 3: Make Them Compete for Your Business

How do you get the best lease deal? The same way you get the best purchase deal—by pitting one leasing team against another and discovering which one wants your business the most. To shop smart, you must get specific offers, including all the details, from at least two or three dealers. Assume that all lease deals are negotiable . . . and shoppable.

If you remember only one thing from this book, it should be: *Make them compete for your business.* It always pays to shop around. Even on an appealing factory-subsidized lease, don't assume that the terms in the ad are as rigid as they seem. Contact several dealers for that make and tell them you're going to lease where you get the best deal. Some dealers are always going to be more desperate than others to get your business.

Dealers have a compelling reason to close every lease deal they can:

higher customer retention. Research shows that about 80 percent of leasing customers return to the same store when they're in the market for their next vehicle. That's more than double the percentage of regular purchasers who return to the same dealerships. This simple fact gives leasing prospects extra leverage.

Rule 4: Beware of the Lowball Lease Offer

The lowball opener has found its way to the leasing side of the business. Whenever you see a "no money down, only $179 a month" offer, read the fine print. You may find that it's for a stripped-down model no one would want. The purpose, of course, is to get you into the showroom, where the salesman will move you to a more profitable model—one with much higher payments.

Rule 5: Examine Each Thread Individually, but Make Your Decision on the Whole Fabric

You should analyze each element of the lease. Have you negotiated a slim-profit capitalized cost? Is the lessor's residual value attractive compared to the number in the *Residual Percentage Guide,* given the supply and demand situation for the vehicle? Is the interest rate favorable compared to the current market rate for auto loans?

But after answering these questions, step back and look at the lease as a whole. If the cap cost is just marginally over the invoice price, the lease rate is an eye-popping 2.9 percent, and the residual is only one or two percentage points above the number in the *Residual Percentage Guide,* it's probably an excellent lease overall. It's unrealistic to expect both a below-cost interest rate and a ten-point inflation of the residual value. Sometimes you have to say, "Two out of three ain't bad."

Rule 6: Read the Fine Print—All of It— Before Your Sign Anything

Signing a lease is like signing a mortgage. You've got to make those payments, or else. Understand exactly what you're signing. If the lessor won't give you a copy to study, there's a reason—one good enough for you to find another, more cooperative lessor.

When you've narrowed your vehicle choices and are almost ready to start negotiating, consider ordering the specific information you need from Fighting Chance. As you now know, you need the same information to lease intelligently as to buy intelligently, and then some. One feature you'll appreciate: a customer service number you can call to talk to us and ask questions as you go through the shopping process. We'll look up residual values for customers in the latest issue of the Automotive Lease Guide's *Residual Percentage Guide,* and even go through the payment calculation with you before you sign the lease. See chapter 25 for details.

Rule 7: Don't Take Possession Until the Leasing Company has Approved the Deal

A Fighting Chance customer drove a leased car home, assured by the dealer that the lease would be approved, though the final documents hadn't been signed by the leasing company. Almost two weeks later, the dealer called to say that there were problems with the customer's credit application, and that the interest rate (and the monthly payment) would be significantly higher.

Don't let this happen to you. A deal isn't a deal until it's a done deal.

There is no substitute for hard work.

—Thomas Alva Edison

We won't say Edison was wrong. But, considering all the better mousetraps he invented, surely he knew there was more than one way to catch a mouse.

23

There Must Be an Easier Way!

T he problem with doing something right is that somebody's got to do it. We recognize that many of you are sitting there now feeling that this task will require more time and effort than you can give it, and wondering if there aren't easier ways to accomplish the objective. You may even be wishing that someone else could do it for you.

As you might expect, we think you should practice what we preach. We're convinced that you can negotiate the best deal yourself, using the methods outlined in this book.

But, yes, there are easier ways to buy or lease new cars and trucks, whether you do it yourself or assign the task to someone else. Some of them are excellent alternatives, and we wouldn't be providing a comprehensive service if we didn't cover them.

EASIER WAYS TO DO IT YOURSELF

Believe it or not, you don't have to enter a car store to negotiate the price of most vehicles. You can do it almost painlessly from home or work by using a telephone or a fax machine. Here's how.

Easier Way 1—The One-Offer Phone Call

In this approach, you make a "take it or leave it" telephone offer of about $500 over invoice, assuming you're shopping for a vehicle in good supply with a sticker price under $25,000.

To best prepare for this phone call, visit a few dealers' lots between 7:00 and 8:00 A.M. on a weekday morning, when there will be no salespeople around to bother you. Check out their inventory to see if they have any cars that fit your specifications. If they do, write down the 17-figure vehicle identification numbers on the manufacturer's window stickers. In addition, you should prepare a two-column worksheet showing dealer invoice and suggested retail prices for the car you want, including all the equipment packages and optional accessories and the destination charge.

Call those dealerships later that morning, starting with the one you'd prefer to buy from. Ask the name of the fleet manager and write it down. (If there's no fleet manager, get the sales manager's name; in many dealerships, it's the same person.) When you get through to him, introduce yourself and tell him you're going to buy a car in the next day or two and you're calling sales managers to make a specific offer. The first one who accepts your offer will sell you a car tomorrow, and he's the first one you've called. Also say that this will be a house sale because you haven't worked with any salesperson at his store (if that's true), so he knows that he won't have to pay a sales commission on the deal.

It will enhance your bargaining position if you can also say you were on his lot that morning and he has one or two vehicles that you'd be happy to drive home today if the price were right. If it's true, tell him you also plan to get all your regular servicing done at his store. (Remember, car stores earn the bulk of their net profits from parts and service.)

Then, just as you would in person, tell him you've done your homework. You know the dealer invoice price. You know about the holdback (if there is any). You know about any rebates or factory-to-dealer cash incentives. (Be specific.) You know how that model's sales have been going. (Be very specific if sales are down.) You also have a good feel for transaction prices among knowledgeable customers. Offer him about $500 over invoice, after subtracting any incentives, and remind him that the ($400) holdback will bring the total profit to ($900) on one of the easiest deals of the month. (You'd offer more for a more expensive car.) Finally, say that if he accepts your offer, you'll be there that afternoon to handle the details, but if you haven't heard from him in 15 minutes, you plan to call the next dealer on your list.

Then bite your tongue. He may buy the offer immediately. He may say he'll call you right back. Or he may turn you down. If he does, you're on to your next call. Either way, this is a hassle-free way to negotiate the price of a car. You're very likely to have a deal before you make the third phone call. When you agree on a deal, fax the dealer your worksheet, to be sure your numbers and his agree. And ask whether there will be any other charges, saying that you don't like last-minute surprises.

This approach can work as well for leasing as for buying. Just say up front that you're planning to lease a new car in the next day or two. Once you've established the capitalized cost, tell him you expect a competitive money factor and residual value, and you understand leasing and can do the monthly payment arithmetic. You'll want to know details of any other costs (dealer advertising association charge, lease acquisition fee, lease-end disposition fee, sales taxes, and so on) before you sign, and also the amount of the drive-off check required (first payment, security deposit, registration fees, and so on). He will quickly realize that you've done your homework.

There are still a few dealers who refuse to make deals over the phone. They want to get you on their turf, in the showroom, where they think they'll have the advantage. But consumers are finding more time-efficient ways to shop for everything, and dealers who won't do business over the phone are losing sales to those who will. Once you've got all the information you need to negotiate effectively, what could be easier than doing it from your own home or office?

Easier Way 2—The Fax Attack

More and more dealers are open to nontraditional ways to sell cars, including responding to faxes from live prospects who are ready to buy. If you live in a market with several dealers for the make you want and you're shopping for a vehicle that's in good supply, there's no reason a fax approach shouldn't work for you. We regularly hear from customers who tell us they faxed seven to ten dealers at 9:00 A.M. and got responses from four or five of them within hours. (This can be an effective approach for women; if you sign the fax "S. G. Smith," the dealers won't know they're dealing with Susan Smith.)

There's another benefit to the fax approach: It enables you to quickly separate the dealers who want to sell you a car from those who want to play games. You will probably get responses from half to two-thirds of those you contact, and they will be the dealers most likely to be flexible on prices.

Start this process by going to your phone book's yellow pages and calling eight to twelve dealerships, asking for the name (and correct spelling) of the fleet manager, if they have one (the sales manager if they don't), and the fax number to reach that person. If they ask why you want that information, say you're planning to buy a car and want to fax them an offer.

Then go to a computer and put together a one-page fax to each person that's similar to the phone conversation outlined above in Easier Way 1. You plan to buy a new (Toyota Camry) in the next few days, and you're contacting several dealers by fax. If they can meet your price, you'd prefer to buy it from (Smithtown Toyota), where you'd also have the car serviced. (Don't lie about this, but use it where it's true.) Then list the specs for the car you want, with columns showing dealer invoice and suggested retail prices, including all the equipment packages and accessories and the destination charge. Tell them you are aware of the current customer or dealer incentives (be specific) and have a feel for transaction prices among knowledgeable customers. If it's true, say you've been on their lot and seen one or two cars you'd drive home tomorrow if the price were right. Then offer a modest but fair profit and remind them of the extra ($400) profit they'll receive in holdback. Give your daytime and evening phone numbers and invite them to contact you soon.

It's difficult to tell you exactly what "modest but fair" profit to offer because it will differ, depending on the supply and demand situation for your vehicle. Use the general target price guidelines in chapter 21, modified by your sense of the supply situation in your market. Our inclination would be to offer a little more than we might have to pay because the purpose of the fax is to start a competitive dialogue with several dealers. It is not unusual for dealers to attempt to close out the bidding by countering with a price that's *less* than a customer offered in his fax. It's strange: Most dealers will ignore a fax offering them just $100 or $200 over invoice, but if you offer a lot more, several dealers will respond and the competition might drive the price to that level or lower.

There's another valid fax approach: Instead of making a specific offer, tell them you're contacting several dealers and will buy from the one that responds with the best price. Sometimes it's difficult to know what price to offer. For example, if there's a factory-to-dealer cash incentive with a range of $1,000 to $3,000, any number you pick is likely to be either too high or too low. But you avoid that problem if you ask the dealers to play the first card. Some are going to bid more aggressively than others, and the result of that competition is likely to deliver the entire dealer incentive to you.

Whichever approach you choose, send all the faxes at the same time on a weekday morning, preferably in the last week of the month. (They're too busy with customers on weekends to respond to faxes, but you'll get their full attention on a slower sales day.) Don't stray too far from your phone for the rest of the day, because it will ring. And don't make the mistake one man made when he sent the fax, then left immediately for a two-week business trip. When he returned, he was back to square one and got little response from the next round of faxes because nobody took him seriously.

If you send several faxes, you might get agreement to a quick, easy deal. Even if you don't, you should get responses that will be the basis for further discussion. Remember, your objective is to start a dialogue that will lead to a deal.

A few final thoughts on the fax attack:

• Faxing can work if you're in a smaller market with few dealers for your make, but you'll have to broaden the geography of your search. Remote dealers might be very willing to deal, since they'll see you as extra business they wouldn't otherwise get. For example, a Fighting Chance customer in Madison, Wisconsin, faxed a dozen midwestern Lexus dealers and saved $3,000 by traveling to St. Louis to buy his LS 400.

• If you don't have access to a fax machine, go to your local Mail Boxes, Etc., or Kinko's or any public faxing facility and pay them a dollar per page to transmit ten faxes. The fax attack is such a powerful tool, it's crazy not to try it. But get back to your phone as soon as the faxes are sent.

• The fax attack also works well for leasing. You modify your fax just as you'd modify a phone conversation (see Easier Way 1).

• If you're shopping for a hot seller in short supply, forget the fax approach. A dealership that is selling every car it can get will ignore your fax.

HAVING SOMEONE ELSE DO IT

Okay, so you can't get up for the task, or you're just too busy. Here are some alternatives to consider.

Easier Way 3—CarBargains

If you like the idea of having someone else do the hard part (negotiating for you), there's a special service you should know about. It's called Car-Bargains, and it's offered by the Center for the Study of Services (CSS), a nonprofit consumer service organization in Washington, D.C. (As noted in chapter 15, CSS publishes *CarDeals,* our source of detailed information on manufacturers' current consumer and dealer incentive programs.)

CarBargains is a systematic process in which CSS gets dealers in your market to bid competitively against each other to sell you the car you want. Here's how it works.

You call CarBargains toll-free at (800) 475–7283 and tell them the make, model, and style of car or truck you wish to buy or lease. If you're buying, they'll charge your credit card $165 for the service; if you're leasing, the charge is $290 for a service they call *LeaseWise,* but they negotiate the entire lease for you. (This book will be in circulation for years, and any prices quoted herein can change over time. Always call for current prices.)

CarBargains then contacts dealers with its own version of the fax attack described above in Easier Way 2. Within about two weeks, they will get at least five dealers in your area—including any specific dealers you request—to bid blind against each other for your business. Each dealer commits to a selling price that's a specific dollar amount above or below the factory invoice price.

The participating dealers know that they're in a competition, and that it will take a low bid to win. They also know that CarBargains has a real customer, since anyone who has paid for this service is almost certain to buy a vehicle very soon from one of them.

The Center for the Study of Services has helped thousands of people save money on new cars and trucks via competitive bidding. In addition to their own data on current transaction prices, they use a solid base of inside information to remind dealers of current factors that give them room to cut prices. Factory-to-dealer incentive programs and manufacturers' holdback could come into play in the bidding, depending on each dealer's specific sales and inventory situation. This is also a house sale for the dealer, with no salesman's commission to pay.

When the bids are in, CSS sends you a report containing a specific price quote sheet for each dealer, showing exactly how far above or below the invoice cost the dealer has agreed to sell the vehicle. The report also includes the name of the sales manager responsible for this commitment. Each dealer's bid must include all the costs involved, including any advertising association fees, processing fees, or other miscellaneous charges. You'll have no last-minute surprises.

Their report also includes a printout showing the dealer invoice price for the base vehicle and for all factory-installed options and equipment packages. You can add the invoice prices for the vehicle and the options you want, then add (or subtract) the amount of the dealer's agreed markup (or markdown). Thus, you know the price you'll pay before you leave home.

You visit one or more of the dealerships, select the car you want, and see the sales manager listed on the quote sheet to purchase the car at the price the dealer has already agreed to. The bidding dealers will honor their commitments; they know they won't get future opportunities to bid if they don't.

Important note: The Center for the Study of Services can get bids anywhere in the country and has no ties to any specific dealers. They are scrupulously honest; for instance, there are always a few hot vehicles that dealers won't bid on competitively, and in those cases, CarBargains will tell you they can't help you. The only income CSS derives from the bidding process comes from the consumers who order the service, which is something many car-buying intermediaries cannot say.

CSS believes that CarBargains frequently results in "the lowest price a dealer will allow" simply because he perceives their phone call as a one-shot, out-of-the-blue opportunity for an incremental sale that he wouldn't normally get.

This strikes us as an attractive, reasonably priced alternative for people who just can't negotiate for themselves. Indeed, CarBargains may be a worthwhile card for any buyer to play. An attractive bid from a relatively unattractive dealership might improve your bargaining leverage with the dealer down the street.

Easier Way 4—Automobile Brokers and Other Middlemen

You have lots of other options if you're willing to pay someone else to do your car shopping. There are buying services and auto brokers and buyers' agents who will do it for you. These people charge you a fee for their service—sometimes (if you can believe it) as little as $50 or $100, sometimes a lot more. They negotiate a price that's supposed to be much lower than you could get without their help, since they move a lot of metal for dealers.

As you surely know by now, we are convinced that you can do the job very well by yourself if you have the right information and use it effectively. If we didn't believe that, we wouldn't have written this book.

Whether you do it yourself or hire someone else do it, there's only one relevant question: How good is the deal? The answer will be based on the total price you pay for the car, including the cost of the helper. We believe in most instances the helper's deal won't be that terrific. The major reason for employing a helper should be simply to avoid doing it yourself. You should decide what that's worth to you, but don't go into it assuming you're going to save a bundle compared to doing it yourself.

In our view, the most attractive helpers are those who work only for you and are compensated only by you. We'd place the CarBargains service (Easier Way 3) at the top of that list because they charge a relatively low fee and you are their only source of income. A growing number of independent buyers' agents are worth considering; they also work only for you and get paid only by you. Their fees are typically higher than that charged by CarBargains, but at least you know whose side they're on.

Then there is the automobile broker, who may charge you $100 or less for his service. But how cheap is that service, and how much does he really save you? Let's consider the low service fee. How do the numbers work for him? Remember, he's got to communicate with you, negotiate with one or more dealers, and coordinate the paperwork and delivery, which he frequently makes himself. All this for only $100?

Assume he sells a car every working day, about 250 a year, giving him a gross income of $25,000, before phone bills. No way, José! Assume he sells two a day, 500 a year, giving him a $50,000 gross. Maybe, but it still seems very skimpy for the work involved.

You won't be surprised to learn that most brokers have another source of income from the deals they make. Brokers are typically in cahoots with dealers and get a silent, undisclosed commission that is often several times the size of the fee they charge the customer. Of course, all of that money ultimately comes from the customer's pocket because it's built into the price he pays. This leaves open the question of how much they really save knowledgeable, disciplined shoppers, who might negotiate equally good or better deals on their own.

As one broker reported in a feature story in *Automotive News,* he "sells" 300 to 500 vehicles in an average year and makes "anywhere from $70 or $80 to more than $1,000 per transaction, depending on the vehicle *and the deal he can cut with a dealer.*" And while all brokers contacted said they always pass along any factory-to-consumer incentives, the factory-to-dealer incentives are a different story. As one put it, "We don't get too involved with the dealer's business, we [just] supply them with the audience."

Let's return to the one relevant question: How good is the deal? Assume the car is a popular mid-priced sedan. If the broker gets a $100 fee from you and another $200 to $300 from the dealer, you're starting off $300 to $400 in the hole. And remember, the dealer still wants to make a profit on the sale—at least as much as he's paying the broker, and probably more. So how good can the broker's deal possibly be—especially considering that Fighting Chance customers routinely report negotiating their own deals on popular mid-priced sedans for just a few hundred dollars over invoice?

When you're dealing with a broker, you may simply be trading one car salesman for another. He may have an alliance with the dealer that increases his compensation as the overall profit increases. Our sources tell us these kickback alliances are common, that many buyers can expect surprises like unwanted add-on options—for example, dealer-applied paint sealant that "lists for $750 but will cost you only $225" (and probably costs the dealer only $50).

Whenever a negotiator gets the bulk of his income from the firm he's negotiating with, there's an inherent conflict of interest. The broker tells you he's working on your behalf, but he's much more dependent on his long-term relationships with specific car dealers. Indeed, he's much more concerned with the dealers' satisfaction than with yours; he may never see you again, but he's got to go back and do business with those dealers the next day.

Many car-buying services operate much like brokers. They charge you a modest fee, positioning themselves as consumer champions, but have a "sweetheart network" of dealers who are a major source of their income. Some disclose this, but many don't.

In sum, you must draw your own conclusions about these hired guns. Maybe some of them are terrific, but others are not. The proof will always be in the result. If the total transaction cost (including the helper's fee) is within the general target price guidelines in chapter 21 for cars in good supply, you can feel pretty good about the deal. In most cases, however, we'd bet that you could negotiate an equally good or better deal yourself, if you're willing to put in the effort.

Even if you're not, we believe that an alternative like CarBargains is likely to save you more money than any broker. Why? Chances are that broker is dealing mainly with one dealer for each make. (Concentrating his business is the key reason he can get good prices, right?) That means, by definition, there's little or no price competition between dealers for your business. And in the retail auto business it's the competitive aspect that enables a buyer to take advantage of price flexibility, which may change dramatically from dealer to dealer . . . and from week to week.

The same principle applies to those fleet purchase referral services that are offered by all kinds of affinity groups. They claim they'll set you up with a nearby participating dealer whose fleet manager will give you a terrific price.

The problem: He's typically not competing against any other fleet manager. That dealer paid for the privilege of being on that referral list. He doesn't want to compete with anyone for your purchase, which means that you will usually pay for the privilege of buying from him.

The solution: If you use one of these referral services, you should ask for at least three different dealer referrals within your driving radius. And make sure each fleet manager knows he's in a competition.

Easier Way 5—Doing It in Cyberspace

The growing popularity of the personal computer and the Internet is enabling more and more people to conduct major commercial transactions without leaving their home or office. Today consumers can shop for and purchase new vehicles on the World Wide Web through the web sites of individual car dealers and car manufacturers or those of national buying and referral services. The best-known referral service at this writing is Auto-By-Tel (www.autobytel.com), but there are many others (AutoVantage, Autoweb, CarPoint), some of which may or may not be in business in a few years.

The problem with these online buying and referral services is that *in most cases there's no competition between dealers for your business*. When you give the service your name, address, and phone number and the specs on the car you want, they forward the information to just one dealer, who has paid a substantial monthly fee for the exclusive right to all leads from your zip code. That dealer may or may not offer you a great deal.

But a deal isn't a great deal until it's a done deal. An online dealer may quote you a great price on the phone, as a way to get you into his store, then renege on the first price and charge much more. As an example, a Fighting Chance customer used the AutoAdvantage online referral service and got a bid of $1,000 over invoice on a Toyota Sienna minivan from a dealer an hour's drive from her home. When she got to the store to complete the deal, the sales manager told her the price would be $2,000 over invoice. We frequently hear stories like this about all kinds of referral services, not just those online.

As you ponder this option, remember that no matter what medium you use to negotiate with dealers, the only relevant issue is the price. To know whether it's good or bad before you agree to it, you still have to do your homework. And even in cyberspace, you have to shop dealers against each other to get the best deal.

The dealers from those online buying services are sitting ducks, just like other "no-dicker" dealers. They close only about 20 percent of the deals they quote, an indication that their prices aren't that great. Once you have a price quote from an online dealer, use it as the place to start negotiating with others. Try to beat it by using Easier Way 1, calling the dealers near home or work—the ones you'd probably rather buy from anyway. You may find that they'll match or beat any online deal.

If we've said it once . . . whether you're negotiating for yourself or having someone else do it for you, the key to getting the best deal will always be having several dealers compete against each other for your business.

24

The buyer needs a hundred eyes, the seller not one.

—George Herbert

Resisting the Final Temptation

Now comes the fun part: uninhibited emotional involvement without financial risk! Driving that new baby home . . . being seen by envious friends and neighbors . . . inhaling that new car smell . . .

Not so fast! There's one more piece of unfinished business, some work to do now to avoid a potential pile of grief next week: *the inspection.* Smart buyers allow at least one extra day at this juncture to ensure that they'll be happy with the car they drive home.

WHAT YOU DON'T SEE IS WHAT YOU GET

That new car or truck belongs to the dealer until the minute you pay him, sign the delivery receipt, and drive the front wheels off the lot. If it's got any problems, they're going to get fixed much quicker while he still owns it, before you've given him the final check. Once you drive away, he can claim that any defect happened after you took delivery.

Prepare the salesman in advance. Tell him that when the car is ready, you plan to inspect it carefully, and that you'll expect him to correct any problems before you take final delivery. Tell him to be sure to leave the dealer's tags on the car because you want to test-drive it while they still own it. That message should motivate the dealer to pay even closer attention to his checklist for the car before you get there.

MAKE THIS A DAY GAME . . . ON A NICE DAY

You can't inspect a new vehicle properly in the dark or in the rain. Put the trip off until you can do it in broad daylight on a reasonably nice day. Take a friend or relative to help; four eyes and ears are better than two.

Carry a pad and make a list of any problems you discover. Here are the things you should do on your inspection trip:

1. Check the odometer. If it shows more than about 300 miles, the dealer better have a good explanation. (Maybe he made an exchange with a dealer 200 miles away. But maybe he's trying to slip you a demonstrator that someone's been driving for a few weeks.)

2. Make sure all the optional equipment you ordered is on the car. Then have the salesman take you through the operation of all the equipment. The air conditioner, cruise control, lights, sliding sunroof, stereo system (the basics only for now), electric windows, washer-wipers, remote side mirrors, remote fuel cap opener . . . everything. Make sure it all works. (Incidentally, this is part of his job.)

3. Use your accomplice to help check all the lights. The turn signals, backup lights and brake lights, dome light and other interior lighting, even the glove compartment, trunk, and engine light (if there is one). Ask whether the manufacturer has set the interior lights to go on briefly when you leave the car at night, and if so, how long they stay on.

4. Go over the interior fabric areas very carefully. On cloth areas, make sure that the fit is perfect everywhere, and that there are no stains or tears. Ditto for the carpets and the headliner (the cloth or plastic covering between your head and the roof), which should show no sloppy glue stains.

5. Pay close attention to the exterior finish, both body and chrome. It should be perfect, without scratches or dents. (New-car owners should be allowed to put the first dings in their own doors.) If there are small scratches, they can be buffed out without too much difficulty. *But if the scratches are long enough and deep enough to require repainting, you should refuse the car, period!* The original factory finish is very difficult for even the best body shop to match, and partial-panel matching is next to impossible. The body shop would probably end up repainting the whole side or panel to fix a small imperfection, and chances are, you'd be unhappy with the result.

6. Check for previous body damage. It's rare with new cars, but it happens—on test drives or in transporting dealer exchanges. Look for mismatched paint on adjacent body parts or ripples in the surface. (Federal law says the buyer must be given a disclosure statement on previous damage.)

7. Check the fit and finish on all things that open and close. Windows, passenger doors, hood, trunk, glove box—and make sure all the tires match.

8. While the hood is up, ask the salesman to show you where all the fluids go and how to use the dipsticks to check the levels. The engine oil. The brake fluid. The automatic transmission fluid. The power steering fluid. The radiator anti-freeze, and even the windshield washing solution. If any of these is not at the proper level, either the dealer has done a poor job of prepping the car or there's a leak.

9. Most important, take the car for a test drive, ideally while the dealer's tags are still on it, not with temporary or permanent tags assigned to you. That way it's still under his insurance coverage, and he can't claim you've taken delivery. Drive the car reasonably aggressively to test it. If it's an automatic transmission, do the gears seem to shift smoothly and at natural progression points? Does the cruise control work? Accelerate to about 30 mph on a straight, flat, dry road with little or no traffic, and take your hands off the wheel. If the vehicle pulls left or right, it may have alignment problems. Slam on the brakes. Does it stop squarely? And find a road with some bumps to drive over to see if there are any annoying squeaks and rattles.

The dealer won't love you for all this, but you will. Give your list of problems to him to copy (keep the original yourself), and tell him you'll come back after he calls to say he's fixed everything. At that time, examine the car again and, if it's perfect, turn over the final check, sign the delivery receipt, and drive it off into the sunset.

An important detail: *Be sure you've communicated with your insurance agent,* so that you're covered the moment the wheels hit the street in front of the dealership.

One last word to the wise: *If you're financing the car, don't drive it home if the loan documents have not been approved and signed by the lender.* More than one buyer has done that, then learned a week or two later that because of a problem with the credit application, the interest rate (and the monthly payment) would be much higher.

25

Going to a dealer without the Fighting Chance information is like going to the beach without sunblock. You're gonna get burned.
—Tom Gargiulo, Westport, Conn.

Tom leased his BMW 5-Series sedan for a capitalized cost just $1,190 over dealer invoice. At the sticker price, the dealer profit would have been $7,000.

Call

1-800-288-

1134

We cannot tell a lie; this chapter is a commercial. It's for something you'll need, something that others have rated the best of its kind. At $21.95 (plus $3.00 handling), it's a fine value. You can order it toll-free anytime. And if you find this book valuable, you'll probably want it.

If you've been paying attention, you know that if you're going to shop smart for that new car or truck, you must arm yourself with current information about the model or models you're considering. That information falls into two different areas.

1. You need the facts about *all* the elements that affect the dealer's bottom-line cost so that you can determine whether the deal is a good one or a bad one before you agree to it. Those elements are (a) the dealer invoice cost, (b) the factory holdback, and (c) any factory-to-dealer cash payments that may be available for selling specific vehicles within a specific time frame. (Of course, you also want to know about any customer rebates, which affect your own bottom-line cost.)

2. You'll bargain from a position of greater strength if you have a feel for how your vehicle is doing in the marketplace and for actual transaction prices among knowledgeable customers. Are sales up or down so far this year? Does the average dealer sell many of that model each month or just a few? Were the most recently reported inventories high or low? Is there a redesigned version of the vehicle coming next fall? And what prices are informed shoppers negotiating in relation to the invoice price?

Fighting Chance is a unique consumer information service that provides all of this information in one package. We created this business because we concluded that the traditional sources of information were not providing consumers with the information they need to fully empower them in their price negotiations with dealers. We know of no other source that has put together a package this complete, priced it as a "best buy" value, and made it so easy to order. (Think of this book as the crossbow you'll use and Fighting Chance as the arrows.)

Fighting Chance has been featured in articles in *Smart Money, Reader's Digest, Road and Track, Good Housekeeping, Business Week,* and *Money* magazine, plus newspapers from coast to coast. When the *San José Mercury-News* rated the major national car-buying information services, Fighting Chance was the only one to receive four stars. (The *Consumer Reports* Auto Pricing Service got just two stars.) That *Mercury-News* article infuriated the local car dealers, who canceled their advertising for a full month, costing the paper over $1 million in lost revenue. It would be fair to say that the dealers don't want you to know about us.

Here are the four key elements of the Fighting Chance package.

1. COMPLETE DEALER INVOICE DATA

For each car or truck, you get a reader-friendly printout showing all the configurations the manufacturer offers, with both the sticker price (MSRP) and the dealer invoice price. That way, you'll be able to make price/value comparisons between different trim levels. (Remember, a higher trim level often represents a better value because it includes standard equipment in the base price that would be extra-cost items in a lower trim level.)

These printouts show the standard equipment included with each trim level. They also include both retail and dealer invoice pricing for all the available preferred equipment packages and convenience groups, as well as the optional accessories and equipment. Note, however, that a couple of import manufacturers don't share information on pricing for dealer-installed options or accessories. That means, for example, that if you buy one of their models without air conditioning as standard equipment, neither we nor any other pricing service can tell you the dealer invoice price for the air conditioner. In those cases, we tell you what other automakers charge for air conditioning for comparable models, to give you some frame of reference.

These reports are compiled and updated regularly by Chek-Chart Publications, a division of Macmillan Publishing USA that has been the definitive source of this data for auto-financing institutions since the 1950s. We get an update every week or two all year.

Our $21.95 package price includes dealer invoice price data for one vehicle. Complete invoice price information for additional vehicles on the same order costs $8 each. (There's a $3 handling fee on the total order.)

Bonuses

When you order the Fighting Chance package, you frequently get a second printout free: the previous pricing data for that same vehicle.

Virtually all manufacturers increase prices during the model year, often more than once and sometimes as late as June or July. As price increases occur, it is common to find identical vehicles on dealers' lots with different sticker prices, reflecting the different prices that were in effect when they purchased the vehicles.

In that situation, it is to your advantage to know the different dealer invoice prices for each vehicle. That's why, if there has been a model-year price increase within recent months, we send you two complete sets of pricing data—the most recent price and the price that immediately preceded it.

Here's another bonus: If you're shopping early in the model year and trying to decide whether to buy the new model or one of last year's leftovers, at your request we include the final dealer invoice price for *last* year's model along with the printout for the new one.

We know of no other new-vehicle pricing service that provides either of these additional price printouts. They can be powerful bargaining tools.

2. *CarDeals*—THE AUTHORITATIVE REPORT ON CURRENT INCENTIVE PROGRAMS

The second element in the Fighting Chance information package is the latest issue of *CarDeals,* a report covering the current manufacturers' incentive programs—both the consumer rebate offers and any factory-to-dealer cash incentive programs in effect. This biweekly report is compiled by the Center for the Study of Services, a nonprofit consumer service organization in Washington, D.C.

As you might guess, we subscribe to just about every publication that covers the retail automobile market, and this is the most comprehensive report available on incentives, by a country mile. *Automotive News,* the weekly newspaper of the industry, has its own incentives section, but *CarDeals* often has twice as many listings—especially in the area of factory-to-dealer cash. (An abridged version of a typical *CarDeals* report is shown in appendix C. The incentives shown there are not current offers, but simply an illustration of the kinds of information these reports contain.)

Often dealers don't tell their salesmen the full details of incentive offers, or they tell them less than the whole truth, because they don't want them to negotiate away the factory-to-dealer cash. (We have pulled out the *CarDeals* report in negotiations and watched salesmen's eyes get as big as silver dollars. They've even asked if they could make a copy.) Since you're the one paying for these incentive programs, you're the one who should benefit from them, and you can't negotiate from strength if you don't know the details.

There's another advantage in having a report covering the current incentive offers for all cars: It can open other attractive options. Reviewing the *CarDeals* report, you might discover there's a significant offer on another vehicle you hadn't considered buying—perhaps even a model more expensive than you thought you could afford.

One caveat: This is a supply and demand business, and manufacturers generally don't have to spend incentive dollars to move hot-selling vehicles. An automaker's retail incentives may *average* $500 to $1,000 or more per vehicle, but many popular cars seldom get incentive dollars. If *CarDeals* shows no incentives for your vehicle, please don't shoot the messenger; we just report the news, we don't create it. Remember, you're also paying us to tell you what *isn't* there so that you don't end up wondering if the dealer made another $1,000 or so on your deal.

3. OUR BIG PICTURE ANALYSIS— A POWERFUL NEGOTIATING TOOL

As we noted in chapter 3, there is real power in knowing how the makes and models you are interested in are doing in the marketplace. That's why each Fighting Chance package includes "The Big Picture," our analysis of the current sales and inventory status for each automaker on your list. Updated monthly, this report enables you to gauge the relative sales strength of different vehicles and determine which are likely to be more flexible on price. You'll also learn whether the average dealer sells thirty of your model every month or just one or two. We'll tell you if there's a major redo of your vehicle scheduled for the next model year. And if there have been changes in a manufacturer's holdback policy, we include the latest information in this summary.

Here's an illustration of how important just one little nugget from this package can be. Assume you want to buy a Honda Prelude. The Prelude is an excellent little sports coupe, but its sales have been minuscule for years; as we're writing this, the average Honda dealer is selling just one per month. Clearly, no one is waiting in line to buy this car. When you walk onto a dealer's lot, there will probably be only two or three Preludes in stock. Yet the car salesman, assuming that you don't know what we've just told you, will walk up to you and say, "This thing is so hot, we can barely keep it in stock." To which your response will be, "Please don't feed me that baloney. The average Honda dealer sells only one per month, and you know it. With sales that low, you'd be fools to stock even five or ten. Now let's talk about the right price for a car that almost no one wants to buy." Guess who just took control of that negotiation! And all you mentioned was one simple little fact that you found in our Honda Big Picture analysis.

Perhaps most important, you'll get the benefit of the actual shopping experiences of other Fighting Chance customers. We get continuous feedback from them on actual transaction prices (in relation to the dealer invoice price), and we include this information in our Big Picture summaries. Understand that this is anecdotal data, not real research. Since we are not your parents, you don't have to send your report card home if you aren't proud of it. But lots of folks do, and if people in several markets report buying a given car for $300 to $400 over invoice, that's strong evidence that you can negotiate a similar deal where you live.

This up-to-date perspective can provide real leverage in the showroom.

With Fighting Chance in hand, you'll be able to walk in and say, "I know the dealer invoice price of the car I want, I'm aware of the holdback you'll get, and I know about the customer rebate and/or the factory-to-dealer cash offer. I also know that sales of this car are down 10 percent this year, and the average dealer is selling just three a month. And I have a good feel for realistic transaction prices among knowledgeable customers. I expect you to make a profit—albeit a modest one—plus your holdback. If you want to sell an extra car this month and you'll deal in a very straightforward manner, we can conclude this in 30 minutes. Otherwise, I'll go somewhere else."

Why is Fighting Chance the only information service for new-car shoppers that provides these kinds of insights? We've asked ourselves that question for years. The automobile industry is the most overreported business in the world, and we read everything. Anyone who took the time to analyze the available information could do what we do. The only extra edge we have comes from our "insider contacts" with thousands of Fighting Chance customers. They make us smarter every day, so we can make you smarter.

The fact that *you* know this information—and 99.99 percent of the other shoppers don't (even the salesman probably doesn't know most of it)—stamps you as a knowledgeable prospect who expects no-nonsense treatment. It also changes the way you feel about what you're doing, bolstering your confidence in your ability to negotiate a good deal. As much as anything else, that feeling is what we're selling.

4. A UNIQUE FEATURE: A REAL PERSON TO TALK TO

Thanks to the miracles of technology, we now live in an automated, computerized, voice-mailed, digitized, impersonal world—a world where you get to talk to machines, not people. That's not our world. The Fighting Chance package comes with an endangered species: someone to talk to as you go through the process of purchasing or leasing a new car.

Puzzled about how to interpret a pricing printout, or by something a car salesman said that doesn't ring true? Call our customer service number, and we'll be happy to answer any questions you have. We work with this information every day, but you use it only every few years, so there's no such thing as a silly question.

If your purchase gets postponed, you may call to ask for updated information on incentive programs or price changes on your vehicle. As long as you're requesting the latest data for models you've previously ordered, we'll provide it at no charge.

If you're negotiating a lease, think of us as your informal "coach." We invite you to call us to go through the numbers before you sign the lease. We'll look up residual values in the latest issue of the Automotive Lease Guide's *Residual Percentage Guide* to make sure no one's trying to lowball you, charging you for phantom depreciation. It'll be a toll call, but it'll save you the cost of purchasing the guide. We'll take out a calculator, go through the monthly payment calculation with you, and tell you whether we'd sign that lease. But we're in loss prevention, not triage, so be sure to call us *before* you sign the agreement. Once you've signed, it's a done deal.

Remember that we're in the Pacific time zone, which may be a few hours behind you. And please note that we provide this service only for customers who have ordered the Fighting Chance package described in this chapter.

Important notes: This is a service for *new vehicles only.* We have no information on used vehicles. Also, we have *no Canadian pricing* data. (For Canadian pricing, call the Auto Hot Line in Toronto at 800–805–2270.) Finally, we have no information on travel trailers, truck campers, motor homes, van conversions, or motorcycles.

TO LEARN MORE, CHECK OUT OUR WEB SITE

If you'd like to learn more about Fighting Chance, you can find us on the Internet at www.fightingchance.com, where there's a more detailed description of the package, including a look at the parts of a typical vehicle pricing printout, a Big Picture analysis, and a *CarDeals* incentive report. You'll also find a current listing of available vehicle pricing, updated as soon as we get new data.

In addition, you can play the "Car Name Game." We invite web site visitors to treat car names as acronyms and submit their ideas on what a make's name really stands for. For example, did you know that Jeep means "Journey Eventually Ends Perpendicularly?"

You may place an order via e-mail from the web site or print out an order form that you can fax to us. And if the price of the package has changed, the web site will always have the current information.

HOW DOES FIGHTING CHANCE COMPARE TO THE *CONSUMER REPORTS* AUTO PRICING SERVICE?

When we created Fighting Chance, our objective was to provide a service that was demonstrably better than the existing alternatives.

The most well-known and probably the largest new-car pricing service is the one offered by *Consumer Reports*. It charges $12 for a printout for one car and $10 for each additional car on the same order. (As with all prices in this book, there can be changes over time.)

That sounds reasonable, but the *Consumer Reports* New Car Price Service treats each different body style and trim level combination as a separate printout. Its ordering instructions state: "Please have the following information ready when you call: Make, model *and trim line* of the vehicle you want to buy, such as Ford Taurus LX 4-door sedan." If you wanted to compare that LX trim level with the higher-level SE model, that would cost an extra $10. And many cars have three or more trim levels—Honda Accord and Civic, Toyota Camry and Corolla, Dodge Caravan, Ford Explorer, Nissan Altima, Maxima, and Sentra, and every pickup truck in captivity, to name just a few. While its reports sometimes show the base invoice price for all available trim levels, *Consumer Reports* provides pricing for the optional equipment packages and groups for only one of those trim levels. To make an apples-to-apples comparison of all trim levels, you must purchase several reports. We think that's a rip-off.

By contrast, our printouts cover all the configurations a manufacturer offers for a given vehicle, making it more efficient for shoppers to compare the relative values and make smarter purchase decisions.

Many Fighting Chance customers have also reported that we frequently have new pricing data well before *Consumer Reports*. For example, one year an automaker introduced a new vehicle in the month of March, and we had the pricing data by the end of that month. But a customer who ordered on May 6 told us he'd called *Consumer Reports* first, and they still didn't have it.

Customers who use both services often tell us that our information is more complete. As an example, one customer reported that *Consumer Reports* told her there was no incentive on the vehicle he wanted, when the *CarDeals* report showed a $1,000 factory-to-dealer cash offer. *Consumer Reports* also told that same customer that his make had no holdback, when in fact that automaker had instituted holdback ten months earlier!

If you have a question, there's no knowledgeable person to talk to at the *Consumer Reports* New Car Price Service. Those operators can take your money, but they can't answer questions about the data they send you or go through the lease payment calculations with you. As with most things in life, you get what you pay for.

Although we believe our service is more timely, more complete, and a better value, we have great respect for some of the other work of *Consumer Reports*. Indeed, the annual April auto issue is probably the best single source of information on vehicle safety, reliability, comfort, convenience, and economy.

ARE THOSE LITTLE AUTO PRICING BOOKS HELPFUL?

They can be. Several publishers, including Edmund's and Pace, do a credible job of compiling new-car pricing data. You'll find their paperbacks in bookstores and on newsstands for about $6 to $7 a copy.

The problem with these sources isn't accuracy, it's timeliness. They each publish several editions every model year, starting in the fall. If there hasn't been a recent price increase, they're fine. But all publishers need a significant amount of lead time to make changes, and the last thing you should do is walk into a dealership to negotiate today's price with yesterday's pricing data. Often increases are announced too late to make one edition, and the next edition may be months away. Also, with the model year starting October 1, many people can't wait for these books to hit the shelves later in the fall; they want the information *now.* That's what they get from Fighting Chance. We get a computer update every week or two, year-round, and the latest information is always in our database.

WHAT ABOUT THE INFORMATION IN CYBERSPACE?

The Internet is a bottomless resource for research, and new-car shoppers can find a lot of information there, much of it free. The automakers have sites that tell you how great their products are and link to their dealers. Some of them provide dealer listings in concentric circles at different distances from your home or work address, enabling you to compile a list of several dealer contacts quite easily. (You'll find their web site addresses listed with their phone numbers in appendix A.)

The publishers of traditional pricing guides like *Edmund's* and the *Kelley Blue Book* have web sites providing prices online. As with their books, the issue here is whether the information is current. We have periodically spot-checked these sites over the years and found pricing data that should have been updated two or three months previously, as well as information on holdback and incentives that was simply wrong. (In our checks, the Edmund's track record has been spottier than Kelley's.) "Free" is a great price for anything, but sometimes it's also an accurate measure of worth.

Even when the information is up-to-date, the pricing in their books and on their web sites is of limited value. As you surely understand by now, if all you have is the correct dealer invoice price, you don't have nearly enough to negotiate from a position of strength. As one Fighting Chance customer put it, "Your service is deeper, more insightful, more interactive and personal, and ultimately more helpful than anything else out there—including the free stuff on the Internet."

HOW DO YOU ORDER?

The Fighting Chance information package is easy to order: Just dial (800) 288–1134, 24 hours a day, 7 days a week. You may also order online from our web site (www.fightingchance.com).

The price of the complete Fighting Chance information package is $21.95, plus $3 for handling, and it includes everything you need to shop for one vehicle. Additional vehicles are just $8 each if you request them on the same order.

Orders are filled within two business days and sent via first-class mail. For an extra $2.00, we'll send the package by priority mail, which the Postal Service advertises heavily as two- to three-day delivery but does not guarantee. We believe it may speed delivery by a day or so, but only if you live east of the Rocky Mountains.

If you need the package sooner, we can send it via Federal Express. FedEx orders must be in by 3:00 P.M. Pacific time to ship the same day. There are four FedEx delivery options: (1) Second Business Day service, which costs $11 (remember, however, that a Thursday order won't be delivered until Monday, and a Friday order won't arrive until Tuesday); (2) Standard FedEx service ($15), which delivers in the afternoon of the next business day; (3) Priority service, which delivers in the morning of the next business day and costs $16; and (4) Saturday service costs $26. If you live in Hawaii or Alaska, the charges are higher. (Everything costs more in Alaska and Hawaii.) Note that FedEx raises rates about once a year, so you need to check with us to see if these rates still apply. If your company has a FedEx account, we'd be happy to use your account number. We are not a big FedEx user and don't get great rates.

The quickest way to get the package is by fax. We offer same-day fax service, weekdays only, for an additional charge of $12. If that sounds high, it's because there's a lot of information. The minimum fax is 25 to 35 pages; depending on the number of vehicles, it can easily be double or triple that. (The average is over 30 pages.) Faxing is not a profit center for us, it's a convenience for you. When a fax exceeds 50 pages, we usually ask if we can please send it via Federal Express instead. (Fax orders must be received by 3:00 P.M. Pacific time for same-day service.)

You may charge the purchase to Visa, MasterCard, or American Express. If you'd rather mail a check, make it payable to Fighting Chance, 5318 East 2nd Street, No. 242, Long Beach, California 90803. (If you live in California, you must add the sales tax of 8.25 percent.)

HOW DO OUR CUSTOMERS RATE US?

The best source of any company's business is customer referrals, and a very high percentage of Fighting Chance's business comes from old customers telling new customers. To illustrate why, here are excerpts from a tiny sampling of the fan mail we receive every day. (We've used initials instead of entire names to insulate the individuals from nuisance or prank phone calls. For the same reason, we don't sell mailing lists of our customers.)

I was initially skeptical about how much your information was really going to help me. But I got my new Camry for $250 over invoice, and I did it in ten minutes with *one* phone call to *one* dealer. My wife's jaw hit the ground! It was the most hassle-free, haggle-free, bickering-free car-buying deal of our life.

M.S., Hinsdale, Ill.

I planned to fax 18 dealers, but before I got the fourth fax out a dealer called to accept my offer of $500 over invoice for a Chevy Suburban. This was by far the most pleasant car-buying experience I've ever had, and I can honestly say that $32.95 was one of the best investments I've ever made.

N.M., Greenville, Ala.

With Fighting Chance, we were able to strip away the salesman's lies and deceptions to get to an excellent final price for our Jeep Grand Cherokee—$275 over dealer invoice. We're very happy. Keep up the good work.

J.F., Augusta, Maine

When I first read the testimonials of others who used your service, I was a little skeptical and a little intimidated by the whole thing. Especially since this was the first new car lease I've negotiated. I thought if I came even close to those results, I'd be satisfied. Well, I got my Saab for $600 over invoice, and it wasn't hard to do. Your advice helped me every step of the way. Spending just $25 and saving thousands of dollars—now that's an exceptional deal! To say that your service delivered is an understatement.

R.S., Santa Monica, Calif.

With the vehicle-specific information from Fighting Chance, selecting and buying a car this time was quite pleasant and not a hassle. Without this information, I would have paid close to $1,000 more for my Cadillac DeVille.

C.W., Richmond, Va.

My wife and I bought an Isuzu Trooper, and the dealer made a net profit of just $600, including his holdback! The information you provided had an enormous influence on the final price we paid. Most significant, however, was the enjoyment I experienced negotiating for a new automobile. Knowledge *is* power, and you are providing an incredible service.

E.W., Atlanta, Ga.

The prospect of buying a new car overwhelmed me, and the Fighting Chance material was a godsend. The information empowered me and transformed the task into a challenging adventure. The result: I bought my new Prizm for just $150 over invoice. Thank you for your major contribution to my achievement.

C.S.W., Wooster, Ohio

I got my Lexus LS 400 for $2,000 over invoice. Your advice on how to use the fax machine to buy a car worked like a charm. I faxed to 16 Midwest dealers and saved over $10,000.

R.S., Green Bay, Wisc.

I probably saved at least $1,000 by doing my homework and following your advice. The Price Club "sweetheart deal" was pretty good—$600 over invoice—but I was able to beat that by $200 with your information.

N.R., Santa Monica, Calif.

We negotiated a deal for $300 over invoice on the Caravan we wanted. The salesman told us that mail-order information isn't always accurate, but your prices matched his invoice to the penny. Easiest deal I ever negotiated.

D.E., Jensen Beach, Fla.

I bought a new Ford Windstar minivan for just $145.15 over invoice, so my modest investment for your service paid off in a big way. You were the only service with information on the new Windstar. (*Consumer Reports* still did not as of May 6, and the vehicle was introduced in March.) I used your information about the upcoming all-new Caravan/Voyager to negotiate this deal; no other service gave me this news. Thank you for the most up-to-date information available.

M.A.S., Walworth, N.Y.

I paid just $200 over invoice for my Chevy Malibu. It was so easy, I couldn't believe it. With your help, I became a seasoned and confident car shopper in one week!

N.B., Cleveland, Ohio

We found your service to be incredibly valuable. Two dealers showed us their invoices, and they matched your information. We got our Pontiac Bonneville for $300 over invoice. We felt good as we drove our new car away, and for the first time, we haven't had buyer's remorse.

M. & L.A., Portland, Oreg.

I paid $536 over invoice for my Camry, and I would never have had the confidence to carry it off if it were not for all the information you sent. Reading about others' experiences let me know what was possible. Your service was worth every penny.

B.S., Tucson, Ariz.

It is a wonderful feeling to buy a new vehicle and drive away knowing you got the best deal possible. I purchased my new red Mustang for $278 above dealer invoice. It was so easy it almost scared me. The information you provide is invaluable.

L.Q., Whitesburg, Ky.

I bought my Sebring LXi coupe at the dealer invoice price. The dealer told me I was the most knowledgeable and informed customer he had ever worked with. Little did he know that I had never bought a car in my life!

N.V., Minneapolis, Minn.

Frugality is the other thing money can't buy.
—W. James Bragg

26

The Used-Car Alternative

Let's start with the caveats.

We are not experts on used cars; our business is helping people buy or lease new cars. But we're not sure a true used-car expert exists. By definition, every used car is different from every other used car. That makes expertise very difficult to attain. When knowledge is harder to come by, nobody knows that much.

The books we've read on the subject seem to do a poor job of focusing the buyer on the best used-car options. Maybe that's because they're trying to talk to everyone, right down to the person with only $2,000 to spend who will end up with a 10-year-old car with over 120,000 miles on the odometer.

This chapter is not for everyone. It's for people who are seriously considering a new vehicle but have a strong left-brain orientation and wonder whether a previously owned vehicle would be a smarter buy. (If your left brain could talk, it would say, "Nobody needs a brand-new car to get from A to B.") These folks understand that every new car becomes a used car very quickly, and that in a sense we're all really driving used cars—it's just a matter of timing. They also know that when it comes to cars and humans, there's more than a dime's worth of difference between "used" and "used up."

THE ECONOMICS ARE COMPELLING

There's a strong dollars-and-sense argument for used over new, especially if you're a relatively young person convinced that you'll live forever but concerned that Social Security won't.

If you're in your twenties or early thirties, the slam-dunk way for you to put an extra $300,000 into your retirement kitty is simply to decide never to buy a new car. Instead, every four years, buy a two-year-old car. Let that first driver take the big depreciation hit. (The average car's wholesale value drops to 60–70 percent of its original sticker price in two years.) On a car with a sticker price of twenty to thirty grand, you'll save a thousand or two a year. For the rest of your life.

You won't be buying someone else's problem either. Today every automaker is building longer-lasting, more reliable cars. And the average two-year-old car even comes with some of its original three-year/36,000-mile bumper-to-bumper warranty. (We've focused on two-year-old cars for that reason. If you're shopping for a used luxury car with a four-year/50,000-mile warranty, you can consider buying a three-year-old. See the table in chapter 19 for warranty specifics by make.)

But saving $1,500 a year won't inflate your retirement kitty unless you invest that money religiously. Pick an aggressive no-load mutual fund. Start when you're 25, and if you average only a 7 percent return after taxes, you'll have an additional $320,000 when you're 65. Average 10 percent, and you'll have an extra $730,000. Doing that will require more financial discipline than most people have, but we told you this chapter isn't for everyone.

ADOPTING THE RIGHT TWO-YEAR-OLD

Whether you want to bolster your retirement savings or just cut your transportation budget, the strategy of buying a two-year-old car every four years makes a lot of sense. People are spending money more carefully these days, and with the average new-car transaction price over $20,000 and climbing, the stigma of driving a used car isn't what it used to be. Since body styles change only every four to eight years, most of your neighbors won't know whether you're driving new or used anyway.

How Do You Choose the Most Desirable Two-Year-Old Car?

By doing a little homework to narrow your choices. Go to the library and check the *Consumer Reports* annual auto issue, published each April. The substantial used-car section contains the key information you need to narrow your choices: (a) lists of the most reliable and least reliable used cars; (b) model-by-model reliability summaries, based on an annual survey of over 500,000 readers; and (c) frequency-of-repair records for several recent model years, with trouble spots detailed. While you're in the library, you may also want to check out the current annual editions of the *Consumer Reports Used Car Buying Guide* and *The Used Car Book* by Jack Gillis.

After you've selected a few likely candidates, ask the reference librarian for the library's copy of the *Kelley Blue Book's Guide to Used Car Values* or the *NADA* (National Automobile Dealers Association) *Official Used Car Guide*. As we've said before, these books purport to show trade-in/wholesale and market/retail used-car values, but don't take them too literally. They usually don't reflect the specific situation in your market, but they'll give you a feel for the percentage differences between what dealers pay for used cars and their retail asking prices. They'll also let you assess the differences between one car and another and one model year and another. You can find similar ballpark numbers on the Internet at the web sites of Kelley Blue Book (www.kbb.com), Edmund's (www.edmunds.com), and Pace Publications (www.carprice.com).

Are All Two-Year-Old Cars of the Same Make and Model Equally Desirable?

We don't think so. Assume two apparently identical cars are side by side on a dealer's lot, each with 25,000 miles on the odometer. One has just returned from a two-year lease to a private individual or family; the other has been in a car rental company's daily rental fleet. Which would you choose?

We'd choose the off-lease car over the rental fleet car in the blink of an eye, and we'd pay a premium for it. It's likely to be the highest-quality used vehicle you'll find. The difference isn't in the way the two cars have been maintained, for both have surely had all the required maintenance work done. The difference is in the number of different drivers they've had and the way they've been driven. The leased car probably had one or two regular drivers who treated it lovingly because they knew at lease-end they'd have to pay to fix anything beyond normal wear and tear on the vehicle. By contrast, the daily rental car had 300 to 500 different drivers, none of whom spent even one minute worrying about wear and tear. Some accelerated quickly and screeched to a halt at every light or stop sign, maximizing the strain on the powertrain and brake systems. Others drove it on rough roads and over potholes, bottoming out the suspension system. For many car renters, anything goes as long as there's no visible damage when they return the car.

The major car rental companies sell their own used cars at facilities similar to new-car dealerships, where the prices are non-negotiable. The smaller rental outfits send theirs cars to wholesale auctions, where they are sold to franchised new-car dealers and independent used-car dealers. In our view, these are cars to avoid.

Here's an experience that brings the point home. Returning our daily rental to the local office of a major national car rental company, we asked the manager of the office if he'd rather buy that Ford Taurus with 25,000 miles on it or an identical one with the same mileage that we had leased for two years. His immediate answer: "I'd rather have yours with 45,000 miles on it than ours with 25,000." Now, there's a testimonial worth remembering!

Where Do You Find Your Target Vehicle?

The two-year-old used car you want is most likely to be on the lot of a franchised new-car dealer who sells the same make. Remember, most new-car dealers sell as many used cars as new cars. But since they don't get all the late-model trade-ins they need, they must look elsewhere to stock their used-car operations. The two-year-old cars you'll find on a new-car dealer's lot come from several sources:

- Some are the better ones he's taken as trade-ins on new vehicles or purchased from private individuals who know they'll get the highest wholesale price from a dealer who sells the same make.

• Others are cars the dealer has purchased from leasing companies when customers returned them at the end of the lease term. A dealer will buy them if the price is close to the wholesale value, but he'll pass on cars from highly-subsidized leases with sky-high, non-negotiable buyout prices. Three to four million vehicles come off leases every year, split about equally between two- and three-year-olds. If a leased car is not purchased by the lessee or the leasing dealer, the leasing company will have it trucked to a wholesale auction. (As many as 80 percent of off-lease units on two-year leases end up in the hands of the leasing company.)

• Most of the other cars on a new-car dealer's used-car lot come from those wholesale auctions, where 2.5 to 3.5 million cars of all ages and backgrounds are sold to dealers each year at prices 20 percent or more off retail prices. Some auctions offer only one automaker's cars, sent there by the company's captive finance arm, and only that manufacturer's dealers are invited to attend. Other auctions are open to all dealers and offer cars from many different sources.

Most late-model cars from wholesale auctions fall into four categories:

1. Some are excellent cars coming off leases to private individuals, mostly those that dealers decided not to buy at lease-end because the residual values were too high. These cars sell for significantly less at auction.

2. Others come to the auctions from daily rental company fleets. These are typically less than two years old and have high mileage for their age. They are frequently called "program cars" because they're programmed to leave the rental fleet at a certain age and mileage.

3. Some are finance company repossessions from buyers who failed to make the required payments.

4. And some are refugees from corporate auto fleets. These can be high-mileage, high-wear-and-tear vehicles that have been poorly maintained. They can also be attractive lower-mileage cars driven by auto company executives.

The car you want, of course, is one that's been driven by an individual or family as a personal car. These are more likely to be off-lease cars, since relatively few car buyers trade cars after only two years.

What About Those Chains of Used-Car Superstores?

You're less likely to find the car of your dreams there. What you will find is a lot of cars from daily rental fleets at "no-dicker" prices. For example, Republic Industries, which owns AutoNation USA, also owns several car rental companies. One key reason for buying those companies was to provide AutoNation stores with a steady stream of late-model used cars. These stores don't get to buy the best cars leased through an automaker's captive finance company; the manufacturer's franchised new-car dealers get first crack at those. Superstores do, however, get cars from leases financed by third-party lenders.

These no-dicker used-car superstores are good places to shop prices, but we think your local new-car dealer will have better late-model used cars. You'll probably pay less there, too, because the prices will be negotiable. (See the research findings on comparative transaction prices on page 71 in chapter 14.)

BACKGROUND CHECKING

How Can You Tell Where a Late-Model Used Car Has Been?

For openers, the dealer who bought it has the previous title document, so he knows where it came from. Ask for the car's history, in writing; if he won't give it to you, that's a signal that he has something to hide and you should buy from someone else. And don't sign a "power of attorney" form when you buy a used car. That enables a dealer to process the title transfer papers without showing you the certificate of title.

Some states require that a dealer disclose whether a used car is a former rental or salvage vehicle or a "lemon law buyback." But those laws aren't universal. Fortunately, there's a universal source you can use to check any vehicle's background.

The Carfax® Vehicle History Report

To reduce your risk when buying a used vehicle, order a report on the car from Carfax, a database firm with over 550 million vehicle records. You give them the 17-character vehicle identification number (VIN) found on title documents and on the driver's side of the dashboard, near the edge of the windshield. With that number, Carfax can generate a detailed history report on virtually any used car or light truck built since 1981.

This report helps you answer these questions.

- Has the vehicle ever been declared a total loss by an insurance company, been sold at a salvage auction, or been damaged extensively in a flood?

- Has the odometer been rolled back?

- Has the manufacturer ever bought it back under the lemon laws?

- Was it used as a rental vehicle?

Carfax says it finds a red flag for one of nine cars.

The Carfax database may not have the history of every vehicle. The information on any given car depends on how long it has been on the road, how many times it's been titled, and where it's been driven. Carfax obtains its information from state motor vehicle departments (except Rhode Island and Vermont), auto auctions, used-car wholesalers, and emission inspection stations. It does not collect the names of vehicle owners, repair service records, stolen vehicle data, or the dollar value of vehicles.

We ordered a report for a 1995 Toyota Camry that was purchased as a used car from Avis several years ago in California. The four records it contained showed that:

- The car was registered in California as a rental vehicle by a major rental car company on October 1, 1994. (Avis was not identified by name.)

- The original title or registration was issued on October 13, 1994.

- A new title was issued on August 18, 1995, which is when the new owner borrowed money to buy the car from the rental company and a California financial institution put a lien on the vehicle. The odometer reading then was 20,674.

- A California inspection station performed an emissions inspection on September 14, 1996, when the odometer reading was 29,809.

- There were no problems found for the vehicle.

You may order a Carfax report on the Internet (at www.carfax.com). The price is $19.50. You enter the vehicle identification number and your credit card number on a form and receive the report moments later online. You may also order toll-free by calling (888) 4–CARFAX (422–7329). You'll get the report by fax or e-mail in less than 30 minutes. (*Note:* Many dealers use Carfax regularly and may order a report for you if you ask.)

GIVE THAT CAR A COMPLETE PHYSICAL

Have a mechanic look before you leap. When you find a car you're serious about buying, any offer you make should be contingent on the vehicle passing a thorough inspection by an independent mechanic, ideally one who knows the model well. The service department of another dealership that sells the same make would be a good choice. Tell them exactly what you're doing, and make it clear that you don't own the car and won't buy it if it has mechanical problems. That will eliminate any incentive for them to recommend unnecessary repairs.

Many dealers will do a thorough used-car inspection for $50 to $150. This should include a compression test on all cylinders, a body integrity check for accident damage, a brake inspection, and checks of the front wheel bearings and suspension system, the transmission, and the exhaust, cooling, and electrical systems. Ask them to road-test the car for you. And get a cost estimate for any repairs they recommend.

This may seem to be overkill for a nearly new car with plenty of its original bumper-to-bumper warranty remaining, but it's not. If it's a car headed for mechanical trouble, you don't want it. If the selling dealer won't let the car off his lot for an inspection, and if you can't find one of those traveling inspection outfits that will do it there, find another dealer.

SHOULD YOU BUY A "DEMO"?

Several times a month, customers call us and say they've got an opportunity to buy a dealer's "demo" vehicle; they wonder whether that's a good idea and ask how they should negotiate a realistic price. This is a gray area with no established guidelines, but here's an approach to dealing with the question.

Strictly speaking, a demo is not a used car. It's a "used new vehicle" that's owned by the dealership and has never been sold. It might be the current year's model or last year's. It typically has from 1,000 to 10,000 miles on the odometer—most often 4,000 to 6,000.

You need to know who put those miles on the car. These are seldom true "demos," in the sense that they've been used mainly for test drives with prospective customers. Usually the vehicle has been driven for a few months by someone in the business or the dealer's family—perhaps a spouse, the sales manager, or the salesperson-of-the-month. Those are not tough miles; they're the same kind any individual would put on the vehicle. But if a car has been rented or loaned to service customers, and if 6,000 miles means 300 different people have driven it 20 miles each, those are not wonderful miles. (It's rare for a brand-new car to be used for this purpose, but it happens.)

Assuming you're comfortable with the car's history, there are three key issues to consider when you're trying to put a price on one of these cars.

1. Loss of Warranty Protection—Assume you find a demo with 6,000 miles on the odometer, and the car's original bumper-to-bumper warranty was 3 years or 36,000 miles. The mileage count started with the first demo mile driven, so one-sixth of the car's original warranty is gone. If you drive only 12,000 miles a year, you'll be out of warranty after two and a half years, and any big repairs in the following six months will come from your checkbook instead of the automaker's.

The time clock may also have been ticking on that warranty. Ask the dealer whether he established an "in-service" date on the car when he started using it as a demo. He may have, since he can't make warranty repairs on a car that's not yet in service. You need to know that in-service date, because that's the day the three-year warranty started. Ask him to print out a warranty history on the car. If warranty work has been done, an in-service date has been established.

A dealer might say he'll extend that original warranty by 6,000 miles or 6 months, but don't fall for that. That warranty is between you and the manufacturer, period. No dealer has the authority to extend any manufacturer's warranty.

2. Loss of Trade-in Value—Someday, years from now, you'll sell that car or trade it in on another new one. It will have an extra 6,000 miles on it that you didn't put there, and it'll be worth less because of those miles. That loss must be factored into the price you pay.

3. The Cost of the Same Car with No Miles on It—This must be your reference point. There are two relevant questions: (a) What would you have to pay for an "unused" version of the same new car? (b) How much would you have to save to make the used version a smart buy?

So What's the Right Price for a Demo?

The dealership has driven significant value off the vehicle; it must compensate the buyer for those miles. Our rough rule of thumb is 25 to 30 cents per mile—$1,500 to $1,800 on a car driven 6,000 miles. Why? Because 10 or 15 cents isn't enough, and they'd never agree to anything like 50 cents. (If it had 20,000 miles, you wouldn't get a $10,000 price reduction.) Assuming you could buy an "unused" version of the same model for $500 over invoice, you'd want to pay $1,500 to $1,800 less—or $1,000 to $1,300 *below* invoice—for one with 6,000 miles.

And if that 6,000-mile demo is last year's model? Figure that five years down the road, you'll get about $1,000 more for this year's model than for last year's with the same mileage. That's *another* $1,000 you'd have to save just to break even. So your total purchase price would have to be $2,500 to $2,800 below what you'd pay for this year's "unused" model to make it a smart buy.

One more concession you should ask for: an extended warranty at dealer cost. Emphasize that you are very concerned about buying a car with a chunk of its original warranty gone, and the only way you'll do that is if they'll sell you the extended warranty at cost. They just might.

THE PICK OF THE USED-CAR LITTER: MANUFACTURER-CERTIFIED CARS

There's another alternative you should consider strongly: a "certified" used car. These are typically cars coming off lease that are inspected and reconditioned according to the automaker's specifications and come with a manufacturer's warranty. They cost an extra $500 to $1,500 compared to "uncertified" cars, but that modest upcharge buys a lot of long-term peace of mind. (With these cars, you don't need a Carfax vehicle history report or a separate mechanic's inspection.)

Automakers initiated these certification programs to deal with the glut of late-model used cars spawned by the leasing craze. It all started with the high-end luxury cars, but today everyone from Toyota and Ford to Lexus and Mercedes has a certification plan that runs quality exams on used cars. Depending on the manufacturer, these cars must undergo a 75- to 150-point inspection. Dealers fix whatever needs to be fixed, and the cars are sold with relatively comprehensive manufacturers' warranties.

Most used cars are sold "as is" and carry the dealer's 30-day or 1,000-mile warranty. But the manufacturer-backed warranties on certified cars typically run at least one year or 12,000 miles and come with roadside assistance. (Lexus backs some certified cars with 2-year/20,000-mile coverage.) And this extra protection is often added to the end of any new-car warranty still in effect.

Not all franchised dealers sell certified cars. The ones that do tend to be large dealerships in major markets. At this writing, about half of Toyota's dealers, one-third of Ford's, and just one-tenth of GM's participate. We'd expect participation to increase dramatically, especially as the competitive used-car superstore chains expand nationally. Manufacturer certification programs are a potent weapon for traditional dealers in the battle for used-car market share—a weapon the superstores can't match. Only franchised new-car dealers can get these cars.

USED CARS ARE FOR LEASING, TOO

If you're a candidate to lease, you should consider leasing a used car. This alternative makes the most sense for someone who'd rather be driving a luxury or semiluxury car, but can't afford a new one.

You reference point should always be the cost of leasing the current model of the same car. After determining that number, check the cost of leasing a two- or three-year-old version. In most cases, you won't save much leasing a car that listed for under $20,000 when new. With all the subsidized new-car leases for vehicles in that price range, a used-car lease might save you only $20 a month. But leasing a three-year-old, factory-certified BMW 5-Series sedan might save you $200 a month compared to a new one.

TALKING TURKEY

Okay, you've done your homework and chosen the car you want. You've checked the logical sources of estimated trade-in/wholesale and market/retail used-car values, recognizing that those sources aren't perfect. You've also checked local asking prices for your car on dealers' lots and in the classified ad section.

There's no "dealer invoice price" for used cars. But we know that dealers make a lot more profit selling used cars than new ones, and they build a 20 to 30 percent gross margin into their asking prices.

Once you've located the car you want, tell the salesperson you have a feel for both the wholesale prices and the asking prices in your market.

You expect him to make a profit, but you're not going to finance his next trip to the Super Bowl by yourself. Then offer 15 percent below the asking price and bite your tongue; the next person who talks will lose. When he counters with a higher number, bump your offer to 90 percent of the asking price. If he turns that down, say you've got an appointment at a competitor who has the same car and leave. But leave your phone number; he'll probably call.

Education is what you have left over after you have forgotten everything you have learned.
—Anonymous

27

The Executive Summary

Our objective is to make this guidebook the most comprehensive and useful information package available to people shopping for new vehicles. While it would be impossible to compress it into a pocket-size checklist, we have tried to highlight below the major points covered, for use as a memory trigger as you go through the shopping and negotiating process.

• **For openers, have a current overview of the automobile business.**

What's the sales and inventory picture for the vehicles you're shopping? The poorer the sales and the higher the inventories, the better the deal is likely to be (chapter 3).

- **Adjust your attitude.** Project total emotional detachment around car salesmen ("A car is a car"). Be ready to walk out if you don't like what's happening. Remember, there's always a deal that's as good or better around the next corner. They need you much more than you need them (chapter 4).

- **Watch all three ways the car store can make money on you:** (1) the price you pay for the new car, (2) the financing and other back-end add-ons they try to sell, most of which are of little value, and (3) the real price they pay for your trade-in vehicle (chapter 5).

- **Develop a smart buyer's plan.** Learn what your current car is really worth at wholesale and retail. Decide whether you'll trade it or sell it yourself. Shop for money before you shop for cars. Visit car stores to narrow your choices. Gather information on dealer costs. Understand the overall state of the automobile market, including current consumer and dealer incentive offers. Do some homework to choose your dealer finalists. Make timing work for you. Put all the pieces together to approach car stores with an aggressive offer. Play them off against each other to maximize your leverage. And resolve to let them do the stewing (chapter 6).

- **If you're going to trade, keep the discussion of the price you pay for the new car separate from the discussion of the price they pay for your current car** (chapter 7).

- **Learn the true wholesale value of your current car before you talk with any car salesman about a trade-in** (chapter 8). And sell it yourself if you expect to get top dollar for it (chapter 9).

- **Deal with the key financing issues before you deal with the dealer.** Shop smart for money, to provide a basis for determining if the dealer's financing proposal is attractive (chapter 10).

- **As you consider your vehicle choices, give serious weight to the safety differences between one car and another.** Some vehicles are inherently safer than others in a serious accident, so check the crash test data on all your finalists (chapter 11).

- **Make your tire-kicking and test-driving visits "away games" if you can.** And try to retain two or three equally attractive vehicle alternatives, perhaps by exploring "family relations" (chapter 12).

• **Learn everything you can about what those vehicles really cost the dealer.** Bone up on dealer invoice prices, factory-to-dealer incentives, and dealer holdback. Make a worksheet showing all the elements (chapter 15).

• **Make timing work for you.** Try to buy at the end of a dealer incentive program. And in general, gather data early in the month but negotiate price at the end of the month (chapter 16).

• **Be prepared for the unexpected, both the games salesmen play** (chapter 17) **and the high-profit options they'll try to sell as add-ons** (chapter 18). And determine beforehand if you're a candidate for an extended warranty contract (chapter 19).

• **Pick your dealer finalists based primarily on service considerations and geography, not price.** Research this issue by talking to service managers, not car salesmen (chapter 20).

• **Approach the negotiating sessions in a disciplined, confident manner, using your now-considerable knowledge base as a lever to keep control of the discussion.** Set a target price based on the guidelines in chapter 21, but start lower. You don't know where the bone is until you hit it. Be very direct, letting them know what you know and what you expect from them. Allow for a modest profit in your offer, but show them your heels if they seem unreasonable. There are plenty of other dealers for most makes (chapters 15, 16, and 21).

• **Aim to get all of any dealer cash incentive.** Of course, you'll get all of any direct customer incentives, such as factory rebates. To strengthen your leverage, remind dealers of holdback profits they'll receive later, if appropriate (chapters 15, 16, and 21).

• **Above all, don't be too eager to make a quick deal.** Nobody's first offer will be his best. Play two or three dealers off against each other, using the phone for follow-up negotiations with your dealer finalists. The secret to winning: Make it competitive every step of the way (chapter 21).

• **If you're considering leasing, ask yourself the right questions to determine whether it makes sense for you, learn the language, follow the rules in chapter 22, and read the fine print before you sign anything.**

• **To simplify the negotiation process, do it by phone or fax instead of in person.** And if it still seems like more than you can handle, check out the CarBargains option (chapter 23).

• Be sure to give that car or truck an inspection that would make a marine colonel proud before you give the salesman the final check and sign the delivery receipt (chapter 24).

• Prepare yourself to bargain effectively for the vehicle you want by having (a) up-to-date dealer invoice pricing for the vehicle, including the previous price if there has been an increase, (b) a current overview of its sales performance in the marketplace, including a feel for the actual transaction prices being paid in relation to invoice price by other educated shoppers, and (c) a list of current incentive activity, including factory-to-dealer cash incentives. You may obtain this information directly from us by calling Fighting Chance at (800) 288–1134 or ordering from our web site (www.fightingchance.com), or you may obtain it elsewhere. But be sure to have it. (See ordering details in chapter 25.)

• If you're considering buying or leasing a late-model used vehicle as an alternative to a new one, be just as disciplined in your approach. Do your homework to learn which previously owned cars to covet and which to avoid. And take a long look at factory-certified used vehicles (chapter 26).

Appendices

Auto

Manufacturers'

Addresses

If you can't get all your important questions answered by people at a dealership, try calling the manufacturer. Here's a list of their phone numbers. The 800 numbers are typically for customer assistance and information, including directing you to your nearest dealer, but you may not get someone who can answer all your questions. If you don't, call the other number, which is for corporate headquarters. Identify yourself as a consumer who is considering the purchase of one of their vehicles and say you have a question the dealer can't answer. The automakers have become much more consumer-oriented, and the operators should be able to find someone who can help you. If they can't, perhaps you should consider buying from another company. (Note: A few companies don't have 800 numbers, and a couple have 800 numbers only for consumer information calls.) We're also including manufacturers' web site addresses, where you will find product information and links to their dealers.

Acura Division
American Honda Motor Company, Inc.
Torrance, Calif.
(310) 783-2000
(800) 382-2238
(www.acura.com)

Audi of America, Inc.
Auburn Hills, Mich.
(248) 340-5000
(800) 822-2834
(www.audiusa.com)

BMW of North America, Inc.
Woodcliff Lake, N.J.
(201) 307-4000
(800) 831-1117
(www.bmwusa.com)

Buick Motor Division
General Motors
Flint, Mich.
(800) 521-7300
(www.buick.com)

Cadillac Motor Car Division
Warren, Mich.
(800) 458-8006
(www.cadillac.com)

Chevrolet Motor Division
General Motors
Warren, Mich.
(810) 492-8841

(800) 222-1020
(www.chevrolet.com)

Chrysler Corporation
(Chrysler, Dodge, Jeep, Plymouth)
Highland Park, Mich.
(313) 956-5741
(800) 992-1997
(800) 227-0757 (for news of current consumer incentives)
Chrysler: (www.chryslercars.com)
Dodge: (www.4adodge.com)
Jeep: (www.jeepunpaved.com)
Plymouth: (www.plymouthcars.com)

Ferrari North America, Inc.
Englewood Cliffs, N.J.
(201) 816-2600

Ford Division
Ford Motor Company
Detroit, Mich.
(313) 446-4450 or (313) 322-3000
(800) 392-3673
(www.fordvehicles.com)

GMC Truck Division
General Motors
Pontiac, Mich.
(248) 456-5000 or (313) 556-5000
(800) 462-8782
(www.gmc.com)

Honda Division
American Honda Motor Company, Inc.
Torrance, Calif.
(310) 783-2000
(800) 999-1009
(www.honda.com)

Hyundai Motor America
Fountain Valley, Calif.
(800) 633-5151
(www.hyundaiUSA.com)

Infiniti Division
Nissan Motor Corporation in U.S.A.
Carson, Calif.
(310) 532-3111 or (310) 771-3111
(800) 662-6200
(www.infiniti-usa.com)

American Isuzu Motors, Inc.
City of Industry, Calif.
(562) 699-0500
(800) 726-2700
(www.isuzu.com)

Jaguar Cars
Mahwah, N.J.
(201) 818-8500
(800) 452-4827 or (800) 544-4767
(www.jaguarcars.com/us)

Kia Motors America, Inc.
Irvine, Calif.
(714) 470-7000
(800) 333-4542
(www.kia.com)

Land Rover North America, Inc.
Lanham, Md.
(301) 731-9040
(800) 637-6837
(www.landrover.com)

Lexus Division
Toyota Motor Sales U.S.A., Inc.
Torrance, Calif.
(310) 328-2075
(800) 255-3987
(www.lexus.com)

Lincoln-Mercury Division
Ford Motor Company
Detroit, Mich.
(313) 446-4450
(800) 392-3673
Lincoln: (www.lincolnvehicles.com)
Mercury:
  (www.mercuryvehicles.com)

Lotus Cars U.S.A., Inc.
Lawrenceville, Ga.
(770) 822-4566
(www.lotuscars.com)

Mazda Motors of America, Inc.
Irvine, Calif.
(949) 727-1990
(800) 222-5500
(www.mazdausa.com)

Mercedes-Benz of North America, Inc.
Montvale, N.J.
(201) 573-2246
(800) 367-6372
(www.mbusa.com)

Mitsubishi Motor Sales of America, Inc.
Cypress, Calif.
(714) 372-6000
(800) 222-0037
(www.mitsucars.com)

Nissan Division
Nissan Motor Corporation in
  U.S.A.
Carson, Calif.
(310) 532-3111 or (310) 771-3111
(800) 647-7261
(www.nissan-usa.com)

Oldsmobile Division
General Motors
Lansing, Mich.
(517) 377-5000
(800) 442-6537
(www.oldsmobile.com)

Pontiac Division
General Motors
Pontiac, Mich.
(248) 857-5000
(800) 762-2737
(www.pontiac.com)

Porsche Cars North America, Inc.
Atlanta, Ga.
(770) 290-3500
(www.porsche.com)

Saab Cars U.S.A., Inc.
Norcross, Ga.
(770) 279-0100
(800) 955-9007
(www.saabusa.com)

Saturn Corporation
General Motors
Troy, Mich.
(248) 524-5000
(800) 553-6000
(www.saturn.com)

Subaru of America, Inc.
Cherry Hill, N.J.
(609) 488-8500
(800) 782-2783
(www.subaru.com)

American Suzuki Motor
  Corporation
Brea, Calif.
(714) 996-7040
(800) 934-0934
(www.suzuki.com)

Toyota Division
Toyota Motor Sales U.S.A., Inc.
Torrance, Calif.
(310) 328-2075 or (310) 618-4000
(800) 331-4331
(www.toyota.com)

Volkswagen of America, Inc.
Auburn Hills, Mich.
(248) 340-5000
(800) 822-8987
(www.vw.com)

Volvo Cars of North America, Inc.
Rockleigh, N.J.
(201) 768-7300
(800) 458-1552
(www.volvocars.com)

B

The
All-American
Speedster

THE ALL-AMERICAN SPEEDSTER

Factory Code No.	Model/Trim Level	Dealer Invoice	Retail (MSRP)
S88	AAA 4-door wagon	$15,700	$18,400
S87	AA 4-door wagon	13,000	15,200
S86	A 4-door wagon	12,800	15,000
S85	AAA 4-door sedan	14,300	16,800
S84	AA 4-door sedan	12,200	14,300
S83	A 4-door sedan	11,900	13,900

STANDARD EQUIPMENT BY TRIM LEVEL

A trim level:

Driver-side airbag
Power front disc brakes/rear drum brakes
Dual power mirrors
Digital clock
3.0-liter V-6 EFI engine
Full wheel covers
Fuel cap tether
Lights for ashtray, door courtesy, trunk,
    glove box, under hood, headlight switch,
    cargo area, dome

AM/FM radio w/4 speakers
Split bench seats w/dual recliners;
    65/35 split fold-down rear (wagon)
Power steering
Map pockets
P205/70R14 SBR all-season tires
    (blackwall)
Tinted glass
Cloth upholstery
Luggage rack for wagon

AA trim level (in addition to or in place of A trim level):

Deluxe cloth upholstery
Diagnostic warning lights
Remote release, decklid/liftgate

Pain stripe
Cast aluminum wheels

AAA trim level (in addition to or in place of AA trim level):

Air conditioning
Convenience kit
Illuminated entry system
Reclining front bucket seats w/6-way power
    driver seat and lumbar supports
P205/65R15 SBR blackwall tires

Full console w/armrest and storage
3.8-liter V-6 EFI engine
Automatic on/off/delay headlights
Speed-sensitive power steering
Tachometer
Luxury cloth upholstery

PREFERRED EQUIPMENT PACKAGES

Factory Code No.	Model/Trim Level	Dealer Invoice	Retail (MSRP)
444B	AA	$1,500	$1,800

Includes 725 manual air conditioning; 757 rear window defroster; 211 f&r floor mats; 129 power door locks; 888 AM/FM stereo radio w/cassette; 254 cruise control; 343 power windows; 298 power driver seat; 765 P205/65R15 tires. Prices reflect discounts of $600 dealer invoice and $730 suggested retail.

(continued)

THE ALL-AMERICAN SPEEDSTER *(continued)*

Factory Code No.	Item	Model/ Trim Level	Dealer Invoice	Retail (MSRP)
291	Passenger airbag	All	$400	$500
725	Manual air conditioning	A, AA	700	850
735	Automatic air conditioning	AAA	150	190
525	Anti-lock brakes	All	500	600
754	Cargo cover	Wagons	60	75
254	Cruise control	All	190	225
757	Rear window defroster	All	140	170
129	Power door locks	A, AA	210	250
222	California emissions	All	75	110
947	3.8-liter V-6 EFI engine	AA, AAA	470	560
143	Engine block heater	All	20	30
211	Front and rear floor mats	All	40	50
888	AM/FM stereo/cassette	All	140	175
861	High-level audio system	All	250	300
	(includes controls for bass, treble, balance, fade; seek-scan turning; AM stereo; Dolby noise reduction; 80 watts power)			
862	Compact disc player	All	400	500
	(includes cassette; requires 861 high-level audio system)			
311	Power moonroof	AAA	700	800
	(requires 725 manual air conditioning when 735 automatic air conditioning is not ordered)			
298	6-way power driver seat	AA	250	300
299	Dual 6-way power seats	AAA	250	300
314	Rear-facing third seat	Wagons	130	160
301	Leather bucket seats	AA	500	600
	with console	AAA	400	500
524	Leather steering wheel	AAA	65	90
	(requires 254 cruise control)			
343	Power windows	A, AA	300	360
106	Rear window washer/wiper	Wagons	100	150
	(requires 757 rear window defroster)			
765	P205/65R15 blackwall tires	AA	130	150
608	Conventional spare tire	All	60	75
	(replaces rear-facing third seat on wagons)			
	Destination charges	All	500	500

Note: This chart contains fictitious information about a vehicle and a manufacturer that do not exist. It was created solely as an aid in helping the reader learn to build a new-vehicle worksheet (see chapter 15).

C

CarDeals—
A Sample
Report

Important Note: The sample *CarDeals* report shown here is *not* a listing of current customer rebates or factory-to-dealer cash incentives. It is an abriged version that illustrates the kinds of information these reports typically contain.

The actual *CarDeals* report is published every two weeks, as incentive offers are constantly changing. The Fighting Chance information package always includes the most recent edition of this report.

CarDeals

Rebate and Incentive Programs Offered on New Cars and Light Trucks.

A Newsletter Published by the
Center for the Study of Services/Consumers' CHECKBOOK,
733 15th Street, N.W., Suite 820, Washington, DC 20005, (202) 347–7283

This is information on deals being offered by car manufacturers. Manufacturers sometimes offer *customer* rebates directly to the consumer. You can get the rebate as a check in the mail or you can have the dealer credit the rebate immediately as a discount to reduce the price of your car. A dealer will tell you if any *customer* rebates are available, so you don't have to worry about missing out on something you are entitled to.

Another type of deal offered by car makers is *factory-to-dealer* cash incentive programs. In these programs, the manufacturer gives the dealer a cash payment for every car the dealer sells. Manufacturers sometimes advertise these factory-to-dealer cash incentive programs, but often the programs are secret.

Dealers don't have to tell you about factory-to-dealer cash incentive programs, and a dealer doesn't have to give you any part of the cash incentive payment it receives for selling you a car. Dealers may use these payments for advertising, employee rewards, extra profit, or in other ways. It's up to you to get the dealer to pass all or part of the cash incentive payment along to you. The information this report gives you about ongoing factory-to-dealer cash incentive programs will enable you to negotiate with the dealer.

Here are some tips on using the *CarDeals* information:

• If you are considering several makes/models of cars that seem roughly comparable in value for the dollar, be sure to check whether one carries a rebate or cash incentive program that will significantly drop its cost. It's not unusual for the maker of one car to offer no rebate or incentive program while the maker of a similar car is offering a rebate worth $1,000 or more. That $1,000 may be just what it takes to make the second type of car the best choice for you.

• If a car you want doesn't currently carry any special deals, consider waiting. New programs start all the time.

- To get all or part of the factory-to-dealer cash incentive money that a dealer will receive for selling you a car, you may have to negotiate. Let dealers know that you are aware of the money and that you intend to shop several dealers until you find one that gives you some or all of this factory-supplied cash.

- Some factory-to-dealer cash incentive programs give dealers larger payments per car as the dealers sell more cars during the program period. Unless otherwise noted, when you see a range in our listing (say, $400–800), this means that a dealer gets more cash if it sells more cars. In some programs, all dealers have the same volume targets. In such programs, you can expect large dealerships to get larger cash payments than small dealers, because the large dealers sell more cars. In other programs, larger dealerships have to meet higher-volume targets in order ot qualify for cash than small dealers have to meet, so there's no reason for you to expect to get a better deal at a large dealership. In our listing, we tell you the programs where incentive payments are "based on sales targets set for the dealer," rather than targets that are the same for all dealers.

- In programs that give dealers higher incentive payments as the volume of cars sold increases, you might do well to delay your purchase until nearly the end of the program period so that some dealers are likely to be at the highest cash incentive plateau.

- If the car you want is part of an incentive program in which payments go up as sales volume goes up, be sure to shop at several dealerships in hopes of finding one that is at the highest payment level.

- In some programs, a dealer that meets a sales target gets extra cash for all cars sold earlier in a period, before it met the target. Since meeting its target may get the dealer hundreds of dollars for each previously sold car, the dealer might give dramatic discounts as it gets close to its target.

- Although you can get a *customer* rebate in the form of a check from the manufacturer, you may be better off to have the dealer credit the rebate as a discount to reduce the price of you car; in some states, doing so will reduce your sales tax.

- Some manufacturers offer reduced-rate financing plans as an alternative to a customer cash rebate. These plans are noted in our listing. You must decide whether the rebate or the finance plan is better for you. The answer depends on the size of the rebate, the factory-offered plan's annual percentage rate (APR), the APRs available from other lenders, the amount you'll be borrowing, and how long a period you'll be borrowing for. On a 48-month loan, each percentage point you cut your APR is the equivalent of a care price disount of about $20.50 per $1,000 of loan.

To illustrate, assume you could get a $13,000, 48-month loan from a bank at a 8 percent APR, and that the special factory plan's rebate is 3.9 percent. The savings from using the factory plan would be estimated as follows:

$$(8 - 3.9) \times 13 \times \$20.50 = \$1,093$$

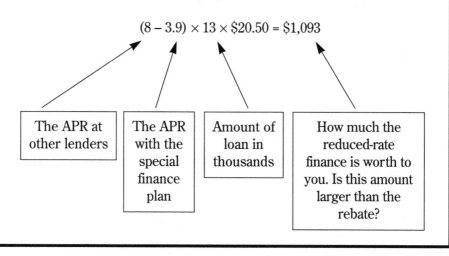

| The APR at other lenders | The APR with the special finance plan | Amount of loan in thousands | How much the reduced-rate finance is worth to you. Is this amount larger than the rebate? |

The sample tables on the following pages represent a shortened version of a typical *CarDeals* report. Customer rebates are followed by a (C) and dealer incentives by a (D).

This is NOT a listing of current incentives. The actual *CarDeals* newsletter, published biweekly, typically lists two to three times as many incentive offers.

CarDeals INCENTIVES PROGRAMS

Model	Cash-to-to-Customer (C) or-Dealer (D) and/or Finance Plan	End
SUBCOMPACTS (current-year models except where noted)		
Chevrolet Prizm	$1,500 (C) or Plan 5	9/23
Ford Escort (last year's model)	$750 (C) or Plan 4	9/23
Ford Escort	$400 (C) or Plan 4	9/23
Honda Civic (4-door)	$400 (D)	9/2
Mazda Protegé	$1,400 (C)	9/8
Mercury Tracer	$400–1,000 (C) (varies by region) or Plan 4	9/23
Nissan Sentra	$1,000 (D)	9/2
Toyota Corolla	$800–1,000 (D) based on sales targets set for individual dealer	9/2
Toyota Tercel	$200–400 (D) based on sales targets set for individual dealer	9/2
COMPACT CARS		
Acura Integra	$500 (D)	9/2
Chevrolet Cavalier	$750 (C) or Plan 5	9/23
Ford Contour	$500 (C) or Plan 4	9/23
Honda Accord	$500 (D)	9/2
Mazda 626	$1,200 (C)	9/8
Mercury Mystique	$500 (C) or Plan 4	9/23
Mitsubishi Galant	$0–1,200 (D)	9/30
Pontiac Grand Am	$500 (C) or Plan 1	9/23
Subaru Legacy	$1,000 (D)	11/3
Volkswagen Jetta	$500	9/30
MID-SIZE CARS		
Buick Century	$250–1,000 (C) or Plan 3	9/23
Buick Regal	$500–1,250 (C) or Plan	9/23
Chevrolet Lumina	$1,500 (C) or Plan 5	9/23
Chrysler Concorde	$750 (C) or Plan 2	8/31
Dodge Intrepid	$750 (C) or Plan 2	8/31
Ford Taurus	$750 (C) or Plan 4 plus $0–180 (D)** based on sales targets set for individual dealer (varies by region)	9/23
Hyundai Sonata	$2,000 (C)	10/2
Lincoln Continental	$2,000 (C)	
Mercury Cougar	$0–1,500 (C) or Plan 4 (varies by state)	9/23
Mercury Sable	$750–1,000 (C) or Plan 4 (varies by state)	9/23
Nissan Maxima	$1,000–1,500 (D) based on sales targets set for individual dealer	9/2
Oldsmobile Cutlass	$1,000 (C) or Plan 3	9/23
Pontiac Grand Prix	$500–750 (C) (varies by region) or Plan 1	9/23

(continued)

CarDeals INCENTIVES PROGRAMS *(continued)*

Model	Cash-to-to-Customer (C) or-Dealer (D) and/or Finance Plan	End
LARGE CARS (current-year models except where noted)		
Buick LeSabre	$250-1,000 (C) or Plan 3	9/23
Buick Park Avenue	$1,000 (C) or Plan 3	9/23
Cadillac DeVille	$1,500 (C)	9/23
Ford Crown Victoria (last year's model)	$1,000 (D)	9/23
Ford Crown Victoria	$500 (c) or Plan 4	9/23
Lincoln Town Car	$2,000 (C)	9/23
Mercury Grand Marquis	$500 (C) or Plan 4	9/23
Oldsmobile Eighty-eight	$500–1,000 (C) (varies by region) or Plan 3	9/23
Pontiac Bonneville	$750 (C) or Plan 1	9/23
SMALL VANS		
Chevrolet G-Van	$500 (C) or Plan 5	9/23
Chrysler Town & Country	$500 (C) or Plan 2	8/31
Dodge Caravan	$500 (C) or Plan 2	8/31
Dodge Ram (wagon, van, conversion)	$1,000 (C) or Plan 2	8/31
Ford Econoline	$1,000 (C) or Plan 4	9/23
GMC Safari	$500 (C) or Plan 1	9/23
Mazda MPV	$1,000 (C)	9/8
Plymouth Voyager	$500 (C) or Plan 2	8/31
PICKUPS		
Chevrolet S-10 Pickup	$750 (C) or Plan 5	9/23
Dodge Dakota	$500 (C) or Plan 2	8/31
Dodge Ram Pickup	$1,500 (C) or Plan 2	8/31
Ford F-Series Pickup	$300 (C) or Plan 4 plus $0–180 (D)** based on sales target set for individual dealer	9/23
Ford Ranger	$750–1,000 (C) or Plan 4 (varies by state)	9/23
GMC Sonoma	$750 (C) or Plan 1	9/23
Isuzu Pickup	$800–1,600 (D)	9/30
Mazda Pickup	$0–1,400 (C) (varies by region)	9/8
Nissan Pickup	$750 (D) based on sales targets set for individual dealer	9/2
Toyota Tacoma Pickup	$800–1,200 (D) based on sales targets set for individual dealer	9/2
SPORT UTILITY VEHICLES		
Chevrolet Blazer	$1,000 (C) or Plan 5	9/23
Chevrolet Tracker (2WD models)	$750 (C) or Plan 5	9/23
Chevrolet Tracker (4WD models)	$1,000 (C) or Plan 5	9/23
	(continued)	

CarDeals INCENTIVES PROGRAMS *(continued)*

Model	Cash-to-to-Customer (C) or-Dealer (D) and/or Finance Plan	End
SPORT UTILITY VEHICLES *(continued)*		
GMC Jimmy	$1,000 (C) or Plan 1	9/23
Isuzu Rodeo (2WD)	$400 (D)	9/30
Isuzu Rodeo (4WD)	$950 (D) or $800–1,400 (D) (dealer chooses)	9/30
Jeep Cherokee	$500 (C) or Plan 2	8/31
Jeep Wrangler	$500 (C) or Plan 2	8/31
Nissan Pathfinder	$1,000 (D)	9/2
SPORTY CARS		**9/23**
Chevrolet Camero	$500 (C) or Plan 5	9/23
Chevrolet Corvette	$1,000 (D)	9/23
Ford Mustang	$500–1,000 (C) or Plan 4 (varies by state)	9/23
Mitsubishi Eclipse	$0–1,200 (D)	9/30
Pontiac Firebird	$750–1,000 (C) (varies by region) or Plan 1	9/23
Toyota Celica	$600–800 (D) based on sales targets set for individual dealer	9/2

Finance Plans:

Plan 1: 6.9% APR up to 48 mos.

Plan 2: 4.9% APR up to 24 mos., 6.9% up to 36 mos., 7.9% up to 48 mos., 9.9% up to 60 mos. (Minivans: 6.9% APR up to 24 mos., 7.9% APR up to 36 mos., 8.9% up to 48 mos., 9.9% APR up to 60 mos. The lower rates that may be available on some models vary by region)

Plan 3: 2.9% APR up to 24 mos., 4.9% APR up to 36 mos., 6.9% APR up to 48 mos.

Plan 4: 7.9% APR up to 48 mos. (The lower rates that may be available on some models vary by region)

Plan 5: 6.9% APR up to 48 mos.

*If dealer meets targets by the end of the period he gets cash for all cars sold in the period.

D

Dollar Savings per $1,000 of Loan Amount

DOLLAR SAVINGS PER $1,000 OF LOAN AMOUNT

Prevailing Market Rate (APR)

Dealer's Factory-Subsidized Interest Rate

2-Year Loan	3%	4%	5%	6%	7%	8%	9%
7%	40.01	30.10	20.13	10.09	—	—	—
8%	49.66	39.85	29.98	20.05	10.05	—	—
9%	59.18	49.47	39.69	29.86	19.97	10.01	—
10%	68.56	58.94	49.27	39.53	29.74	19.89	9.97
11%	77.81	68.29	58.71	49.07	39.38	29.62	19.81
12%	86.93	77.51	68.02	58.48	48.88	39.22	29.50
13%	95.93	86.60	77.20	67.76	58.25	46.68	39.06
14%	104.80	95.56	86.26	76.90	67.49	58.02	48.49
15%	113.55	104.39	95.19	85.92	76.60	67.22	57.79

3-Year Loan	3%	4%	5%	6%	7%	8%	9%
7%	58.16	43.82	29.35	14.74	—	—	—
8%	71.97	57.84	43.57	29.18	14.66	—	—
9%	85.49	71.56	57.51	48.33	29.01	14.57	—
10%	98.74	85.01	71.16	57.19	43.08	28.85	14.49
11%	111.72	98.19	84.54	70.77	56.86	42.83	28.68
12%	124.44	111.11	97.65	84.07	70.37	56.54	42.59
13%	136.90	123.76	110.50	97.11	83.60	69.97	56.22
14%	149.11	136.16	123.08	109.89	96.57	83.13	69.57
15%	161.09	148.31	135.42	122.41	109.28	96.03	82.66

4-Year Loan	3%	4%	5%	6%	7%	8%	9%
7%	75.67	57.09	38.29	19.26	—	—	—
8%	93.34	75.12	56.68	38.01	19.12	—	—
9%	110.54	92.67	74.57	56.26	37.73	18.97	—
10%	127.28	109.75	92.00	74.03	55.84	37.44	18.83
11%	143.59	126.38	108.96	91.33	73.49	55.43	37.16
12%	159.47	142.58	125.49	108.18	90.67	72.94	55.02
13%	174.94	158.36	141.58	124.59	107.40	90.00	72.41
14%	190.00	173.73	157.25	140.57	123.70	106.62	89.34
15%	204.68	188.70	172.52	156.15	139.58	122.81	105.84

5-Year Loan	3%	4%	5%	6%	7%	8%	9%
7%	92.55	69.93	46.97	23.65	—	—	—
8%	113.81	91.73	69.30	46.54	23.44	—	—
9%	134.39	112.81	90.91	68.67	46.11	23.22	—
10%	154.30	133.22	111.82	90.02	68.05	45.68	23.00
11%	173.57	152.97	132.05	110.83	89.28	67.43	45.26
12%	192.22	172.08	151.64	130.89	109.84	88.47	66.81
13%	210.27	190.59	170.61	150.32	129.74	108.85	87.67
14%	227.76	208.51	188.97	169.13	149.00	128.58	107.87
15%	244.69	225.87	206.76	187.35	167.66	147.69	127.43

Prepared by William Bryan, Bureau of Economic and Business Research, University of Illinois at Urbana-Champaign.

Index

additional dealer markup (ADM), 103, 104, 116–17

additional dealer profit (ADP), 116–17

additional market value (AMV), 104, 116–17

add-on options. *See* Optional equipment and accessories

advanced payment leases, 162

advertising charge, 147, 150–51

African-American buyers. *See also* minority buyers

price discrimination and, 8

airbags, 2, 52–53

alternatives to negotiating in person, 143, 179–89, 221

brokers and other middlemen, 185–88

CarBargains, 184–86

by fax, 181–83

one-offer phone call, 180–81

on-line computer services and the Internet, 188–89

psychological aspects of, 16–17
summary of, 219–22
walking out as tactic in, 17–18
warranties, 126–28
women and, 10
New Car Cost Guide, The (Chek-Chart Publications), 83
new-car dealers. *See also* Saturn
choosing finalists, 129–36
within competitive geography, 142–43
estimating how long a car has been in inventory of, 121
one-price, "no-dicker," 64–66, 68, 70–77
relatively farther from your home or office, 56
new cars. *See also* buyers; negotiation; new-car dealers
bugs in new models, 105
depreciation of. *See* depreciation
price discrimination against women and minority buyers of, 6–11
separating used-car sale from purchase of, 29, 138, 220
in short supply, 119, 142
special ordering, 118–20
newspaper ads, 91
Nissan holdback, 96
Nissan Motors Acceptance Corporation, 164

odometer, checking the, 191
one-price selling, 64–66, 68, 70–77
on-line computer services. *See* Internet
optional equipment and accessories, 20, 24, 114–21, 221
checking, 191
leasing and, 176
protection package, 115–16

Pace Publications, 32, 202, 209

paint sealant, 115, 116
personal information requested by salespeople, 111–12, 145
pickup trucks
Monroney label on, 84
special ordering, 118
Porsche holdback, 96
powertrain warranty, 123–26
price discrimination, 6–11
prices. *See also* negotiating (bargaining)
increases in, 2
inflation and, 103
"no-dicker," 64–66, 68, 70–77
special ordering, 119
target price, 139–41, 182, 221
value pricing, 76–77
window sticker (Monroney label), 83–84
pricing books
for new cars, 202
for used cars, 31–32
profit
of "no-dicker" dealers, 65–66, 68
ranges, 140–41
slim-profit deals, 78–79, 138, 141, 151
program cars, 211
psychology of negotiating, 16–17

race discrimination, 7–8
rebates (direct-to-consumer incentives), 43, 84–85, 87–88, 142, 221
recalls, 125
referral services, 188–89
registration fees, 160, 162
rental cars, 210, 211
finalist cars, 62
Republic Industries, 71, 75, 212
residual value, 161, 168–72, 177
depreciation and, 160
purchase option and, 162–63
Road and Track, 56

timing of leases, 175–76, 221
timing of purchase, 99–107
  beginning of model year, 104
  carryover allowances, 100–103
  end of the model year, 100–103
  factory-to-dealer incentives and, 100
  January and February, 106
  last hour of the last day of December, 106
  last week of the month, 105–6
  new models and, 104–5
  special sales events, 106–7
  "the middles," 106
title fees, 46, 82, 160
Toyota
  certified cars, 217
  dealer advertising charge, 150
  holdback, 96
Toyota Motor Credit Corporation, 159
trade-ins, 20, 25–28. *See also* used cars
  not talking to salespeople about, 111
  separating new-car purchase from, 29, 138, 220
trim levels, 196, 201

under-the-table money, 98
United Auto Workers, 2, 120
"upside down" financing, 44–46
Used Car Book, The (Gillis), 209
used-car dealers, 27
  number of, 75
used cars, 207–18. *See also* trade- ins
  background checking on, 212–17
  certified, 216–17
  classified ads for, 36, 37
  consumer confidence and demand for, 32
  demo cars, 214–16
  detailing, 37
  down payment and, 23
  keys to, held as hostage by salesperson, 112

leased cars as, 154, 217
pricing books for, 31–32
profit of new-car dealers in sales of, 25–27
retailed by new-car dealers, 27
selling to individuals, 35–40
shopping for offers, 32–34
superstores, 212
telephone research on price of, 36–37
two-year-old, 209–11
wholesale value of, 30–34, 220
wholesaling by new-car dealers, 27, 28

value pricing, 76–77
VIN (vehicle identification number), 84, 212–13
Volkswagen
  Beetle, 104
  holdback, 96
Volvo holdback, 96

Wall Street Journal, 53, 87
warranties, 20
  basic, 61, 123–25
  corrosion, 123, 124
  demo cars, 215, 216
  extended, 20, 122–29, 151, 164, 221
  factory-backed, 126, 127, 130–31
  leasing and, 126, 164
  negotiating, 126–28
  powertrain, 123–26
  secret, 125–26
warranty parts, 130–31
wholesale auctions, 211
wholesale value of currently owned car, 30–34, 220
wholesaling of used cars by new-car dealers, 27, 28
window sticker (Monroney label), 80, 83–84